To Tell a Black Story of Miami

UNIVERSITY PRESS OF FLORIDA

Florida A&M University, Tallahassee
Florida Atlantic University, Boca Raton
Florida Gulf Coast University, Ft. Myers
Florida International University, Miami
Florida State University, Tallahassee
New College of Florida, Sarasota
University of Central Florida, Orlando
University of Florida, Gainesville
University of North Florida, Jacksonville
University of South Florida, Tampa
University of West Florida, Pensacola

TO TELL
A BLACK STORY
OF MIAMI

Tatiana D. McInnis

University Press of Florida

Gainesville · Tallahassee · Tampa · Boca Raton
Pensacola · Orlando · Miami · Jacksonville · Ft. Myers · Sarasota

Publication of this work is made possible by a Sustaining the Humanities through the American Rescue Plan grant from the National Endowment for the Humanities.

27 26 25 24 23 22   6 5 4 3 2 1

Library of Congress Cataloging-in-Publication Data
Names: McInnis, Tatiana Danielle, author.
Title: To tell a black story of Miami / Tatiana D. McInnis.
Description: Gainesville : University Press of Florida, [2022] | Includes
    bibliographical references and index. | Summary: "In this book, Tatiana
    McInnis examines literary and cultural representations of Miami
    alongside the city's material realities to challenge the image of South
    Florida as a diverse cosmopolitan paradise"— Provided by publisher.
Identifiers: LCCN 2022020658 (print) | LCCN 2022020659 (ebook) | ISBN
    9780813069579 (cloth) | ISBN 9780813068954 (pbk) | ISBN 9780813070315 (pdf) | ISBN
    9780813072555 (epub)
Subjects: LCSH: Black people in literature. | African Americans in
    literature. | Black people—Florida—Miami—Social conditions. | African
    Americans—Florida—Miami—Social conditions. | Miami (Fla.)—Race
    relations. | BISAC: LITERARY CRITICISM / American / African American &
    Black | SOCIAL SCIENCE / Ethnic Studies / American / African American &
    Black Studies
Classification: LCC PS173.B53 M35 2022 (print) | LCC PS173.B53 (ebook) |
    DDC 810.9/352996073075938—dc23/eng/20220810
LC record available at https://lccn.loc.gov/2022020658
LC ebook record available at https://lccn.loc.gov/2022020659

The University Press of Florida is the scholarly publishing agency for the State University System of Florida, comprising Florida A&M University, Florida Atlantic University, Florida Gulf Coast University, Florida International University, Florida State University, New College of Florida, University of Central Florida, University of Florida, University of North Florida, University of South Florida, and University of West Florida.

University Press of Florida
2046 NE Waldo Road
Suite 2100
Gainesville, FL 32609
http://upress.ufl.edu

For the McInnis family and for Miami

Contents

Figures

Acknowledgments

A book is a communal effort and there are so many people I must thank for how they helped me bring this project to fruition. I am indebted in every imaginable way to my father, my mother, and my sister who are steadfast in their support, and to every member of the McInnis family for trusting me with our stories. To my colleagues: Annie, you are a master of self-care, a brilliant mind, and the one person whose encouraging words make all the difference. To Ro: to ten years, and beyond in whatever form that takes; thank you always for believing in me. To members of Dr. Kutzinski's reading group: Thank you for your kindness, attention, and close reading and for putting up with my headstrong defense of my work. Thank you, Vera, for opening your home to us, for the various baked goods, and for how you continue to support me so much time after I completed graduate work. To the many interlocutors and mentors I have encountered while developing *To Tell a Black Story of Miami,* thank you—when you were right, I learned volumes, when you were wrong, I learned how to argue. To my fellow fellows at the Robert Penn Warren Center for the Humanities, your attention to detail and suggestions have made this project the interdisciplinary cultural study that I hope it is.

To the staff at the Florida State Archives, the Black Archives of South Florida, University of Miami Cuban Heritage Collection, and Florida International University Special Collections: thank you for your curiosity about my project. For wanting to talk to me and listen to me, and for using our conversations to guide me to resources I had not even thought of.

To Drs. Vera Kutzinski, Michael Kreyling, Candice Amich, and Alex Stepick: you oversaw this project because it is your job as professors to teach the next generation of scholars, but how you oversaw, guided, and nurtured me through this process can only be described as a labor of love. Thank you endlessly for supporting this project, for never doubting its stakes and importance, for envisioning the stakes long before I could. Thank you for asking questions (even when I just wanted answers) that pushed my thinking, for your editing skills, for your "big-picture" questions, for encouragement and patience, and for never, not once, forcing me to make changes that I did not want to. Thank you to Drs. N.D.B. Connolly, Scott Kurashige, Brandon Manning, Stacie McCormick, Ianna Hawkins Owen (nar), Kailani Polzak, Randa Tawil, Nino Testa, and for your interest, patience, and grace in engaging this work and giving me boundless space to talk about it and share it with students. Thank you, Kelan O'Brien and nar for your workie sessions, humor, and encouragement in taking this to the finish line.

I am especially thankful for Dr. Connolly's time and his words, especially what he offered in his recent essay, "Speculating in History":

> I was told more than once by well-meaning white urban historians that [Miami] didn't have enough—archivally—to sustain a proper book-length treatment. I learned, though, that if you cross a few residential color lines and violate a few disciplinary boundaries (a little field work, more-than-a-little archival work, sprinkled, perhaps, with some Black Power analytics), Miami can absolutely be a valuable place to think with. You may even get a book out of it. (2)

The lessons you learned in sticking and thinking with Miami were foundational to my courage to take on this work. Thank you for the reminder of Miami's import always, but maybe especially during unprecedented times.

Thank you, thank you, thank you.

Introduction

But we all know that Miami is
America. is Now what it always
was: a sunbleached monument to Obese brutality
a vicious incarnation reservation of
sand and bleeding money and murdered
Indians and lost refugees
lynched niggers flying from religious
trees

—from "POEM FOR ARTHUR MCDUFFIE: MAY, 1980" by Kofi Natambu

Miami's the special-that-ain't-*that*-special . . . This so-called capital of the Caribbean home, but, Lord, if Miami's "Diversity" ain't been one of the biggest bait-and-switches in our sun-drenched history of selling points, swindles, and snake-oil.

—from "Speculating in History" by N.D.B. Connolly

Black storytellers' examinations of South Florida are largely missing from literary studies. Like Natambu and Connolly, other poets, scholars, novelists, memoirists, and filmmakers have identified and countered the mythic construction of Miami, and South Florida generally, as somehow magically distinct from the remainder of the United States because of its "diversity." Instead, Black creators have outlined legacies of anti-Blackness and racialized violence that continuously shape and reshape South Florida's cultural terrain to the detriment of Black people. These creators have called out anti-Blackness either subtlely and shadily, or boldly and explicitly, refuting the region's widespread reputation as a cosmopolitan mecca. This project holds the rich culture inspired by Miami's position as a transnational "contact zone" in tandem with the violent and virulent anti-Blackness that constitutes the region.[1]

To Tell a Black Story of Miami integrates Black voices into "the story we tell" about South Florida. I provide examples of how Black creators name and reject South Florida's winter playground reputation to argue that the region's casting as a diverse cultural mecca overlooks and is dependent on anti-Blackness. In what follows, I treat anti-Blackness both as an ideology or set of values and ideas that inform the master narratives of South Florida, and a methodology that dictates the space-making practices evident in South Florida's terrain. I use Miami as a microcosm to discuss transnational racial hierarchies and suggest that this examination facilitates an intersectional analysis of cross-cultural interaction and tension. My analysis treats anti-Blackness as not only a global phenomenon, but also a transnational problem.

In its focus on space-making and storytelling, my analysis of South Florida is relying on Katherine McKittrick's foundational work on how racist ideologies make space in *Demonic Grounds*. Like McKittrick, I reject any neutral interpretation of space that relies on self-evident assumptions. I assert that our constructions, destructions, and "developments" naturalize unjustly asymmetrical hierarchies that are in turn inscribed into our cartographies and geographies; put simply, "we produce space, we produce its meaning, we work very hard to make geography what it is."[2] The storytellers I include in this manuscript present South Floridian cartographies that echo Monika Gosin's claim that despite the city's diversity and boosters' efforts to sell the winter playground, "Miami remains among one of the nation's most segregated cities."[3] The "maps" in *To Tell a Black Story of Miami* expose regional, national, and international politics of diasporic subjectivity, violent, and at times deadly, detention of émigrés, other instances of racialized violence, and increasing wealth gaps among Miami inhabitants, most of which occur across racial/cultural/ethnic lines.

The celebrations of Miami as a city of a multiracial future dangerously obfuscate myriad social inequalities that disproportionately affect the city's Black residents, regardless of nation of origin. Dismantling this myth reveals the state-sanctioned mistreatment of many of Miami's residents (who are in turn used to support its reputation for diversity), and throws into relief the rigid racial, socioeconomic, and political stratifications that sometimes make massive waves of immigration (like those that have shaped Miami's demographic) a disproportionate burden to already marginalized communities.

Which Miami? Whose South?

Throughout, I variously use "Miami" and "South Florida" as metonyms for the cities and neighborhoods within and beyond the City of Miami, and even Miami-Dade County proper. These areas have been influenced by massive waves of immigration and have shaped and carry a variety of produced meanings: the nation's winter playground, a contact zone of linguistic and cultural diversity, an extension of the Caribbean. For a close friend, Miami is a bachata cover of a Beatles song played at The Cheesecake Factory. She had moved to Tennessee and when asked for clarification, she offered that "Miami is geographically, but not culturally, Southern." I have heard this assessment elsewhere, and there are many reasons why it may appear to be true.

The mythic South has been constructed as backward, politically conservative, and culturally homogenous with a Manichean hierarchy of white supremacy and Black enslavement.[4] Debatably the ground zero for settler colonialism in the U.S., the South bears legacies of Indigenous and Black genocide, displacement, dispossession, and exploited labor.[5] In South Florida, Black and Indigenous people built up a region they would be systemically kept from enjoying the benefits of. Investigations of Black Miami reveal a long history of degradation, limited citizenship, labor exploitation, and resistance that predate the city's inception in 1896. As Jafari S. Allen writes:

> Miami could not have become what it has—or any of the things it is imagined to be or aspires to today—without many generations of Black folks' aliveness in this space, from the moment of pirates and privateers, and slave traders bringing kidnapped Africans to these swampy shores that were stolen from the Tequesta and other Indian nations.[6]

The patterns of the past reverberate to the present, and white supremacist erasures continuously inform the stories we tell about South Florida. Any examination of the construction of the city must acknowledge exploited and usurped Black American and Black Bahamian labor as foundational to Miami's modern development.[7] George Merrick, a prominent real estate developer, the namesake of Merrick Park in Coral Gables, and a prime beneficiary of Black labor noted: "all of our heavy laborers were Bahamian negroes . . . [Bahamians] knew how to plant [on this land]" and brought with them "their own commonly used trees, vegetables, and fruits."[8] South Floridian terrain is a challenging amalgam of swamp and rock, and Bahamian insight made possible visions of a habitable, and profitable, South Florida, just as the labor of the enslaved, formerly enslaved, and dispossessed made possible visions of the United States.

It is unlikely that we can ever overstate the impact that enslavement and its afterlives continue to have on the U.S. South. However, the same could and should be said for the imagined community of the U.S., and the world.[9] To view the South otherwise is a reductive displacement that overlooks what is national and global. As Barbara Ladd notes in her meditation on the monolith of the South, we must revisit the region as a site of "cultural dynamism" where plantation cultures are formative foci, but not exclusive ones.[10] Ladd's reflections in 2000 seem prescient given the radical changes the South has undergone in the past two decades as industry has capitalized on lower prices in the Southeast (Amazon is moving to the Raleigh-Durham area, for example) and the increased Latinization of the rural U.S. generally, specifically in the Southeastern states.[11]

Though the region has evolved or as Ladd might suggest, has always been more than the reductive monolithic myth, the South gets a bad rep from which South Florida is often held apart. This is in part a consequence of the region's demographic and the use of multiculturalism to interpret its changes; more than half of the city's residents (approximately 51.7%) were born outside of the U.S., primarily in the Caribbean, and in Central and South America.[12] This demographic is the consequence of widespread political unrest; although by no means a comprehensive list, Fidel Castro's Communist revolution in Cuba (beginning in 1959), François Duvalier's regime (1957–1971), and his son, Jean-Claude Duvalier's succession (1971–1986), and the overthrow of the Somoza dynasty by the Sandinistas in Nicaragua (1970s–1990s) each triggered massive waves of emigration that radically altered Miami's racial and ethnic demographic.

It is perhaps unsurprising then that Miami is often lauded for its diversity and has even been nicknamed a "global" or "international" city, the "Capital of the Caribbean," and the "Gateway to Latin America." Given the history of tourism in Miami, and the widespread *marketing* of the city, cultural analysis of myriad representations of Miami yields insight into its cultural construction.[13] Miami's official tourist guide markets the city as an "international hub of cultural diversity and world-class offerings."[14] Google's description of Miami reads, "Miami is an international city at Florida's southeastern tip. Its Cuban influence is reflected in the cafes and cigar shops that line Calle Ocho in Little Havana." This description is striking in its implicit conflation of "international" with "Cuban," which references massive waves of immigration from Cuba to Miami in the latter half of the twentieth century. The travel-booking website TripAdvisor's site on Miami boasts "scorching" nightlife "thanks to a strong Latin influence and spicy salsa culture." Sociologist Saskia Sassen, examining both Miami's residential demographic and the representation of international industries in the port city has dubbed Miami a "global city," while Colin Woodard included Miami in the Spanish Caribbean region in his book, *American Nations: A History of the Eleven Rival Regional Cultures of North America* (2011). As these various assessments of Miami might reflect, "international," "global," "Caribbean," and "Cuban" are variously used, in some cases interchangeably, to describe Miami's cultural topography.

Scholars, tourists, beneficiaries of the Miami tourist industry, and city officials capitalize on claims of the city's Caribbeanness, cultural diversity, and/or internationality.[15] Even the renaming of Dade County, the county within which the City of Miami is located, to Miami-Dade County, implicitly indexes the displacement of the city's "Southernness." The county, founded in 1836, was originally named after Southern Major Francis Langhorne Dade who died in the Second Seminole War, a conflict whose express purpose was the displacement of Seminoles in the interest of expanding the spatial parameters of the Southern United States. In 1997, Mayor Alex Penelas successfully advocated for renaming the county Miami-Dade, asserting, "There is a magic to the name Miami . . . quite frankly no one knows what Dade County is. By adding Miami to our county's name we will be able to better identify and market our community *throughout the world.*"[16] Historian Gregory Bush highlights the marketability of this renaming, suggesting that we view "Miami-Dade" as a promotional effort that relies on Miami's reputations as a lush, tropical, and cosmopolitan paradise as opposed to a Southern town.[17]

What Black Stories Reveal

I contend, in concert with many of the creators whom I cite herein, that there is limited benefit to contesting or defending Miami's Southernness, Caribbeanness, or internationalism—to do so fosters only tautological or binaristic conclusions that the authors I take up are largely uninterested in. Instead, this book identifies larger stakes geo-narratives put forth in enabling or suppressing discourse around how race makes place in South Florida. The mythmaking monikers about South Florida disguise the pervasive, adaptive nature of white supremacy and anti-Blackness in diverse locales that renders darker-complected people vulnerable to premature death while providing lighter-complected people disproportionate access to various resources that prolong and enhance their quality of life, regardless of nation of origin. In short, the South Florida myth of diversity belies the complexities, tensions, and the violence that constitute the city and that underlie any diverse, but not equitable, society.

In what follows, I demonstrate that the widespread narrative of South Florida's appealing diversity functions to silence and invalidate the lived experiences of the region's Black inhabitants. Most of the creators I have chosen to engage for this project have generated book- or film-length responses to being told in any number of ways that they do not exist, that they do not matter. Largely, the histories and examples that have justified Miami's cosmopolitan reputation reveal a hyper-focus on South Florida's post-1959 demographic shifts, neglecting the formative role Black people have had on Miami as it exists today. I revisit the post-1959 period, centering Black reflections to enhance the scope and scale of the changes South Florida has undergone in the past sixty years. To do so, *To Tell a Black Story of Miami* investigates the following questions: What circumstances, issues, and cultures shape Miami, its inhabitants, and representations? What is at stake for Black creators in the stories we tell about South Florida? What do various descriptions and selective historiographies reveal about the city's racial politics and cultural climate? What do they hide? This project also takes up a question that N.D.B. Connolly posed in "Speculating in History": "What does it mean to live under multicultural forms of white supremacy, indeed, to understand multiculturalism as white supremacy?"[18] To answer this question, I turn to the neglected stories of the region's Black inhabitants.

Storytelling and Memoir as Archive

By focusing on literary and filmic representations by and/or about Afro-Diasporic storytellers, *To Tell a Black Story of Miami* offers an investigation of race, ethnicity, and nation of origin through an interdisciplinary and intersectional examination of Miami's cultural topography. Literature enables an imperative analysis of representation, especially when we consider who, in an unjust, inequitable power dynamic, gets to represent the city, its residents, and how they represent them. As my project's focus on memoirs might suggest, literature enables examinations of *self*-representations and *self*-fashioning.[19]

I primarily center memoirs published by authors who live or have lived in Miami and justify this focus by asserting the ethical imperative of learning about Black people who comprise the most obfuscated populations within Miami's mythic diversity. The Black women, Black Cuban men, Black Haitian women, Black Bahamian men, and Black queer men that structure this manuscript tell a different story of Miami that exposes compounding exclusions, state-sanctioned violence, and present South Floridian cartographies that make visible the mechanics of anti-Black oppression.

Often, these creators are responding directly to their own erasure, and I examine these responses with specific attention to their rhetorical strategies and concurrent address of contemporary sociopolitical issues. In many cases, the literature I analyze corroborates the findings of systemic anti-Blackness, but also provides additional insight into how authors adapt the form and style of their writing in response to these material realities. As Jewel Amoah argues, storytelling in Black culture is rooted in resistance and cultural survival.[20] In South Florida's ever-changing natural and built environments, the region's Black inhabitants have documented their manufactured vulnerability to threatened qualities of life and premature death resulting from state-sanctioned violence, limited employment opportunities, divestment in their communities, gentrification, and climate change. *To Tell a Black Story of Miami* seeks to amplify and treasure their stories in accordance with the gravity of the events, treatment, and trauma the works bear witness to.

These storytellers invite readers to sit with uncomfortable questions about Miami's cultural diversity: What does it mean, how does it feel, and how does one represent living in an increasingly diverse Miami during the 1950s and 1960s as a Black woman civil rights activist, fighting for racial equity, while your contributions are elided in favor of Black male voices? What does it mean, how does it feel, and how does one represent living in a "diverse" city after your uncle is subjected to premature death for, it would seem, the alleged crimes of being Black and Haitian and seeking asylum in Miami? What does it mean, how does it feel, and how does one represent being told that Miami is a "Cuban" city, only to arrive as an Afro-Cuban and be persecuted for your observation of continuities of anti-Blackness from Cuba to Miami? What are the consequences of projecting anxieties about immigration onto criminalized Brownface performances? What does it mean and how does it feel to "harden" yourself because your Blackness and queerness render you invisible and silent to your community, your family?

Roadmap

Each chapter is devoted to one of these questions and centers a prominent cultural group in South Florida to challenge the homogeneity implicit in descriptors like "global city" or "melting pot" by focusing on the multiplicity of Blackness as it is represented in the texts I analyze. I hold apart and treat these groups separately to more clearly highlight how mechanisms of anti-Blackness distinctly affect each group. I work to be as specific and grounded in place and history as possible, but do not present my work as comprehensive. As Allen reminds us:

> There is richness and heterogeneity at the creative edges of societies and cultural spaces, yes. This does not make boundary-crossing any less fraught with epistemic violence and material danger. Neither the concept of diaspora, nor the current disciplinary divisions of academe are capacious enough to hold all of this.[21]

Moving within and between disciplines, spaces, and stories is a fraught enterprise as Allen notes; what follows reflects my belief in the duty to try. The project moves from uncovering what I view as the most understudied, or missing, narratives of Miami, to problematizing the prominent narratives disseminated in and about the city.

I begin with what until recently, with Chanelle N. Rose's *The Struggle for Black Freedom in Miami: Civil Rights and America's Tourist Paradise, 1896–1968* (2015), was an egregiously underrepresented history of Miami: its role during the Civil Rights Movement. In my first chapter, "To Tell a Black Story of Miami: Civil Rights and the Reverberations of History in *Freedom in The Family*," I explore this history, relying on the recollections of civil rights activist and Florida native, Patricia Stephens Due, and her daughter, speculative fiction author, Tananarive Due, in their collaboratively authored memoir, *Freedom in the Family: A Mother-Daughter Memoir of the Fight for Civil Rights*. I focus on the form of the memoir and argue that its alternating chapters signal a cyclical chronology that metaphorizes the perpetuity of the struggle for Black equality. I contextualize the memoir within local, national, and international histories, expounding on its address of police brutality, residential segregation, urban renewal, and Overtown as a center for Black organizers. I trace Stephens Due's and Due's reflections of the influx of émigrés of Cuban descent during the early 1960s, and émigrés of Haitian descent in the early 1970s to illustrate how Black American activists variously adjusted their tactics to address racial differences within South Florida's communities.

In the second chapter, I discuss a cultural group for which Patricia Stephens Due and Tananarive Due advocate in Miami: Haitian émigrés. In "The Anti-Haitian Hydra: Remapping Haitian Spaces in Miami," I argue that literary works by Haitian Americans who live or have lived in Miami present alternate cartographies of the city that map methods of repelling, repatriating, containing, and even killing Haitians across economic and political strata. Centering the state-sanctioned disenfranchisement of Haitian Americans in Miami, and South Florida more broadly reveals the region as contested territory, characterized by cross-cultural conflicts for space and other resources. Though the procedures differ, these mechanized strategies of subjugation all share the objective of rendering Haitian people unseen in a supposedly "diverse" city. I focus on national and international policies that make Miami inaccessible to Haitian émigrés through an analysis of Edwidge Danticat's short story, "Children of the Sea" (1995) alongside her later work, *Brother, I'm Dying* (2007), which details the use of the detention center as a site of population control that disproportionately prosecutes and contains Haitian émigrés. I put Danticat in conversation with M. J. Fièvre's more recent short story, "Sinkhole" (2014), which metaphorizes gentrification through its depiction of a sinkhole swallowing up a prominent Haitian enclave in Miami.

The third chapter offers a comparative analysis of racial and ethnic differences within Miami's Cuban American populations. In "Becoming Whiteness, Rejecting Blackness: Genre, Castro, and Transnational Identity in Carlos Moore's *Pichón* and Carlos Eire's *Learning to Die in Miami*," I compare the authors' experiences as represented in their respective memoirs. I use the insights from both authors to trace the various assimilation routes available to lighter-complected émigrés as compared to those available to émigrés with darker skin. I argue that Moore and Eire represent these different routes through the form of their memoirs; Eire, a white-passing émigré embraces the fluidity of the postmodern, which emblematizes his "life on the hyphen" wherein he can variously embrace and reject his Cubanness to pass as white American because of his light skin. Moore, on the other hand, replicates prominent tropes from the slave narrative to situate his experiences as an Afro-Cuban within a longer history, and broader geographic space, of violence against Afro-Diasporic peoples.

In chapter 4, I intentionally deviate from the project's primary focus on Black creators to devote more attention to Cuban Miami. This is arguably the focus readers of any examination of Miami expect, and the Cuban influence in South Florida has yielded countless cinematic and literary representations. In "Who Speaks for Miami?" I analyze how the racial demographic of the Mariel Boatlift, the War on Drugs, and anxieties about queerness are represented in *Miami Vice* and *Scarface*. I assert that their hyperbolic conflation of violence, drugs, illicit economic ascent, and immigration codified Miami as a white American nightmare during the 1980s. Both the film and series rely on a strategic Brownness to entertain, entice, and approximate documenting, while simultaneously avoiding anxieties around the Black and mixed-race Mariel émigrés.

In the last chapter, I focus on Billy Corben's documentary, *Dawg Fight* (2015), which explores a bareknuckle fighting ring in West Perrine and the Academy Award–winning film, *Moonlight* (2017), which focuses on protagonist Chiron's experiences as a gay Black man in Liberty City. I argue that both films thematize how men who live in low-income Black neighborhoods develop an ethic around their masculinity that prioritizes a dearth of vulnerability and impenetrability that is often coupled with violence. I link this ethic of masculinity to a toxic combination of limited economic opportunities and the entrapment of poverty in a diverse, but still white supremacist culture.

To provide a broader scope beyond the manuscript's anchor texts, I concurrently consider localized cultures and surroundings that shape, limit, and contain these cultures, be they statewide, national, or international debates, discourses, and desires. Therefore, my archive extends beyond literary works to include the language of immigration policies, the policies, and corresponding operations of detention centers, and municipal ordinances that structure the topography of the city. *To Tell a Black Story of Miami* thus lies within and investigates the tension between material realities and the representations of such realities put forth in the works I analyze.

I bolster my close readings with concurrent attention to the various mechanisms of white supremacy and anti-Blackness to which the authors I have selected are responding. I further use strategies of close reading on all of the texts I engage, driven by the principle "that literary and 'non-literary texts' circulate inseparably" and are mutually illuminating.[22] To provide an example, in my second chapter, "The Anti-Haitian Hydra," I analyze municipal ordinances alongside the fictional and non-fictional literary texts to expose how race-neutral legislation contributes to the gradual elimination of Little Haiti that Danticat and Fièvre document in their work.

Miami's Scholarly Genealogy

Given this methodology, and the various contexts and cultural groups that anchor this project, *To Tell a Black Story of Miami* departs from and contributes to various fields of study, including the interdisciplinary fields of American Studies, Southern Studies, Caribbean Studies, Transnational Studies, and Global South Studies. I imagine these interventions in expanding, concentric circles that metaphorize my treatment of Miami within local, regional, national, and transnational frameworks. Primarily, what follows builds on earlier studies of Miami through its treatment of literature as a primary archive. This focus enables a thick description of cross-cultural interactions and thus complements previously published foundational historical, anthropological, and sociological research that analyzes Miami's demographic. *To Tell a Black Story of Miami* is indebted to and builds upon work by Alex Stepick, Alejandro Portes, Guillermo Grenier, and Marvin Dunn. Their work about Miami in the late 1990s and early 2000s prioritized interethnic relations and power in Miami to illuminate how racial and ethnic diversity often did little to shift sociopolitical and economic hierarchies that privileged lighter-complected people in the city.

Recent work has revealed renewed interest in questions of racial inequity in Miami. Work by Chanelle N. Rose, N.D.B. Connolly, Alan Aja, Monika Gosin, and Gregory Bush has taken up the role Blackness plays in the lived experiences and architecture of South Florida. Rose's work fiercely writes South Florida into the Civil Rights Movement, and chronologically reframes the region's demographic shifts with attention to Black emigration. N.D.B. Connolly addresses the overt and insidious ways real estate practices inhibited Black people from accruing property and capital in Miami in *A World More Concrete: Real Estate and the Remaking of Jim Crow South Florida* (2014). I was privileged to discuss parts of *To Tell a Black Story* with Connolly, whose work is foundational to this project's undertaking. During our conversation, we explained to peers that many take up the idea that immigration "put Miami on the map." South Florida's legacies precede the twentieth century, and Connolly concluded by saying that suggesting otherwise is a practice of anti-Blackness; I take him up on this claim throughout this book. Gregory Bush explores the contentious access to public space and related segregation of Miami's beaches in *White Sand Black Beach: Civil Rights, Public Space, and Miami's Virginia Key* (2016). Alan Aja's *Miami's Forgotten Cubans Race, Racialization, and the Miami Afro-Cuban Experience* (2016) outlines how Afro-Cubans navigate rejections and alienations in the racially bifurcated U.S. and compounding experiences of racism within and between the U.S. and Cuba. Monika Gosin's *The Racial Politics of Division: Interethnic Struggles for Legitimacy in Multicultural Miami* (2019) asserts that white supremacy has fractured Miami's various Latinx and Black communities by purporting notions of "worthy citizenship," and outlines demonstrations of interethnic solidarity that make clear that a different, more just world is possible. This book joins this genealogy of explorations of race, place, and the stories we tell about South Florida.

Personal Stakes, Collective Futures

I have my own story of South Florida that led me to this book. For me, Miami is one of the most anti-Black places I have ever experienced—its saltwater air, zoning, poverty, humidity, ostentatious wealth, and flouted inhibitions. I came to this interpretation of South Florida having lived there for the first twenty-one years of my life and visiting frequently after moving away for graduate study. *To Tell a Black Story of Miami* offers histories of some neighborhoods I knew of, but seldom visited, when I was younger, even as they came to shape my experiences.

Devoting scholarly attention to the question of anti-Blackness in South Florida is especially important to me as a Black woman who was born and raised there. I grew up without learning about the contributions and complexities of Black life in my hometown as I "[navigated] the anti-Black terrain of *whitino* hegemony in Miami."[23] Working through this project has helped me grapple with my own experiences of anti-Blackness ranging from elementary school to undergrad at Florida International University. Through this book, I am just beginning to reconcile those traumas with recollections of growing up in what others celebrated as a culturally rich environment. I have joked that readers can interpret my project as a response to the representations of Miami found on tourist websites: an anti-tourist guide. But this book does not emerge from a place of disdain or resentment—I love Miami "more than any place in the world, and exactly for this reason, I insist on the right to criticize [it] perpetually."[24]

Because of my fraught love for Miami, the personal motivations behind this project are two-fold: First, I write about what was missing from my education and the stories I was told about my hometown. I left South Florida for Tennessee in 2012 to commence graduate work, and while navigating the culture shock of Nashville I took "Ideas of Black Culture," "Southern

Studies," "Caribbean Studies," and "Global South Studies" courses. In each of these classes, Miami was missing. I often urge my students to find themselves in the stories we engage in our classes or to receive stories that are not theirs to expand their worldview, and throughout my graduate education, I could only do the latter as I struggled to find myself in the academy.

It can be a monstrous thing to witness one's own erasure, and Edwidge Danticat, Tarell Alvin McCraney, Barry Jenkins, Carlos Moore, Patricia Stephens Due, and countless others have written against their own disappearance.[25] The creators of the cultural artifacts analyzed herein equate this erasure with ontological violence and grapple with it in several ways: some with concerted efforts to reclaim and document lost voices and add them to master narratives of local and national history in acts of literary resistance. My stakes throughout my research are simultaneously lower, and equally urgent—I just wondered why Miami was missing.

Secondly, I am writing about a bruising hometown that I deeply miss and yearn for, even as I acknowledge that the South Florida of my childhood no longer exists. These stories help me commemorate and reconcile the Miamis that will never be again. With each visit, I note recent changes that take me further away from the sights, sounds, and smells that came to shape who I am. The rhythmic cacophony of the city used to stress me out; it is now welcome ambient noise. The food is unmatched, and there's no place else where Uncle Luke's "Scarred" will blast on the Power 96 mix and remind me of middle-school dances with inappropriate soundtracks. "Where are you *really* from?" that incessant inquiry for Black people, means something different there and sometimes (not always) functions as a reminder of the region's position as a satellite to Haiti, Cuba, Jamaica, the Bahamas, the world. It's unlikely, given the nature of our academic job market, that I will ever live there again, but I feel deeply seen when I revisit the stories these authors have shared.

There is an urgency to this project that exceeds its personal stakes for me. Deep investigations of Miami are timely and imperative in analyzing and anticipating the destiny of the U.S. as a whole; by 2060, the U.S., especially its major cities will closely resemble Miami's demographic with most residents claiming a birthplace outside of the nation's borders. If we sit with Miami, we might glean imperative understanding of the political, social, and economic regulation of racial and ethnic difference in the U.S. This insight will help us interpret cultural transformations on a national scale, especially with respect to assimilation and the reconstruction of racial hierarchies.

If we take seriously reminders that Miami is a city of the future, a harbinger of what is to come as multiracialism upholds white supremacy, as climate change wreaks havoc on the ecosystems upon which we are dependent to survive, then Miami-as-future does not bode well. Miami troubles borders demographically, ecologically, and politically with its compounding, palimpsestic legacies of displacement and imminent vulnerability to sinking into the sea like a contemporary Atlantis. I reflect more on what it means to turn to Miami now while anticipating a bleak future, in the wake of protests against police brutality (responded to with brutality), gentrification, and sea level rise in the coda.

For now, I reiterate the importance of addressing the exclusion of Black Miami through the examinations of stories that capture visceral, subtle, and material experiences of erasure, and how it manifests "on the ground." The imperative stakes of Miami remind me of a particularly striking passage in James Clifford's introduction to *The Predicament of Culture* (1988): "it is more than ever crucial for different peoples to form complex concrete images of one another, as well as of the relationships of knowledge and power that connect them." There is no better archive to enable complex, concrete images of the world and its inhabitants than our stories, and attention to the material conditions in which they were produced.

Of course, written, and published stories always index class stratification and access to resources and audiences that limit the scope of the implications of this study. As Alejandro de la Fuente reminds us: "what we frequently perceive as black discourse is, in fact, black middle-class discourse."[26] I have, of course, missed things in this effort to integrate Black stories into our engagement with South Florida and I am humbled with every word on each page by the reminder that "there is always already heterogeneity in Blackness, wherever one finds it—including among American English speaking urban folks whose ancestors raised themselves 'up from slavery' in the US."[27] What a beautiful, fraught, boundless Blackness.

I have labored over this book with the ethical imperative of keeping our stories and honoring boundless Blackness driving me forward. Still, I return to Clifford and his conclusory, cautionary note about the truthfulness of the images we create and accept of one another: "no sovereign scientific method or ethical stance can guarantee the truth of such images. They are constituted—the critique of colonial modes of representation has shown at least this much—in specific historical relations of dominance and dialogue."[28] I take Clifford's words as a firm reminder of my own privileged positionality as the curator of this book, and further, my accountability as a scholar for the blind spots that necessarily punctuate this project despite my goal of amplifying the stories and cartographies the creators have offered through their texts—many of which, as I argue document historical relations of power and erasure. I am hopeful that scholars will continuously think with Miami, its aspirations, beauty, and discontents to dismantle its myths and build a more equitable home for so many. Our future depends on it.

1

To Tell a Black Story of Miami

Civil Rights and the Reverberations of Black Floridian History in *Freedom in the Family*

I was *there!*

—from *Freedom in the Family: A Mother-Daughter Memoir
of Fight for Civil Rights*, by Patricia Stephens Due

In this project of excavations, Patricia Stephens Due's declaration to a textbook committee, ignorant of her work in the Florida leg of the Civil Rights Movement, captures the erasures *To Tell a Black Story* seeks to redress and how Black storytellers have resisted their elision. Through their collaboratively authored 2003 memoir, *Freedom in the Family: A Mother-Daughter Memoir of the Fight for Civil Rights,* former reporter, and esteemed novelist, Tananarive Due, and Patricia Stephens Due write themselves as Black women into a series of histories and cultural topographies from which they have been historically excluded.

Written in thirty-three alternating chapters, Patricia Stephens Due's and Tananarive Due's memoir historicizes approximately fifty years of personal narratives, seamlessly blending personal recollections with historical records ranging from the late 1950s to the 2000s. Footnotes to historical records punctuate the memoir, and authenticate the authors' experiences, posturing the memoir protectively against onslaughts of Black women's subjectivity and testimony. *Freedom in the Family* contributes to a genealogy of Black women's work to recuperate themselves in history—the Dues words are monuments to disappeared stories, places, and people and practice what Angela Ards describes as "the black feminist mode of reading power," and I would add, writing power, that provides a theoretical basis for re-examining the stakes and strategies of the long and ongoing Civil Rights Movement in South Florida.[1]

I argue that *Freedom in the Family* tells a Black story of South Florida and reveals anti-Blackness as an integral thread of Miami's cultural fabric and an ongoing political, economic, and social problem even after immigration increased the city's diversity. The Dues articulate South Florida not as a winter playground or cultural mecca, but a site of erasures, exclusions, and contestations—for Stephens Due, this is what makes South Florida an integral satellite in the Civil Rights Movement. The memoir recasts South Florida as an Afro-Diasporic stronghold that examines the collisions and collusions between minoritized Black Americans and white and non-white émigrés within the context of what some have described as the region's Caribbeanization and/or Latinization during and after the 1960s and 1970s.[2]

In this chapter I contextualize analysis of *Freedom in the Family* within Civil Rights and South Florida histories to show how the collaborative memoir refutes and recuperates national and local narratives of progress toward racial equality during the Civil Rights Movement. The authors notably resist progressive chronology and a myopic focus on singular leaders, organizers, or locales. The achronological format of the memoir metaphorizes the struggle for Black freedom as both cyclical and compounding, rather than progressive, and as a challenge to contemporary timebound representations of the Civil Rights Movement, finished.

The stakes of the Dues' refutations and recuperations are temporal, spatial, and political: *Freedom in the Family,* in form, bends time to demonstrate that the recovery and preservation of Black women's stories are an integral part of shaping the present. The memoir's structural and thematic attention to the interrelatedness of past, present, and future emulates what Christel N. Temple has described as the "Diasporan practice" of Sankofa, a part of the Adinkra philosophical system which "in conventional translation means 'go back and fetch it,' 'return to your past,' and 'it is not taboo to go back and retrieve what you have forgotten or lost,'" (Temple 127). Reading Sankofa into the structure of the memoir and the Dues' invitation to return to the past to understand and address the needs of the present disrupts ideas of chronological progress and misplaced assumptions that anti-Blackness is time bound.

In the memoir, the past and present needs manifest spatially, and the Dues read place to remap South Florida, placing buildings, neighborhoods, and movements within the context of anti-Black legacies that shape who lives where and whose stories are told. The memoir exposes that, as Katherine McKittrick argues, "existing cartographic rules unjustly organize human hierarchies *in place* and reify uneven geographies in familiar, seemingly natural ways."[3] The Dues refute the naturalization of Black life and space as inferior and impoverished as they grapple with their own aspirations of homeownership and what they perceive as the protections of middle-class life.

For the Dues, telling their stories is a political imperative for posterity that should shape decisions about the distribution of resources and how we build our world. Given the stakes, the Dues approach their storytelling as "telling the whole truth" about women's labor that was kept behind the scenes and dismantling the "cult of personality" Ella Baker observed in the intended upkeep of celebrity status for prominent male activists, like Martin Luther King Jr.[4] These exclusions and cults of male personalities structure the contemporary stories we tell about the movement, which the Dues take to task through at-times traumatic exercises of excavation.[5] They revisit psychological and physical attacks on themselves and encourage others to do the same. These stories are a bequest to readers to unearth a future by examining the past.

Contesting Erasure, Reclaiming Stories

Freedom in the Family emphasizes the danger of disappearing and disappeared stories, and from the first page of the memoir proper, notes that the construction of master narratives is a gendered practice. The Dues memoir encourage readers to move beyond the prominent deification of (mostly male) Civil Rights figures, especially Martin Luther King Jr., Stephens Due writes: "Dr. Martin Luther King wasn't the only one lighting the fire. He had a lot of influence, but he was only one man. It concerns me when I hear people say *If only we had Martin Luther King today*, as if we are helpless without him" (1). Stephens Due names the singular, male figure at the outset of her story, contrasting King with the plural "we" to emphasize the collaborative work of Civil Rights activists. She introduces this exclusionary narrative to foreground her story to write herself into a long and ongoing legacy of the struggle for Black freedom.

The presumption of contemporary helplessness without a single, Black male leader belies Black women's often-longitudinal contributions. Stephens Due's reflections of the past and examinations of the present signal a lifelong devotion to protest, civil disobedience, and the documentation of Black histories. In their work on Black women's role in what they describe as "long Civil Rights Movement" or "long Black radical tradition," Dayo Gore, Jeanne Theoharis, and Komozi Woodard frequently describe Black women Civil Rights activists and organizers as "'long distance runners' who produced pioneering gendered analyses of economic, social, and political conditions that proved crucial to advancing the black struggle." In this vein, Due's strategic prowess results in crucial innovations to the movement.

Emboldened by her observation of systemic racism and drawing on her training from and the criminalization of resistance to it, Stephens Due and seven other protestors decide to stay in jail, pioneering the "jail-in" strategy after her arrest for a sit-in at Woolworth's on February 20, 1960. Drawing on the training she undertook from the Congress on Racial Equality (CORE) in Miami, Stephens Due explains why she and others, when given the choice between paying a $300 fine and serving a sixty-day jail sentence, "would not pay a fine to support a system that did not treat us as equal human beings" (68–69). Beyond the punitive implications of the fine, Stephens Due describes the fine as a monetary enablement of further prosecution. She asserts that were it not for segregation, they "would have been served without incident" (68). Stephens Due reframes her arrest, rejecting any notion of illegality in her behavior and highlighting the unjust policy of the lunch counter. She and her sister, Priscilla Stephens, are jailed for forty-nine days. As Stephens Due notes, "not only was this the first time we had been jailed, but it was the first time any activists in the student sit-in movement had chosen jail rather than pay their fine. We pioneered a tactic, becoming the first 'jail-in' of the student protest movement of the 1960s" (70). Stephens Due's and the other activists' determination was a critical part of highlighting segregation in the South, and violence in Southern jails.

The jail-in received national attention and the students received letters from many sympathetic to their cause. Notably, Martin Luther King Jr. wrote the students on March 19, 1960, explaining, "I have just learned of your courageous willingness to go to jail instead of paying fines for your righteous protest against segregated eating facilities" (75). He encourages the students, asserting that "going to jail for a righteous cause is a badge of honor and a symbol of dignity" (76). Like Stephens Due's earlier language explaining her rationale behind refusing to pay the fine, Dr. King's language challenges negative connotations of going to jail by emphasizing the righteousness of resisting oppression.[6]

CORE, capitalizing on the revelatory power of the Tallahassee chapter's jail-in sends its members on a national tour to "bring attention to what happened in Tallahassee" (95). During this time, Stephens Due gave testimony of her experiences across the country, visiting Chicago, Washington, D.C., St. Louis, Philadelphia, New York, and Ann Arbor. CORE thus provides a platform for student activists, especially Black female activists, to become authoritative voices on oppression and resistance in the South.

Despite the attention afforded to Tallahassee CORE, and specifically Priscilla Stephens and Patricia Stephens Due, the latter activist's reflections highlight the omission of women from more widely publicized Civil Rights moments. Stephens Due cites the 1963 March on Washington as a prime example of how Civil Rights leaders privileged the voices of straight (thinking specifically about the sidelining of Bayard Rustin, the openly gay strategist credited with organizing the march) Black men, and white allies, over the contributions of Black women. Stephens Due recalls that after arriving in Washington, D.C.: "I was told that there had been some discussion that Priscilla and I, and some of the others who had spent forty-nine days in jail, should be permitted to speak at the march. In the end, though, we were not given a spotlighted role, as were John Lewis and Dr. King, not to mention Hollywood celebrities like Marlon Brando and Charlton Heston" (181). Stephens Due writes that she and her sister needed permission to speak, rendering themselves passive and subject to the will of the organizers who privileged other insights over those of the Stephens sisters. Repeating that they had spent forty-nine traumatizing days in jail, Stephens Due imperatively outlines her contributions to the movement, criticizing her and her sister's omission from the national stage and citing both male-domination and celebrity culture.

It is worthwhile to wonder how the Dues' story might have been taken up had they been given a platform at the March on Washington—their exclusion signals a hierarchal curation of the movement to the detriment of Black women with far- and future-reaching implications. In detailing her own exclusion from prominent platforms or being forbidden from becoming a representative voice of the movement contextualizes Stephens Due's demand that the Florida movement, and her place within it, be documented—and she knows she must do it herself. In no place is this more evident than the scene from which the opening epigraph—"I was there!"—is taken.

During a meeting sometime in the late 1990s/early 2000s with a "textbook committee for schoolchildren in Miami-Dade County," Stephens Due recalls asking other members of the committee "why the social studies books under consideration mentioned nothing about Tallahassee's civil rights struggle" (1). Stephens Due is exasperated as the committee members render her efforts invisible, stating that "nothing of note happened in Florida" (1). Stephens Due's anecdote details her response to a two-fold erasure of Florida's Civil Rights history: First, she captures the committee's attempt to silence her, bolstered in part by their ignorance of her participation in sit-ins and jail-ins. Their dismissal of Stephens Due's testimony also joins legacies of dismissing and ignoring Black women's truths and storytelling. The exclusion, derision, and silencing of Black women are the subjects of ample scholarship that is foundational to the explorations of this project in its work to center those elided in stories about South Florida.[7]

Echoing Stephens Due's exasperation, Patricia Hill Collins poses a question in the first chapter of *Black Feminist Thought: Knowledge, Consciousness, and the Politics of Empowerment:* "why are African American women and our ideas not known or believed in?" (5). Her answer, evident in her oeuvre, is that the compounding hegemony of white supremacist patriarchy inhibits, restricts, and/or devalues Black feminist knowledge production. As Stephens Due suggests, telling, and believing Black women's stories stands to enhance, transform, contradict, and/or disprove the prominent narratives of "what really happened" with imperative attention to intersecting systems that disappear Black women and their contributions.

Secondly, that Stephens Due endeavors to make these stories, her stories, accessible and available to students renders this introductory anecdote a synecdoche for the memoir's overall objective: disrupting the ignorance or willful erasure of Black histories now, and in the future. Stephens Due suggests that the other committee members devalue her physical (Black, woman) presence, role as a living witness, and spoken testimony in lieu of the constructed authority of the written word.[8] She writes:

A living witness didn't matter to [the committee members]. Without written documentation, I was told, the forty-nine days my sister and I spent in jail, the tear gas that burned my eyes, and the people I knew could not be included. As if we had never existed . . . *History belongs to those who write it.* I have to write ours. (1)

By describing the written word and the concurrent devaluation of other mediums of preservation, Due implicitly references the historical interrogation of Black experience and authenticity, an especially prominent debate within studies of Black literature.[9] Given the setting, Stephens Due links the written word to the dissemination of histories to educate young children in the Miami-Dade school system and suggests that her testimony as a Black woman Civil Rights activist will never circulate unless she writes and publishes it.

Storytelling to children, both via textbook and oral histories, bind the first two chapters, highlighting the future imperatives of stories of the past. For Due, a visit to the Holocaust Memorial on Miami Beach in 1996 clarified the need for posterity. At this commemorative site, Due witnesses a Holocaust survivor urgently telling young Jewish children of her time in a concentration camp. Due describes the "fervor of a survivor's voice," which she recognizes from her mother's stories, and notes that the woman described the dehumanizing experiences in detail, "anything to help the children understand. To help them remember" (4). Due's use of "remember" is striking, as the children cannot remember what they did not experience, but her language gestures toward an empathetic, collective memory that Due characterizes as imperative to cultural progress. Although adverts now list the Holocaust Memorial as a prominent tourist attraction, locals and government officials initially rejected and delayed the memorial's establishment, lamenting that "Miami Beach was a place for 'sun and fun' and the memorial would be too somber for the vacation destination" and would turn a "bright spot into a cemetery" (Holocaust Memorial). This phrasing suggests that recollections of the Holocaust necessarily conflict with Miami's reputation as a vacation destination, and further signal a prioritization of "fun" (in the present) over the work of historical commemoration and preservation. Watching the Holocaust survivor desperately tell her story, Due ponders, "*She is such an old woman . . . Soon, she will be gone, and all of her stories will go with her*" (5). She continues by referencing *The Diary of Anne Frank,* which "helped [her] understand the importance of simply telling a personal story and thus, the importance of writing (and reading) her memoir (5).

The compounding racial, gendered, and spatial erasures at stake in the text are matched with a spectral attention to mortality and posterity—made more poignant in the wake of Stephens Due's death in 2012. By referencing the old woman's inevitable death and Anne Frank's during the Holocaust from her contemporary moment in 1996, Tananarive Due suggests that the past informs the present and emphasizes the imperative of preserving these histories. She extrapolates the disappearance of stories to her family—Tananarive Due describes her familiarity with her parents' stories and still, she laments, "so few people remember. So few of the storytellers remain" (4).

Due and Stephens Due labor to document their stories, driven by the prospect of failing to include their experiences in the archive before they become inaccessible.

This imperative and its stakes are evident in the memoir's dedication to Stephens Due's parents, and the foot soldiers "who died before the book was published" and those "who died before they could tell us their stories." The Dues categorize the dedicatees, now deceased, into four groups, with their names presented in clear columns that emphasize the length of the lists and collaborative nature of the memoir, and by extension, the movement. The authors describe fellow activists as "warriors" and "foot soldiers," who fight domestically for equal rights. The Dues present their labor as a service to the country, that is, as she outlines, often unrecognized. Underneath the listed names is a reminder of the untold stories from unnamed storytellers of the movement, and encouragement from readers to "ask" about these stories so that this history is not lost. It is striking, and perhaps intentional on Stephens Due's part, that the list of storytellers "who died before they could tell us their stories" far exceeds those who the Dues were able to consult while constructing the memoir. This visual reminder of how many activists have died before their stories were preserved symbolizes the urgent need to document Civil Rights stories from a diverse pool of storytellers.

Remapping Place: South Florida in the Movement

The Dues' imperative to tell their own stories in concert with others' offers insight into the shifting cultural terrain of South Florida during the latter half of the twentieth century.[10] Despite the shifts in South Florida's demographic as a result of political unrest in and beyond the Caribbean, the Dues' memoir suggests that massive influxes expanded categories of whiteness and blackness in the city; they did not alter fundamental hierarchies that privilege lighter-complected people, regardless of citizenship status. The Dues contend with the erasure of both anti-Blackness and Black resistance in South Florida and represent the spatial stakes of this erasure by re-authoring South Florida as a stronghold within the Civil Rights Movement, situating the region within Afro-Caribbean exoduses, and contesting the paradisal reputation of the region through their focus on residential and commercial segregation, police brutality, and the historical erasure of Black contributions to Miami history. The Dues address what Angela Ards describes as "geographies, that is how place and history contextualize ideas" in our engagement with Black women's intellectual histories.[11]

The Dues contend with Florida's exclusion from Civil Rights discourse by depicting Miami as an epicenter for training and a testing ground for sit-ins.[12] Patricia Stephens Due situates Overtown, Miami, particularly, as the origin site of her career as an organizer and strategist and a point of departure for her critical work to desegregate Florida. There, she attends a CORE training, the Miami Interracial Action Institute, in 1959 with her sister, Priscilla Stephens, and compares the training to an "Army boot camp" where she "receive[d] instruction . . . [on] the Gandhian principles of nonviolent protest" with the expectation that she would subsequently "be sent into Miami's community for real-life desegregation efforts" (42). Stephens Due echoes her comparison of Civil Rights activists to soldiers and emphasizes the practical application of the skills she hones during this training on Miami's cultural terrain. Stephens Due suggests that the stakes exceed the geopolitical boundaries of Miami and draws on "the tactics [she had] learned in Miami" in Tallahassee during her time at FAMU to teach "potential sit-in volunteers about how to react in the face of taunts or violence that might ensue in the next sit-in" (48). Her iteration suggests that her training in Overtown initiates and enables the spread of nonviolent methods statewide.

Stephens Due's descriptions of Overtown provide a literary archive of systemic divestment in the neighborhood and subjection of Black people, and its simultaneous role as a site of Black life and community-building. As she asserts, "Overtown had its own tempo and rhythm back then, and I was excited to be part of it" (35). She goes on to describe her interpretation of what segregation enabled in the neighborhood:

> Because of segregation, Overtown . . . [provided] a full spectrum of Negro life; educated and uneducated, professional class and working class, well-to-do and struggling. They all had their skin color and discrimination in common, and they lived side by side. Overtown also boasted several renowned Negro-owned hotels, where celebrities like Billie Holiday and Dizzy Gillespie stayed . . . because they were not permitted to live in the segregated hotels in Miami Beach, . . . But Overtown benefitted from segregation because that was the place to be in black Miami. (35)

Figure 1. CORE members during a sit-in at Woolworth's lunch counter in Tallahassee. Patricia Stephens Due is the second person from the camera, wearing dark glasses. Reproduced with permission from the State Archives of Florida.

Stephens Due suggests that the forced proximal relationality of a Black neighborhood enabled community building in Overtown. She refers to an interview with fellow organizer, Benjamin Cowins, to further her point about what she perceives as the benefits of Black neighborhoods in that they potentially spare inhabitants the indignity and violence of encounters with white people. Cowins had similarly moved from Miami to Tallahassee, and states that "in Miami . . . he had everything he needed at his fingertips: a movie theater, a shopping center, everything. There was no need to venture into white neighborhoods to be subjected to the insult of a WHITE ONLY sign." He asserts that in Miami, "he'd been very sheltered" and concludes "that Tallahassee was different . . . Negroes had to patronize the white downtown area because Frenchtown, the hub of Negro life in Tallahassee, did not offer nearly the same range of goods and services" (132). In his comparative cartography of Miami and Tallahassee, Cowins suggests that venturing into white spaces rendered Black people particularly vulnerable. The comparison to Tallahassee's sparse offerings for Black people casts a positive light on Overtown and the life that was possible there for Black inhabitants.

While the daily experience of frequent proximity to Black people and availability of resources should not be overlooked, Stephens Due's description of the benefits of segregation as well as her incorporation of Cowins' reflections rely on nostalgia, which Houston Baker describes as "a purposive construction of the past filled with golden virtues, golden men, and sterling events," which he holds as antithetical to "critical memory" that "renders hard ethical evaluations of the past that it never defines as well passed."[13] The representation of the benefits of segregation especially overlooks Overtown's inception as a repository for exploited Black laborers who were restricted in their ability to occupy space in the region they were developing. As Chanelle Rose writes of the development of present-day Overtown: "The Flagler administration purchased a tract of land on the west side of the railroad tracks, which housed the early southern blacks who came as laborers to work on the Florida East Coast railroad."[14] Stephens Due emphasizes Overtown's popularity and class diversity; however, her celebration of Overtown belies its history of horrific, congested living conditions of the area and the historical class tensions in the neighborhood that ultimately facilitated the displacement of its poorer inhabitants during the 1930s and 40s. Chanelle Rose pinpoints the position papers written by Richard Toomey, Miami's first Black lawyer, as a reflection of class tension in Overtown, citing them as evidence of middle-class Black people's leverage of political power over impoverished Black Overtownians, or "Towners." Toomey, writing on behalf of other Black business leaders in 1933, criticized the deplorable living conditions in Miami, and implored government officials to remove low-income families so "wealthier black families and their businesses could continue to thrive near downtown" (Stuart 193). Rather than advocate for the allocation of resources to assist lower-income families with skill development, and job placement, Toomey endorses the capitalist project of displacing people to promote business.

Stephens Due's description of the Sir John Hotel, read alongside its history, reputation, and significantly, its proprietorship, emblematize the precarity of Black spaces within white supremacist social/spatial formations. The Sir John, the site of the Miami Interracial Institute, was formerly known as the Lord Calvert hotel, described in *JET* magazine as an "all Negro Hotel," and was often where Black celebrities stayed after performing for white venues that exploited Black arts while rejecting Black performers in living quarters.[15] Notably, however, though open to Black folks and advertised as "all Negro," the hotel was built as the Lord Calvert Hotel by Ben Danbaum and managed by his son-in-law, Sam Rabin, between 1953 and 1963; both men were white.[16] The hotel is an example of white property owners as benefactors of the racial practices that establish Black spaces. Describing the Sir John, Stephens Due merges her recollections of the past with an examination of the present:

> The workshop was held at Overtown's Sir John Hotel (now long gone, like so much in Overtown) which had nicknamed itself "Resort of the Stars" and was best known for its luxuries: a saltwater pool, barber shop, beauty parlor, health center, and shopping center. (39)

Stephens Due's parenthetical phrase highlights the decline of Overtown; by describing the luxurious hotel and its disappearance, she suggests that Towners now have limited access to the world-class amenities, implicitly signaling the devaluation of Black life, and more precisely, Black people's pleasure in the wake of the neighborhood's deterioration.

Today, the corner of NW 3rd Avenue and 6th Street in Overtown that was once the home of the Sir John Hotel offers a post office, parking garage, and a view of a leg of the I-95, the project that destroyed the neighborhood. Recapping the devastating impact of interstate construction in Miami, N.D.B. Connolly writes: "When interstate 95 opened its southernmost leg in 1968, the highway had caused the direct expulsion of eighty-five hundred households from Miami's Central Negro District and encouraged the flight of thousands more" (282). Connolly identifies both governmental disregard for Black life and, more maliciously, intentional dismantlement of Black communities in plans for the interstate's construction, noting: "every proposal included some version of interstate 95 connecting to one or two east-west expressways running right through the Central Negro District" (214). The targeted onslaughts against Black communities, themselves a product of white supremacist spatial organization that dictated where Black folks could live, evince the stakes of Stephens Due undertaking her training in Overtown; the neighborhood is an absent presence given her overview of its deterioration.

Elsewhere Stephens Due acknowledges Overtown's precarity through her provision of historical context of the neighborhood to situate her experiences more holistically: "In the 1960s, Overtown was a thriving Negro community. (Despite the black community's recent efforts at improvement, such as the renovation of the historical Lyric Theater, and other proposed changes, Overtown today is one of the poorest areas in Miami-Dade County" (35). Stephens Due's parenthetically shifts time, a microcosmic example of the memoir's structure that inextricably links past and present.

Her temporal transition illustrates Overtown's boom and swift decline after state-sanctioned urban renewal, slum clearance, and the related construction of interstate highways through the neighborhood.[17]

Stephens Due's description of the Lyric Theater and the now-completed renovations to the building, is emblematic of contemporary efforts to preserve Miami's Black history in the wake of Overtown's systematic destruction. The theater, built in 1913, played a central role in Black Miami social life, and "anchored the district known as 'Little Broadway,' an area alive with hotels, restaurants, and nightclubs frequented by black and white tourists and residents."[18] City boosters described the theater as "probably the most beautiful and costly playhouse owned by (Colored) people in all the Southland."[19] The theater operated as a movie and vaudeville theater before closing during the deterioration of Overtown.

During the 2010s, the theater was renovated, reflecting efforts to preserve Miami's Black history, however, it stands in stark contrast to the dilapidated buildings both residential and commercial, that surround it. The contrast between the renovated theater and the state of Overtown more broadly maps a notable investment in Black history as detached from Black people's daily lived experiences in the neighborhood.[20] The Black Archives History and Research Foundation of South Florida, Inc., a non-profit organization started by Dr. Dorothy Jenkins Field, acquired the theater in 1989 and gradually undertook its rehabilitation; Lyric Theater officially reopened in February 2014, and now houses the Black Archives of South Florida Collection. As important as the Theater and Archive are to the preservation of Black histories and accomplishments, it is much easier to preserve and restore a building and artifacts rather than systemically invest in protecting Black lives, wealth, and land/spatial access.

Stephens Due's oeuvre and personal archive reveals a general preoccupation with both the material realities of Black people and communities in South Florida, and the region's reputation as a winter playground and informal capital of the circum-Caribbean. Stephens Due saved the welcome newsletter from the Sir John Hotel; her family donated her papers to the Florida State Archives in Tallahassee after her death in early 2012. The image welcomes CORE members, and features a stylized outline of a head, half black, and half white, to represent the harmonious coexistence of Black and white people and their collaborative work in fulfillment of racial justice. The stylized head outline is set to a backdrop of a leisurely beach scene, highlighting the paradoxical coexistence of Miami's beach reputation with Black oppression, a tension I will examine in further detail shortly.

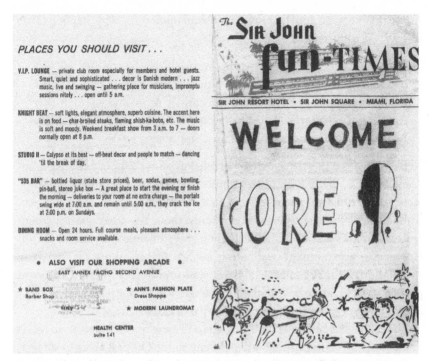

Figure 2. The welcome letter from the Sir John Hotel to CORE, includes a beach image and recommendations of things to do in South Florida. Reproduced with permission from the State Archives of Florida.

Miami's cultural terrain and its place within the circum-Caribbean rendered the city an imperative site to examine and test emerging racial and ethnic hierarchies. CORE's field secretary, Gordon Carey, identified the need for the organizations sustained presence in the city, asserting, "Miami is a city of changing racial practices where there is no lack of potential action projects."[21] Miami's potential leads to the organization of the training Stephens Due attended with her sister, and informs her utilization and experience of CORE strategies. In particular, she narrates an instance of lunch-counter testing at an unspecified Royal Castle wherein Stephens Due's racial ambiguity and South Florida's fluid cultural topography of the city are thrown into relief.[22] She writes:

> When I sat at the counter and asked for food with a group of several Negroes, the manager looked at us closely ... I noticed that the manager looked nervous, with his jaw tight, but to my surprise, he actually took my order and served me a hamburger. None of the other Negroes were served. (42–43)

Another observing activist provides an explanation for why Stephens Due was served while others were not:

> After they left, a white guy got up and went to the counter. He was just red with fury, and he said, "Why did you serve her?" And the manager kind of gently pushed the cashier aside and said, *"If they pay taxes, I can't serve them—, but if they come in and speak Spanish, I have to serve them by law."* (43; my emphasis)

Stephens Due's experience reveals a collision of overlapping cultural phenomena. First, the manager's assumption and rationalization of legal protections in violating social norms that prohibited Black consumerism, while inviting Spanish-speakers (implicitly, though not necessarily, recent émigrés) marks a shift in formal policy and informal practice as Miami emerged as a prominent destination for Spanish-speaking émigrés. The speculation of the organizers' taxpayer status reinforces Miami's historical position as a vacation spot that encouraged local business owners to challenge, however tenuously and temporarily, the color line.

The manager's rationale as presented to the angry, white patron suggests that even in an economy that is dependent on the Other it seeks to subject, dark-complected Black Americans occupy the lowest social standing and the manager denies service because they are tax-paying citizens. Stephens Due expresses befuddlement at this explanation:

> Now I had spoken nothing but my usual Southern accent—and I certainly hadn't said a single word in Spanish—but I was wearing large hoop earrings and had long hair and olive-colored skin, so the manager had apparently decided to pretend he thought I was Hispanic rather than an American Negro. He then had an excuse to treat me like a human being. (43)

As Stephens Due recalls the manager closely examining the group in the excerpt above, her later reflections on her appearance suggest that he was identifying the lightest-complected individual to serve. From what Stephens Due describes of the interaction, including the manager's visible anxiety, it is difficult to speculate what, precisely he was weighing—was he trying to avoid and extinguish the precise drama sit-ins are meant to incite? Was he offering a compromise between the white patrons and the Black organizers by serving Due, who he perceived as landing somewhere in the middle?

In this context, service for Black people was contingent on their proxim-

ity to whiteness; Stephens Due thus illustrates her own privilege founded
on her complexion. She identifies and reinscribes stereotypes of "Hispanic,"
or Latinx women, and does so to gesture toward a racial, or more accu-
rately, colorist or complexion-based and nationalistic hierarchy that privileges lighter skin tones and ideas of a potentially temporary visitor from
"somewhere else."[23] Both the manager's assumptions and Stephens Due's
stereotypes of lighter-skinned Latinx people indexes misconceptions of
"Hispanic" as lighter complected, thus belying the racial diversity of Hispanic and/or Latinx people. Stephens Due also reveals other assumptions
about Latinx people through her emphasis on her citizenship as an "American Negro." Implicitly, this contrast reveals Stephens Due's association of
"Hispanic" with foreign-born, and bolsters Stephens Due's attention to a
hierarchy wherein darker-complected people are disproportionately oppressed.

What is perhaps most notable about this exchange goes unmentioned
by Stephens Due: the likelihood that the manager may have been responding in part to the recent surge of Cuban immigration following Castro's
consolidation of power in February of the same year (1959), and the subsequent exponential expansion of Cuban population and influence in South
Florida. Castro's self-declared position of prime minister after Fulgencio
Batista's overthrow triggered a mass exodus from Cuba to the U.S., especially Miami, from 1959 to approximately 1963. These émigrés were prominently called "Golden Exiles," a moniker reflective of the class, racial, and
political leanings of the mostly white, upper-middle-class professionals
who fled Cuba in response to Castro's direct challenge to capitalism and
white supremacy.[24]

Stephens Due maintains her criticism and rejection of Miami's paradisal
reputation. While taking part in an April demonstration at the 1964 World's
Fair in New York:

> Our voter registration workers were suffering daily harassment and
> intimidation, but the governor of Florida, C. Farris Bryant was plan-
> ning to tout Florida as a "paradise" at the World's Fair, hoping to drum
> up tourism. *Paradise?* Florida might have been a paradise to whites
> on vacation, but it was hell to the Negroes who lived there. (226)[25]

Juxtaposing Black and white people, Stephens Due explicitly pinpoints the
state's paradisal reputation, an integral image to fulfill the state-wide reliance on tourism, especially in Miami. Staging a protest at a world fair is
emblematic of her efforts to take the Civil Rights Movement in Florida to

a broader scale—in many ways, given Miami's characterization as a global city, Stephens Due's work was always implicated socioeconomic and political shifts in the global South.

In other chapters, Tananarive Due suggests that Cuban in-migration to South Florida contributes to the overall volatility of South Florida and the compounding experiences of anti-Blackness, especially as it relates to the notorious murder of Arthur McDuffie, a Black man, by Officers Ira Diggs, Michael Watts, William Hanlon, and Alex Marrero. Due devotes nearly an entire chapter to Arthur McDuffie's murder, describing his death as a formative event in her life, and to "all of the black people in Dade County . . . [and] everywhere" (84). Due presents the impact of Arthur McDuffie's murder in expanding, concentric circles, beginning with herself and then refracting outward to include Black people everywhere. She describes the highly publicized act of state violence as an end to her childhood innocence, writing:

> I was fourteen years old . . . at the precise moment my childhood ended. It was May 17, 1980, and the local television station began scrolling a silent announcement across the bottom of the screen "AFTER DELIBERATING FOR LESS THAN THREE HOURS, A TAMPA JURY . . ." (83)[26]

By introducing the acquittal of the officers first, before delving into the circumstances of McDuffie's death, she encourages primary attention to the failures of the criminal justice system to prosecute officers of the law.

In her detailed, painstaking, and painful description of Due writes McDuffie's death in a longer legacy of anti-Black police violence in the U.S. South. She implicitly writes Miami, a city often held apart from the Deep South, into a region disproportionately characterized as inhospitable and unsafe for Black people:

> The thirty-three-year-old insurance executive had been beaten to death by Dade County police after he had led them on an eight-minute high-speed chase on his motorcycle. His beating was so severe, his skull had been cracked in half, from front to back . . . Realizing they'd killed McDuffie, police had tried to cover up the crime by bashing the motorcycle with "Kel-lites," heavy police-issue iron flashlights, to make it appear that it had crashed. Officially his death had been called an accident: He'd cracked his head open after flying off his

motorcycle, police lied, just as they had for generations from Mississippi swamps to Florida back roads. Such lies have a long history. (83)

Due's experience as a reporter is evident in her outline of the gruesome circumstances of McDuffie's death, including the destruction of his body, and the deceitful efforts of the police officers to disguise their crimes.

Her description of the officers elucidates Miami's cultural shift during the latter half of the twentieth century. She writes "Arthur McDuffie was black. The four police officers on trial were not" (83). Rather than specify the racial identities of the officers, she oppositionally defines them against McDuffie's clear labelling, highlighting the perceived immovable racial, economic, and social position of being Black as opposed to the ambiguous quality of unnamed whiteness, an expanding category given Miami's recent cultural shifts that often aligns white Cubanidad with Anglo whiteness. The ambiguity of Due's gesture mirrors controversy surrounding one of the officers, Alex Marrero, a white-Cuban American, who in local media, was frequently labeled as white, or "Anglo." The other officers ultimately testified against Marrero—he was charged with second-degree murder (as opposed to manslaughter and assault as was the case for the other officers).

Antonio Lopez offers a succinct criticism of reporters' hesitation to expound on Marrero's Cuban background:

> Marrero's Cuban American whiteness was aligned with the Anglo whiteness of his fellow officers in a physical expression of state sponsored, white-supremacist violence; and that over and over in the historical record, this Anglo-Latino alignment is elided, reappearing simply as "white." Merely to cite "four white cops" in the greater narrative of Miami around 1979 is to waste the specific, troubling Cuban American value of that time. (157)

Lopez pinpoints the alignment of white Cubans in Miami with white supremacy in the U.S. and gestures toward the shifting racial order in South Florida. The McDuffie case became emblematic of the asymmetrical treatment, experiences, and distribution of resources between recent white émigrés and Black Americans, even as Marrero's supporters cited the harsher charges against Marrero as indication of anti-Cuban sentiment. Lopez describes the support of Marrero and allegations of anti-Cuban discrimination as "a mockery of minority-rights discourse" that signaled an unwillingness to acknowledge his whiteness, and, going further, his alignment with the white supremacist state via his position as a police officer. South Florida's police departments have historically surveilled, attacked, and targeted Black communities, allegedly "protecting" the boundaries of white neighborhoods (and preserving property values) from the perceived threat of Black encroachment.

More recently, Monika Gosin has analyzed interethnic struggles in Miami, identifying the white supremacist logic of scarcity as the foundation of conflicts between, for example, Cuban Americans and Black Americans. A central conceit of Gosin's work identifies and contributes to investigations of "Cuban American whiteness, or 'off whiteness'—its hegemony and its precariousness" within a racial logic that constructs and protects whiteness to the exclusion and derision of the Other (14). She explains that while white Cubans benefited from the largely unchanged white supremacist systems in Miami (and the U.S. more broadly), their precarity was evident in how "local Anglos began to disparage Cubans in the local media, demonstrated they did not want to live with them by moving away from the area, and characterized them as foreign invaders" (53).

The McDuffie-Marrero example challenges notions of precarity—when Gosin discusses the McDuffie case, she makes brief mention of the lone Cuban police officer without attending to his whiteness, Cubanness, eventual acquittal, and later prosecution for the separate, and unrelated charge of conspiracy to distribute cocaine and to commit bribery. In its extremity, Marrero's death-dealing interaction with McDuffie demonstrates that white people, regardless of nationality, language, and other cultural affiliations are benefactors of whiteness, even if they are not formal signatories of the racial contract that declares and maintains white supremacy. What Charles Mills has called racial contracts, or what might best be understood as tacit agreements to construct practices and policies that create and protect whiteness, are especially pertinent in analyses of Marrero, Arthur McDuffie, and the culturally fraught backdrop of McDuffie's murder and the trial of the officers who (according to the ruling, did not) kill(ed) him.

Due implicitly addresses this cultural collision while contextualizing the McDuffie case, situating it as a challenge to Miami's popular image. She writes, after describing the circumstances of McDuffie's death: "Meanwhile, more and more Cubans were welcomed when they came to make Miami their home—thousands upon thousands in the Mariel Boatlift—while Haitians were still sent away. Arthur McDuffie was still dead. His killers were still free" (88). The overlapping events—the Mariel Boatlift can be loosely bracketed between April and October of 1980, while the trial of the officers charged in connection with McDuffie's death took place between February and April of 1980, leading to the destructive riots between May 17 and May 20, 1980—indicate that even as Miami's population was shifting in the wake of permitted immigration, the white supremacist structure remained largely unchanged. To add insult to the rage expressed at McDuffie's death, Cuban Americans "along with Anglo whites, were among those to receive "most of the federal money to deal with the riot," another way Cuban Americans benefitted from the unjust conditions of Black Americans in Miami.[27]

Cuban exoduses, as well as emigration from other Caribbean countries, are often cited as transforming Miami into a diverse mecca, even as these histories bely the Black foundations of the region I discuss in the manuscript's introduction. Due asserts that cultural shifts and political assimilation of white émigrés in Miami had a continuous, direct impact on the Due family. She recalls that her father, attorney John Due, received a layoff notice in 1997, ending his tenure as the director of the Office of Black Affairs in Miami-Dade County. Even though John Due had committed nearly twenty-five years of service to local government (seven years in the Office of Black Affairs, seventeen years as program officer of the Community Relations Board of Miami-Dade County), John Due "was among 158 people who received pink slips. No new job had been offered to him. Two years before retirement, it seemed, my father was being put out to pasture" (316). Due recalls her father's contributions to the city, contrasting this with his dismissive treatment, writing "he'd been on the streets trying to ease the lives of people in the county since I could remember, braving riots, frustration, and bureaucracy . . . he'd spent twenty-five years trying to keep a lid on such an emotionally volatile place" (316). Her concurrent mention of riots (specifically the destructive riots between May 17 and May 20, 1980 in response to the acquittal of the police officers who murdered Arthur McDuffie) and bureaucracy is striking, and traces white supremacy's effects on intentionally disruptive outcries and mundane bureaucracy.

The cuts were made at the behest of contemporary white Cuban American mayor Alex Penelas, whose power Due takes to represent the assimilative power white Cubans exercise in South Florida. Due notes that "newer voices from different communities were vying for recognition" (316). While the emergence of new voices might exemplify inclusive civic engagement, Due suggests that these voices overrode the input of Black Americans. In her telling, Due highlights how immigrant influx into Miami, and the corresponding diversification of Miami comes at the expense of Black

Americans, especially those employed by local government. Describing the members of these new communities, Due asserts that some

> had not lived in Miami during the 1980 riots and had no memory of a time some years earlier, when black people had to carry passes to work on Miami Beach—or, like my father, were constantly followed by police when they crossed the causeway. Miami is a city of newcomers who bring memories of their histories from other places, which gives the region both its amazing vitality and a kind of collective community amnesia. (316)[28]

Due recaps the history of Black oppression in Miami, situating her father's firing within this history. She asserts that the influx of people, cultures, and histories that the city's tourism boosters often celebrate comes at the expense of the city's Black communities, usually through the forgetting and erasure of their experiences, contributions, and histories. Indeed, although historian Marvin Dunn has devoted his career to researching Black Miami, only recently have multiple scholars turned their attention to the disproportionately high rates of poverty, unemployment, and limited access to health care experienced by Miami's Black communities without couching these examinations in broader assertions of Miami's cultural diversity.[29]

John Due's firing triggers a flood of support from Miami's Black community, demonstrated during a community meeting at the Joseph Caleb Center in Liberty City. The center is named after Black union labor leader, Joseph Caleb, who is known for spearheading projects that nearly quadrupled wages for union members between 1963 and 1972.[30] The center is thus a fitting location for a meeting to protest the widespread job cuts within Miami-Dade's government. With the mayor in attendance, attention turned specifically to the loss of John Due's position. While Mayor Penelas declares that the "meeting should not become about particular people"— betraying his intention to dehumanize the recently unemployed into a generalized mass—Bishop Victor T. Curry, pastor of the Newbirth Baptist Church in Opa-Locka, Miami (a Black majority neighborhood) interrupts, declaring:

> Mr. Mayor, I think you miss the point of why it's personalized . . . see, this is part of the problem with many of our Hispanic brothers and sisters. You all don't know the history. You all don't know the history of the black community. You don't know and you don't care . . . that's

what many of our wonderful Cuban brothers and sisters are missing. You have no respect. You've got to respect us, Mr. Mayor . . . People are upset because we're not being respected *as a people.* (321)

Bishop Curry, protecting himself with complimentary language, reiterates Due's description of collective community amnesia, criticizing Latinx ignorance to these histories and conflating this ignorance with disrespect— ignorance is a generous reading given how white Cubans benefited and upheld white supremacy. He pinpoints Cuban ignorance, once again highlighting the privileged position of Cubans, especially white Cubans, in relation to Black Americans. While Curry does not explicitly accuse Penelas and other Cuban officials of anti-Blackness, his appeal for John Due highlights the erasure of Black history in Miami, and the power differential between white Latinxs and Black Miamians that empowers the former group to further disenfranchise the latter. About a week after the forum, and the community's impassioned defense, John Due is given a new job with Miami-Dade County (Due 322).

The Dues couple their attention to Cuban newcomers and the power they can exercise against Black community members with examinations of and contributions to Haitian emigration. They explicitly challenge the diversity-via-immigration logic and dispute Miami's reputation as a hospitable location for Caribbean immigrants by pinpointing anti-Blackness in immigration policy and its implication for Haitian émigrés to Miami. Due opens her examination of Haiti-U.S. politics with a chant: "hey, U.S.A.— *Stop supporting Duvalier!* Hey, hey, U.S.A. . . . " She describes the scene of the protest, illustrating that federal spaces in Miami metonymically reference international geopolitics and are an appropriate site of their demonstration of transnational Afro-solidarity. She writes:

It was the 1970s, and my sisters and I walked in a purposeful circle with a handful of other protesters with hand-written placards in front of the Dade County federal building in Miami, chanting loudly in opposition to U.S.-backed Haitian dictator Jean Claude Duvalier . . . It was just another day in the Due family. (56)

The "purposeful" movements illuminate the normalization of Black resistance in the Due family, and a capacious inclusion of Black émigrés in their politic. Within the context of *Freedom in the Family*'s memoirization of the fight for Civil Rights, situating advocacy for Haitian émigrés as a continuation of her mother's work rather than a disruption functions to expand the traditional parameters of the Civil Rights Movement, temporally, demographically, and geographically.

Due's description further situates Haitian emigration within a broader understanding of anti-Blackness both globally and transnationally:

> Our parents explained to us that Haiti was a very poor country, that most of its inhabitants were black, and that the United States government discriminated against Haitian refugees who tried to come here for a better life while refugees from Cuba were welcomed . . . Worse, we were told, the United States was supporting a terrible Haitian dictator names Jean-Claude Duvalier, who was corrupt and violent. That was all we needed to hear. (56)

Due emphasizes the stakes of Miami as a global city for Black émigrés. Due's focus on the racial composition in Haiti highlights the discriminatory creation and enforcement of the U.S.'s immigration policies. Due indirectly cites the Cuban Adjustment Act that allowed Cuban émigrés easier access to asylum processes on account of the U.S.'s anti-Communist platform, and corresponding belief that all Cuban exiles/refugees were necessarily fleeing political persecution. Immigration and Naturalization Services (INS) officials often categorized Haitian émigrés as economic refugees, which barred or severely restricted their access to asylum processes.[31] The U.S.'s support of Duvalier (which waned during President Reagan's administration) justified the almost unanimous repatriation of Haitian exiles/refugees; to accept and accommodate Haitian refugees would implicitly condemn Duvalier's regime.[32] I devote more sustained attention to discriminatory treatment of Haitians and their resulting experiences as a refutation of Miami's melting pot myth in the following chapter.

Tananarive Due describes her childhood inheritance of her mother's concerns for Black Civil Rights even as her home life presented challenges, the majority of which were consequences of residential segregation and its effects on the Due's efforts to build equity. She writes that while her parents had not "set out on purpose to raise us in a nearly all-white setting . . . that was the end result." She goes on to outline the value of property ownership to Black families to whom "it was denied for so long," before explaining the challenges in finding homes for sale in mostly Black neighborhoods." She concludes, "instead, they took their home search to suburbia, and we ended up in the land of whites" (20). The Dues end up in the contemporary Cutler Bay area.[33]

Due's explication elucidates the rigid segregation of Miami's neighborhoods, contrasting Black neighborhoods to the implicitly vast land of whites. Given the neighborhood delineations and determined property ownership by Black inhabitants, the Dues undertake a coerced form of integration by buying a house in a predominantly white neighborhood.

Due's experiences in the neighborhood harken back to and reaffirm her mother's outline of the protections and daily experience of majority-Black neighborhoods, despite the less-visible exercise of white domination within those spaces. In her description, Due implicitly writes Miami into legacies associated with staunch anti-Black violence in the U.S. South. Writing about her reception in white suburbia, Due explains:

> We did not feel welcome there. My parents shielded us from the direct threats some of our neighbors made—like one in particular who dumped his garbage in our backyard and vowed to shoot me or my sisters if he saw us walking on his grass . . . I was also subjected to the pain of the word "nigger," for which I never had a comeback. That was a word that had been used by slaveholders and murderous mobs. "Nigger" was not a word I took lightly. (21)

The property that is so highly sought by the Due family, and by Black families yearning for economic stability via real estate acquisition, becomes the most vulnerable front in the "land of whites," and is treated with no more respect than a dumping ground. Due's focus on the use of anti-Black hate speech is particularly jarring to Due given the slur's perceived anachronism. By linking the term to slave holding and murderous mobs (likely recalling violence inflicted upon Black Americans by the Ku Klux Klan), Due suggests a temporal stalling in white Miami that undermines the progress implicit in Stephens Due's earlier descriptions of movement building in Black Miami.

Due's movements between white and Black Miami reify the manifestations of de facto segregation, and, as she suggests, contribute to her internalization of stereotypes of Black poverty. While traveling between Miami's neighborhoods, including Overtown and Liberty City, Due writes that she "noticed the stark contrast between those neighborhoods and the ones where my more affluent friends from the Horizon School lived. I saw black children playing barefoot in the street and it troubled me. 'Are all black people poor?' I asked my parents" (23). Her parents contextualize Due's observations, explaining that "because of discrimination there has always been more poverty in the black community. In fact, I remember my parents specifically taking me to black neighborhoods in disrepair to show me how many blacks live ('The *real* Miami,' my mother always called it), so I would know how fortunate we were" (23). Although the Dues introduce Tananarive to systemic anti-Blackness and its consequences, they engage in an unsettling voyeurism, wherein impoverished Black people become a spectacle that reinforces the family's middle-class positionality and reincribes the class tension that was exploited by wealthy Black business and property owners to the detriment of impoverished Black communities. Beyond a lesson to practice gratitude for middle-class status, Stephens Due's description of the real Miami highlights the tension between Miami's paradisal, pseudo-Caribbean reputation and the reality of poverty that disproportionately impacts Black Miamians.

Due also describes the internalization of Eurocentric/white beauty standards and presents it as inextricable from the geospatial politics of Black people in white neighborhoods.[34] She explains that she "hated driving into West Perrine . . . where some of the homes were unsettling to me in their shabbiness, to go to a beauty shop . . . where she cried out in pain, either from a sharp yank or, sometimes, a burn from [the hairdresser's] pressing comb" (22). She bemoans: "I couldn't stand having kinky hair" and describes her "hair envy" of white women's long, straight hair. She contrasts the shabbiness of the majority-Black neighborhood with the impossible-to-meet beauty standards of whiteness in which she is immersed in Cutler Bay.

The regular travels across racial lines to beauty shops provide a map of the spatialization of anti-Blackness in South Florida—Due suggests that these cartographies are thrown into relief during crises. In 1992, Hurricane Andrew wrought utter devastation on the southernmost parts of Miami-Dade County, especially Homestead, Cutler Ridge, and Cutler Bay. Due explains that the storm destroys everything, and "all that remained was splintered plywood, crumbling concrete, littered streets, billows of smoke, uprooted trees, twisted street signs, and the silent anguish of collective loss" (210). Due's list moves from the destruction of the material world into the abstract, disorienting grief of losing all indications of their former lives. Although Due suggests the loss is collective, the racial structures of South Florida society remain untouched and compound to render Black people more vulnerable to the impact of natural disasters:

The hurricane itself had already brought its own injustices. My parents and NAACP observers believed white neighborhoods like affluent Country Walk were receiving more attention than equally battered poor black areas in Goulds, Naranja, West Perrine, and Richmond Heights. It was already painfully clear to my parents while insurance claims could repair damage to their waterfront home, there were so many uninsured and under-insured poorer families—often *black* families—who would never fully recover. (214)

Stephens Due personifies the hurricane as it unveils pre-existing social injustices, including a Black cartography of post-Andrew Miami that traced the remnants of residential segregation. This segregation enabled (and enables) media outlets to ignore Black areas and the inhabitants who were permanently displaced by the storm. Due emphasizes her parents' vulnerability to the storm as Black people with waterfront property, but she also notes their class privilege as insured property owners that allowed them to rebuild and keep their home.

Tananarive Due's recollection of Hurricane Andrew reframes the Civil Rights Movement as an ongoing effort. She makes clear that the issues at hand for her mother during CORE testing and sit-ins continue into the 1990s and evolve to include the impacts of transnational anti-Blackness as they manifest in immigration policy and enforcement. In Due's telling, the knowledge of racial disparities galvanizes Patricia Stephens Due when the police shine a bright light into her home in the wake of Hurricane Andrew's devastation. The police had mistakenly traced a tip to the Due household and surrounded the remnants of the house, armed in riot gear. For Stephens Due, the police presence added threatening insult to calamitous injury:

> After all of the outrages suffered by blacks in . . . Dade County for so many years, this intrusion was the final outrage, the last indecency . . . All that fueled the anger and indignation my mother battered those police officers with at her front gate that night. Here, in the midst of this chaos, in a city with a history like Miami's, a pack of police would descend upon her home simply because of a vague coincidence. (214)

A culmination of the many years Stephens Due fought racial injustice in and beyond Miami, Due stresses the flagrancy of this violation of the family's home space by a "pack" of police, emphasizing the mob-like show of force, jarring even without the immediate backdrop of Andrew's devastation.[35]

Due's language also empowers her mother; although Stephens Due, relying on her training concerning interactions with police, approaches them with her hands raised, and keeps her hands visible to avoid any escalation of violence, she "batters" them with her words, reminding them of the history of Black disenfranchisement and state-sanctioned violence in Miami. Although the circumstances and time had changed, Stephens Due's reliance on Civil Rights training highlights perpetual threats to Black life in Miami.

The Temporality of Black Trauma

Threats against and consequential trauma experienced by Black people are foundational themes of *Freedom in the Family* that collapse time to metaphorize the permanence of anti-Blackness. The Dues detail both the physical and psychic harm they experience and carry in their minds and bodies because of their lifelong work as activists. Further, they outline the painful imperative of revisiting and documenting their traumas to combat their erasure and advocate for Black life.

Patricia Stephens Due's eyes are a literal and metaphorical symbol of both how the body keeps the score of state-sanctioned anti-Black violence and how South Florida's "newcomers" neglect the Black women's bodies and testimonies as evidence. After being shot in the face at point-blank range with a tear-gas canister during a demonstration in 1960, Stephens Due is plagued by a lifetime of light sensitivity and "she has to wear darkened glasses even in a movie theater" (55). Although Stephens Due's disabled body bears scars-as-evidence in the struggle for Black liberation, it is not "admissible" in the textbook about Florida history, as she notes at the outset of the memoir. The dismissal of her embodied experiences signals the devaluation of Black women's testimony, especially in recollections of the Civil Rights Movement. Stephens Due asserts that this devaluation cements her imperative for posterity through the written word, delivered through the memoir itself.

The Dues couple their concern for documenting for posterity with telling a collective story of the movement—this motivates what they call "The Gathering," capitalized throughout the text to emphasize its significance. Stephens Due, witnessing increased rates of illness and death among other movement leaders, declares to her daughter "it's time to have a civil rights reunion" (276). The Due family successfully contacts as many willing former Civil Rights activists as possible and hosting them at her home, where Due describes her experiences of racialized violence just twenty years

A Gathering...

John Due and Patricia Stephens Due are looking forward to hosting an informal get-together of foot soldiers in Florida's civil rights movement.

We will share a day of fellowship and remembrances while we get reacquainted.

Please bring any photographs, articles, music, or other items you would like to share.

We are looking forward to seeing you August 23.

"Florida's Foot Soldiers"
August 23, 1997
8 a.m. until--?

19620 Bel Aire Drive
Miami, Florida 33157
(305) 235-9205

Take the Turnpike (874) to Eureka Drive and turn left to get to South Dixie Hwy. (US1) Turn right (south) and drive a half-mile to Marlin Road. Turn left and cross bridge--first street after bridge is Bel Aire Drive--make left--house is first house on the left.

Please RSVP as soon as possible. Deadline: Aug. 10.

• Accommodations

Guests are responsible for their own accommodations. Group-rate rooms have been reserved at a nearby Budgetel Inn, but call the hotel as soon as possible to confirm with a credit card if you will be arriving after 6 p.m. on Friday, August 22.

Room rate: $44.95 per night (King-sized beds or double-bed rooms available.) Free continental breakfast. Call (305) 278-0001. Ask for rooms reserved for "Due Reunion." Hotel will provide directions.

Double rooms sleep up to four. If you would like to share a room, please let us know as soon as possible.

Figure 3. The invitation created by the Dues advertising "The Gathering." Reproduced with permission from the State Archives of Florida.

before, on August 23, 1997. The Gathering, as detailed by the invitation, was an "informal get-together of foot soldiers in Florida's civil rights movement," and helped the Dues in their composition of the memoir. The Dues encouraged those invited to bring "photographs, articles, music, or other items" to facilitate the communal remembrance of the movement.

While Stephens Due's beginning chapters introduce Miami as an integral site in the germination and dissemination of Civil Rights training and efforts, the concluding chapters set South Florida as a site of critical reflection, and corresponding exhaustion, of the work accomplished, the harm experienced, and the remaining work to be done. The Dues conducted interviews during The Gathering; many of the histories and recollections form the backbone of the memoir. As Tananarive Due recalls:

My mother envisioned a reunion where they could share the stories behind the stories: what had the personal price of their activism been? What did their children and grandchildren know about what they had done during the Civil Rights Movement? What did they think of present day race-relations? She wanted to follow through, even if it meant she and my father had to host it in their home. (277)

The questions that structured the interviews/oral histories conducted with The Gathering's attendees model the memoir's overarching themes and structure: recalling the past and using these reflections to analyze the present day. The second question is most striking as it suggests that these activists may not have told their family members about their involvement in the movement. Even with intimate familial ties, these stories are at risk of disappearing.

Attendees testified to their anxiety-inducing experience of watching family members demonstrate, physical and psychological violence, and realizing their work has not been memorialized, either through monuments or policies. Patricia Stephens Due encourages her mother, Lottie Sears Houston, to open The Gathering with her experience, reflecting her desire to have an elders' testimony introduce early memories of anti-Black oppression, and resistance. Although Houston did not participate in the Civil Rights demonstrations, she asserts that knowing about her daughters' involvement induced its own kind of trauma. Due, paraphrasing Houston's memories as presented at The Gathering, writes:

> Even all these years later, if her telephone rang late at night, she still felt a quickening of her heart, leftover anxiety from the era when a phone call at such an hour was likely to bring tragic news about her two daughters. All over the South, parents regularly received heartbreaking calls that their children had been jailed, beaten, killed, or that they'd simply vanished. (282)

Events that might otherwise be mundane rehash memories of state-sanctioned terrorism that physically affect Houston, even in 1997. Her description also highlights the widespread effects of the movement, and reactionary violence toward activists all over the South.[36] Houston does not specify the actors who may be beating, killing, or disappearing these freedom fighters and this vague referent highlights the various vulnerabilities for Civil Rights activists. While Houston discusses the murder and literal disappearance of Black and white activists in the South, Tananarive Due highlights the equally grave disappearance of stories when recalling her mother's urgency in planning the event:

> "Unsung heroes" is a term my mother uses often and was most of the reason she'd planned The Gathering in the first place. Telling and

retelling the stories of heroes, she must have reasoned, would help ensure that the next generations would not forget. I heard her fear echoed time and again that day. In fact, many of the activists said they could already see their fears coming to pass. (285)

The Dues depict The Gathering as an almost necessary trauma—picking at scabs so that future generations can know how past generations have bled. Others describe how residual trauma from their activism lingers. As Stephens Due surmises, "life was not kind to many of the people I knew from the Movement" (288). She recalls high rates of suicide, mental illness, and other ailments that disproportionately affect the movement's survivors. Tananarive Due, who attends The Gathering as an observer, notes that "just as her eyes were injured by tear gas in 1960, every single person my mother had invited to The Gathering had scars of their own, whether visible or not" (280). Due makes an important distinction between embodied and invisible traces of the violence of the Civil Rights Movement. While her mother's scars are visible, and shape how she views the world, the prevalence of invisible, emotional, and psychological injuries further exemplifies why many of these stories have been lost.

Due continues by noting that daily, mundane interactions and experiences revealed her parents' trauma-related paranoia:

Over the years, my sisters and I have seen the toll civil rights has had on our parents, too. To this day, both my father and mother have a distrust of the telephone. Important names and information like bank account numbers are never revealed on the phone, and during any given conversation my mother is likely to lapse into incomprehensible code . . . but then again, why shouldn't they be paranoid? Our family discovered that my mother and father each have FBI files 400 pages long, presumably from the civil rights era, when they could hear the clicking of wiretaps on their telephones. (279)

Due details the intense surveillance of her family, emphasizing how Black people, and their investments and efforts in fulfillment of full citizenship were viewed as antagonists to the white supremacist nation-state.[37] The discussion of residual trauma problematizes the selective and flat hero worship of Civil Rights activists—usually the deification of cisgender, heterosexual men. Instead, the testimony presented, and welcomed, at The Gathering focuses on the aftermath of the movement and trauma experienced by those who survived. Participants cry, shake, and hold each other:

Figure 4. A photograph taken of "The Gathering" attendees. *First row, left to right*: Miles McCray, Mrs. Athea Hayling, Doris Rutledge Hart, Patricia Stephens Due, Mrs. Lottie Hamilton Sears Houston, and Priscilla Stephens Kruize. *Second row, left to right*: Johnita Patricia Due, Jeff Greenup, Clarence Edwards, Ulysses Baety, John D. Due Jr., Dan Harmeling, Tananarive Priscilla Due, Mrs. Vivian Kelly, and Dr. Robert Hayling. Reproduced with permission from the State Archives of Florida.

Dr. Robert Hayling struggles to discuss "his severe beating at a Ku Klux Klan rally," and Priscilla Due, Patricia's sister, explains that the trauma of the movement drove her into exile, and she spent several years in Ghana to recover (282–283).

Although several people came to The Gathering, others refused to come, unwilling to relive the trauma of their experiences. As Due notes, "my mother has not been able to reach one woman on her list in several tries over the years . . . she wanted nothing to do with those memories" (278). This inclusion reflects one of many challenges to fulfilling the memoir's objective; the Dues must overcome a host of silences: the silencing of Black women, the silencing impact of diversity myths that do not attend to, or intentionally exclude anti-Blackness, and the traumatic silence of those who do not, and cannot, relive their trauma for the sake of historical records. The unnamed woman's refusal makes clear that the recollection of Black trauma is itself an induction of trauma, a harm the Dues willingly undertake in hopes, as they say in their introduction, of changing the present day.

Conclusion

Producing this chapter has been traumatic in its own ways; I have had to take long breaks after reading about the points of impact on Arthur McDuffie's body; I have had to put the memoir down when reading about frequent, violent Ku Klux Klan attacks; I have had to meditate after realizing that the version of Miami history, my hometown, that prominently features people who look like me has been intentionally elided. Most significantly, however, I have had to write, revisit, revise this chapter in an age of rampant, highly publicized police brutality, where I have had to avoid social media for fear of seeing another video of state-sanctioned murder, shared ad infinitum, and remind myself that Arthur McDuffie could have died the same way yesterday; we can see traces of Alex Marrero's white Cubanness in George Zimmerman's. If Patricia Stephens Due were still alive, she could have been blinded by tear gas today. And if that had happened, she still would have been on the front lines with Black Lives Matter (BLM) activists tomorrow. Though she might be disappointed with media coverage of the movement; even now, as during the peak of Stephens Due's Civil Rights activism, BLM's three women founders, Alicia Garza, Opal Tometi, and Patrisse Cullors, are seldom named in discussion of the group, suggesting an ongoing elision of Black women's contributions to social movements. Relatedly, young Black men murdered by police are more likely to receive mainstream attention as opposed to young Black women, who are disproportionately vulnerable to police violence compared to their white counterparts.[38]

The memoir invites consideration of the tragic cycles that are inevitable in a nation that has yet to name and reconcile its foundational anti-Blackness. When discussing McDuffie's death, and the corresponding acquittal of the four officers who killed him, Tananarive Due asserts:

> McDuffie doesn't *matter*, I remember thinking. White people don't think he *matters*. My mind could barely comprehend it . . . Yes, my parents were civil rights activists, and I'd been brought up on a steady diet of black history lessons. I'd known all too well that there was a time, *long ago*, when such trials were commonplace. Lynchings didn't matter. Beatings didn't matter. Rapes didn't matter . . . Black people didn't matter in the 1960s. But in 1980? In the world I live in? (85–86)

While she poses these questions rhetorically and expresses disbelief in the perpetual anti-Black violence she observes, her memoir centers these continuities, and even speaks to the contemporary cultural moment, long after the memoir's original publication. Her words eerily foreshadow BLM's platform, which works to ensure that Black lives matter, too. If we take seriously Sankofa and the need for the past to understand the present, we can see, indisputably, how *Freedom in the Family* exposes the devastating predictability of perpetual anti-Black violence.

The most notable takeaway for Due in The Gathering is how the project of equality and dismantling structures of Black oppression is unfinished. Due specifically highlights instances of police brutality:

> Just because today's world shakers and social pioneers aren't all carrying picket signs doesn't mean the struggle is over and we know this. We know that there are horrible discrepancies in school resources and test scores between black and white children. And in arrests and jail time. And in the imposition of the death penalty. And income. And AIDS statistics. We know that police in New York shot Amadou Diallo forty-one times, fueled by a raving fear of black men. There's plenty left to do. (355)

She lists each iteration, writing in short, choppy fragments that call attention to the weightiness of these issues. Due names systemic anti-Blackness: in schools, an issue exacerbated by the rise of private schools, in prisons, how the prison-industrial machine runs off Black and Brown people, made bodies in the eye of the criminal (in)justice system, in health care, where almost all diseases have higher mortality rates for people of color. Finally, with police brutality and the violent murder of unarmed Amadou Diallo in February of 1999. Diallo was reaching for his wallet after officers approached him outside of his apartment. An undocumented immigrant from Guinea, Diallo was likely looking for some form of identification to stop further questioning; Due's reference to Diallo further reiterates the memoir's attention to Afro-Diasporic solidarity and the vulnerabilities of Black émigrés. Like in the Arthur McDuffie case, a jury in Albany acquitted all four officers who killed Diallo.

I began this chapter during the summer of 2016, in the long aftermath of the murders of Trayvon Martin (2012) and Michael Brown (2014) and subsequent acquittal of George Zimmerman and Darren Wilson that once again made police brutality a topic of public discourse and spurred the creation of Black Lives Matter and the Movement for Black Lives. I had come home to Miami to conduct archival research, the fruits of which are reflected at moments in this chapter. While dining with my family in front of the TV, a local anchor briefly mentioned the recent murder of Philando Castile: On July 6, 2016, Officer Jeronimo Yanez pulled Castile over during a routine traffic stop. Castile informed Yanez that he was a licensed gun owner, and that the weapon was in the car. As Castile raised his hands, Officer Yanez shot into the vehicle, hitting Castile four times. Castile's four-year-old stepdaughter and girlfriend were in the car. He died twenty minutes later.

Moments after the brief news segment, my grandfather called. In a reflection of generational trauma akin to that which structures *Freedom in the Family*, he asked to speak to my father, who after a short conversation turned the phone to me to receive the same message: "stay safe. Do not leave the house unless you have to; the police are acting crazy." Had he seen a similar segment on his local six o'clock news? I don't know, but I know that he understood, having grown up in Virginia as a Black man, and raising Black children, that these men could have been my father, that the women killed by the state, Shelly Frey (2012), Tanisha Anderson (2014), Korryn Gaines (2016), could have been me or my sister.

My mother, a white Latina, nodded upon hearing this, but added, "Well, at least in Miami we're okay, don't you think? Since there's a little more diversity?" My father scoffed; I reminded her of the McDuffie case, and how the diversification of Miami had not saved him, that some argued that it had helped kill him. The following day, news broke of a police-involved shooting in North Miami. On July 18, 2016, Charles Kinsey, a Black mental health therapist, was consulting his patient, who had wandered away from a group home when police approached the pair. Without explanation, while Kinsey laid on the ground with his arms up, Officer Johnathan Aledda, a Latino man, shot him in the leg. Officers handcuffed Kinsey, allowing him to bleed on the asphalt for twenty minutes before requesting medical services. Kinsey survived and is suing the police department.

Kinsey's case rehashes critical questions about how interethnic tensions in Miami disproportionately harm Black Miamians. Indeed, Patricia Stephens Due's experience of being served as a perceived Latina, the McDuffie case, along with Kinsey's recent experience, further contextualizes the Black American opposition to immigration Maria Cristina Garcia outlines in her work and illustrates why Miami's informal title as an immigrant city, or the Capital of the Caribbean, might not be embraced universally. I undertake intra-immigrant group analyses in the forthcoming chapters, treating anti-Blackness as foundational to each analysis. Such examination, I think, will reveal the necessity of advocacy for the preservation of

Black space, and Black life, and work to create economic opportunities for historically disenfranchised Black communities. As I told my mother, diversity myths, especially the idea of an immigrant nation, will not, and do not protect vulnerable populations from state-sanctioned violence. Only rigorous, intersectional policy and efforts will change the reality of so many Black Americans. May the work, and movement, continue.

2

The Anti-Haitian Hydra

Remapping Haitian Spaces in Miami

Prevalent anti-Black and anti-Haitian sentiments and stereotypes shape perceptions and receptions of Haitians in South Florida, the United States, and across the world. Haiti's inception as a Black sovereign nation was, as Michel-Rolph Trouillot writes, unthinkable, because "it challenged the very framework within which proponents and opponents had examined race, colonialism, and slavery in the Americas."[1] White supremacist logic required casting Haitian resistance and independence as an impossibility to uphold the tenuous systems that constructed personhood and its rights, entitlements, and protections around white men.

Haiti, and Haitian people, have been punished for centuries for manifesting the impossible and casting doubt on the perceived permanence of white domination and control through Black rebellion. Evident in the dehumanization of Haitian people, the reverberations of Haiti's history provide invaluable insight into the nation's inception, its Diasporas, and contemporary positionality, as well as the formative role anti-Blackness has played in the construction of our world.[2] The experiences of Haitians and Haitian Americans in South Florida, the site of the largest diasporic Haitian population, index the compounding reverberations of this haunting, looming large in the (mis)treatment of émigrés across generations, and socioeconomic and political strata.[3] Repatriation, detention, high rates of unemployment, health crises, and gentrification have structured many experiences and representations of Haitianness in the U.S., and, as others have argued, this treatment is a precedent for shifts in policies and systems that form the backbone of the U.S.'s contemporary "crimmigration" system, wherein "the vast majority of detainees are held in jails or jail-like facilities, where they are subjected to similar treatment as criminal suspects and offenders."[4]

Unsurprisingly, examinations of South Florida offer imperative insight into the inception, evolution, and compounding effects of anti-Black, anti-Haitian, and anti-immigrant sentiment and the methods and justifications for social removal and separation. In a Duboisian dilemma, the stigmatization and criminalization of Haitian people renders them a problem to be dealt with and disappeared through state-sanctioned methods of population control.[5] Beyond the challenges of getting to and staying in the U.S., Haitian people experience disproportionate rates of poverty, and have limited access to affordable housing and economic opportunities.[6] Widely disseminated labels of Haitians as prone to crime and disease-ridden and unclean have resulted in "tremendous discrimination and fear of the community and instigated a plethora of anti-Haitian practices, such as housing evictions and job losses."[7]

Efforts to prevent entry, contain, and curtail the quality of life for Haitian people has resulted in a reconfiguration of the U.S. cultural landscape as U.S. policies and institutions relegate Haitian people to predetermined areas and strive to keep them away from the "public."[8] Detention centers and hospitals have been studied as modes of social separation and mechanisms that perpetuate and maintain Haitian/Haitian American mistreatment.[9] However, less work has put these modes of separation in dialogue with the insidiously mundane ways discriminatory treatment toward Haitians shapes Haitian spaces, such as cultural enclaves, community centers, neighborhoods, and individual homes.

In this chapter, I examine how Edwidge Danticat's and M. J. Fièvre's work documents and represents Haitian and Haitian American voluntary and involuntary movements and occupation of space to reflect long legacies of Haitian exclusion and derision. I argue that literary works by people of Haitian descent who live or have lived in Miami present alternate cartographies of the city that make visible methods of repelling/repatriating, containing, and even killing Haitians across economic and political strata across time. These methods include, but are not limited to, the establishment of immigration policies that resulted in the immediate repatriation of Haitian refugees, urban renewal ordinances that erase established cultural enclaves, and state-sanctioned murder enabled through the withholding of medical care and the violent, unhealthy conditions in detention centers. The title of this chapter originates from this multiplicity of approaches to disappearing people of Haitian descent; I treat and encourage others to view the discrimination of Haitian people as a tireless machine that reproduces, repeats, and evolves.

With this metaphor of mechanized strategies of subjugation, I borrow and expand on Antonio Benítez-Rojo's foundational repeating island, and his theorization of the Caribbean as the "machine of machines," or a compounding of mechanisms, including colonization, designated also as "Columbus's machine," used to exploit and subjugate Caribbean people (6). He argues that the Caribbean machine "exists today, that is, it repeats itself continuously. It's called: the plantation machine . . . [that] in its essential features keeps on operating as oppressively as before."[10] Although Benítez-Rojo focuses on the Caribbean plantation and its afterlives, I suggest that the strategies of oppression I analyze in this chapter repeat and compound colonial and neocolonial modes of oppression and implicate the U.S. in ongoing violence against Haitians.

Haitian scholars (and scholars of Haitian diaspora who are not of Haitian descent) and artists, have similarly called attention to the perpetual entrapment of Haitians within and between Haiti and the U.S.[11] I am most reminded of Joanne Hyppolite, the African Diaspora Curator at the Smithsonian National Museum of African American History and Culture, and her articulation of the repeating island in "Dyaspora": "Your house in Boston is your island . . . Outside of your house, you are forced to sink or swim in American waters." [12] Hyppolite describes the limited ability to bring Haiti and home with you. The sense of cultural affinity does not extend beyond the walls of her home, where she experiences the effects of anti-Blackness, including segregation, white flight, and the callous gaze and judgment of her white neighbors. She explains that they contrast her personality, mannerisms, and preferences with their understanding of Haiti as "the boat people on the news every night. Haiti is where people have tuberculosis. Haiti is where people eat cats" (8). Hyppolite captures how machinations of anti-Blackness, anti-Haitian sentiment, and practice, as inflected by widespread U.S. ignorance to Haiti, compound to shape and limit her experiences in the U.S.

Though the procedures differ, these mechanized strategies of subjugation all share the objective of rendering the Haitian body unseen, a disappearing that is especially notable in a supposedly "diverse" city like Miami. The literary works I examine and the cultural geographies they contain, demonstrate, as Katherine McKittrick asserts, that "existing cartographic rules unjustly organize human hierarchies in place and reify uneven geographies in familiar, seemingly natural ways."[13] I suggest that anti-Haitian and anti-Black policies and sentiments shape and reshape Miami's cartographies materially, and as they are represented in literature produced by authors of Haitian descent.[14] Throughout the chapter, I move between material contexts and analyses of media disseminated during the late twentieth and early twenty-first century, as these works demonstrate the ongoing and evolving persecution of people of Haitian descent. I analyze memoirs, creative fiction, local media, international policies, municipal ordinances, and publications by community-based organizations that document the ongoing spatial manifestations of Haitian discrimination in Miami. Beyond the perpetuity of oppression represented in these literary cartographies, each text presents childbearing, disrupted inheritance, and the impossibility or precarity of future generations as an allegory for the reproduction of oppressive mechanisms that subjugate people of Haitian descent in South Florida. I read the concurrent foci on space and reproduction as symbolizations of endless persecution.

To address the experiences of Haitian refugees, I focus on national and international policies that make Miami inaccessible to Haitian émigrés through an analysis of Edwidge Danticat's short story, "Children of the Sea" (1995). While "Children of the Sea" presents a non-arrival to Miami, Danticat's later work, *Brother, I'm Dying* (2007), details the limited movement of Haitian refugees in Miami through her focus on airports, detention centers, and hospitals. In a more recent publication, M. J. Fièvre's short story, "Sinkhole" (2014) illustrates the figurative and literal destruction of parts of Little Haiti, Miami, as witnessed by an upper-middle-class couple living in the enclave.

Danticat's and Fièvre's storytelling demonstrate the widespread and interrelated effects of anti-Haitian discrimination across sociopolitical and economic strata. Read together, these narratives demonstrate the wide range of governmental mandates that shape experiences of Miami for people of Haitian descent, both before they arrive and even after they have assimilated into the hierarchal economic structure of the city.

Geography of a Non-Place: Unmappable Miami in "Children of the Sea"

In Edwidge Danticat's "Children of the Sea," Miami is a vaguely described and ultimately unattainable space for a young man seeking refuge in the U.S. via boat after experiencing political persecution during the U.S.-facilitated ousting of President Jean-Bertrand Aristide.[15] The young man leaves behind his girlfriend, and the epistolary story follows imagined letters written between the couple detailing the young man's experience at sea and the young woman's violent persecution in Haiti. Although Miami is the young man's destination, the imprecise descriptions of the city in the story reflect both the grueling seafaring journey and the web of U.S. international policies that entrap and repel Haitian refugees. These policies render the city inaccessible and legitimize the devaluation of Haitian lives. The story details not only the violence individuals experience in Haiti, but also the U.S.'s complicity in said violence that make Miami unmappable.

Published first in 1993 and then reprinted as part of Edwidge Danticat's short story collection *Krik? Krak!* (1995), "Children of the Sea" takes place following the overthrow of Haiti's first democratically elected president Jean-Bertrand Aristide by the military in September 1991. During and immediately after the overthrow, "the army and other repressive groups attacked many of . . . Aristide's supporters" rendering the nation a site of political violence and persecution and sparking waves of emigration." As Christopher Mitchell notes, in "October [of 1991], a massive outflow of boat people began, and by November 18th the Coast Guard had intercepted at least 1,800 [refugees]."[16] The unnamed male protagonist in "Children of the Sea" is part of this outflow. The young man ran a pro-Aristide radio show on which he and others "could talk about what [they] wanted from government [sic], what [they wanted] for the future of [their] country" (Danticat 6). Attacks and even assassinations of dissident radio hosts and journalists were, unfortunately, not unheard of, and may have inspired Danticat's personification of the male narrator, and what he sought to escape in Haiti. The danger of critiquing the paramilitary forces that facilitated Aristide's ousting went beyond Haitian borders: in Miami, three radio hosts, Fritz Dor, Jean-Claude Olivier, and Dona St. Plite were assassinated within a few months in 1991. In an interview with the *Columbia Journalism Review*, Serge Simon, a radio journalist who had fled Haiti in 1992, explained that "they were killed because of their radio work . . . we expected something different in the U.S."[17] Simon emphasizes the porous boundaries between Haiti and the U.S., challenging the implicit assumptions of protection and civil liberties, namely the freedom of speech.

In 1994, *The New York Times* reported on "Fears of Assassination" in Little Haiti after Daniel Buron, who was described by community members as "outspoken" and "active in exile politics" was killed on March 9. Reporter Larry Rohter asserted that "the shooting of Mr. Buron, and the official reaction to it here, are frightening proof that the Haitian military's enforcers can act with impunity anywhere, even in a major American city." Haitian community members were displeased with the police handling of the assassinations, and many specifically criticized the refusal to examine the political motivations for the assassinations—to do so would implicate broader immigration politics:

> If the killings here were recognized as political, there could be important implications. Most Haitians arriving in the United States are considered economic refugees; acknowledging that Haiti's military is attacking exiles on American soil could strengthen refugee claims of political persecution.[18]

Compounding systems of anti-Blackness, a selective and deeply prejudiced immigration system, and the extensive reach of Haitian autocracy serves as the backdrop for Danticat's story. Through the characterization of the narrator as an anti-militant radio host, Danticat challenges the idea of the U.S. as a refuge—within the story, Miami does not, cannot, exist given the narrator's well-publicized disapproval of the military overthrow that makes him a target, wherever he is.

He departs Haiti before he is captured, taking with him money, some food, and a notebook to write to the unnamed, female protagonist about his experiences at sea. Through this structure, Danticat's story suggests that while men are active in the political sphere and thus mobile during dangerous mass exoduses, women remain and bear witness to violence in their homelands. While this can be read as a commentary on masculine mobility and freedom seeking, Danticat's concurrent address of the tempestuous sea and political violence emphasizes continuing violence in and beyond Haiti. As Jenny Sharpe explains:

> "Children of the Sea" exposes the male gendering of black Atlantic narratives by extending the uncertainty of undocumented travel to the presumed sanctity of domestic space. The two lovers are not only linked by the unmailed letters they write to each other but also by the parallel circumstances in which they find themselves.[19]

The letters detail instability both on land and at sea, as the young man describes seasickness, sunstroke, and running out of food, the young woman describes violence, including attacks against those opposed to the military coup and wayward bullets. The young woman notes "haiti [sic] est comme to l'as laisse. yes, just the way you left it. bullets day and night" (4). Although written primarily in English, the translation via repetition in the letters highlights the transnational scope of the short story by bridging Haiti and the U.S. and highlighting the Caribbean island's legacies of colonization by the French.

The female narrator's witnessing of Haiti during and after the coup d'etat creates a sense of timelessness that metaphorizes Haiti's perpetual instability. She details the threatening presence of anti-government groups, including the "Cannibal Army," and the National Revolutionary Front for the Liberation and Reconstruction of Haiti that have by default taken power in Haiti after the coup. Throughout the story, the perpetrators of violence against Haitian civilians are not referred to by name nor organization, solely as "they," or "them." The female narrator also writes that no one in her neighborhood "is mentioning the old president's name," contributing to the culture of persecution that surrounded Aristide's supporters and former supporters after he was exiled (4). The anonymization of the perpetrators of violence and Haiti's first democratically elected president creates a sense of timelessness of the story that is at once specific to the early 1990s wave of instability and displacement but can be extrapolated to describe other waves of instability in the country.

Through the female narrator's recollections, Danticat horrifyingly documents the violent repression following Aristide's overthrow. Rebel groups mock her neighbor who carries her son's head "to show what's been done" after he is murdered for propagating pro-Aristide sentiments on the radio (7). This graphic and frightening display and the brutalized Haitian body at the hands of the state highlight the political violence from which refugees were fleeing while the young man's experiences document the political quagmire that limits his access to the U.S.

The young man's departure is concurrent with and shaped by debates among U.S. policymakers about how to manage the high rates of emigration from Haiti. Prior to the post-Aristide surge, the U.S. maintained a rigid interception and repatriation policy that had been formally established in the 1981 U.S.-Haiti Interdiction Agreement between the Reagan Administration (1981–1989), and Haiti's repressive dictator, Jean-Claude Duvalier (1971–1986), whose rule was characterized by violence. The arrangement between the contemporary Haitian and U.S. governments of the 1980s outlines the U.S.'s complicity in the violence of the Duvalier regime, as it severely limited one's ability to emigrate to the U.S.[20] The Bush administration (1989–1993) largely upheld Reagan's policies until Aristide's removal. Christopher Mitchell observes that the resulting "political violence in Haiti seemed palpable enough that the policy of quick return might draw great public criticism in the United States." As a result, instead of immediate repatriation, in September of 1991, the Bush administration established "a tent camp . . . at the U.S. naval base at Guantánamo Bay in

Cuba to house as many as 12,000 Haitian emigrants."[21] The use of Guantánamo to detain Haitian refugees signals a refusal to allow those fleeing Haiti to set foot on U.S. soil, a policy that shaped most of the Bush administration's management of emigration crises in Haiti. Further, in this case, Guantánamo as a U.S.-operated site in Cuba exemplifies an imperial re-mapping of U.S. borders in the interest of repelling Haitians from the U.S. proper.[22] Guantánamo's subsequent use as a prison camp for those suspected of terrorism in the serial Gulf and Afghan wars indicates ongoing use of the space for those marked as criminal and dangerous. Initially presidential aspirant Bill Clinton (who was elected the year Danticat's short story was originally published) described immediate repatriation as a "cruel policy," however, once elected, Clinton declared he would uphold the Bush policy, explaining, "leaving by boat is not the route to freedom."[23] This route, incidentally, was one of the few options available to economically disenfranchised Haitians. Upholding this policy resulted in skyrocketing rates of sea interception.

The young man's letters in Danticat's story become synecdochic of the large groups of Haitian refugees whose lives were at stake in the U.S.'s repatriation policies. While the story describes individual differences among those escaping Haiti, the epistolary form of the short story, coupled with the anonymity of the characters contributes to the story's applicability to the experiences of Haitian refugees following the military overthrow. As the male protagonist writes, "there are thirty-six other deserting souls on this little boat with me." He devotes substantial attention to their experiences in Haiti that have motivated their departure throughout the story, becoming a vehicle through which Danticat can describe the variegated experience of seafaring travel from those fleeing political repression in Haiti. The letters both protagonists write and imagine sending are undated and unaddressed—a timeless and geographically boundless tale suggesting that oppression in Haiti is perpetual and casts uncertainty on the arrival to Miami.

The story's limited descriptions of Miami and the implied non-arrival to the city detail the consequences of the U.S.-Haitian geopolitics. The young man reveals his ignorance of the city, as he wonders: "I am trying to think, to see if I read anything more about Miami. It is sunny. It doesn't snow there like other parts of America" (6). The man's description relies on touristic representations of Miami, and Florida generally, as the sunshine state, the foundation for its role as a prominent winter vacation site.[24] Danticat may even be satirizing this reputation by referencing it from the perspective of a Haitian émigré who will never arrive in the city. The representation of Miami is marked by delays, uncertainty, and a sense of impending doom: the protagonist notes after three days on the boat that he "can't tell exactly how far [they] are from [Miami]. [They] might be barely out of [their] own shores" (6). This is the extent of the description of Miami, the imagined future home, which presents the city as desirable enough to be a destination, yet unapproachable, both through the young man's lack of knowledge of the city and the dangerous method of escape. The young man foreshadows his own demise in the first few lines of the story, explaining, "I don't know how long we'll be at sea . . . *if* you see me again, I'll be so dark" (4; my emphasis). Indeed, the boat never arrives in Miami, and the young woman learns via radio broadcast that because of many "crack[s] at the bottom," it sinks off the coast of the Bahamas (20). Throughout the story, Miami remains unknown, and the boat's non-arrival signals the inaccessibility of the city.

Miami's unavailability symbolizes a sense of hopelessness of a future for the people on the boat, which the narrator emphasizes through his focus on children and pregnancy. He is particularly dismayed to realize that a fifteen-year-old girl, Célianne, on the boat is pregnant and that her unborn child was violently conceived after soldiers "burst into [her] house [and] . . . took turns raping [her]" (23). Célianne's pregnancy thus operates to remind the reader, narrator, and Célianne herself of the violent military takeover of the nation and the hopelessness of Haiti—in perpetuity. He notes that though Célianne is pregnant, he is grateful that there are "no young children on board" as it would "break [his] heart watching some little boy or girl every single day on this sea, looking into their empty faces to remind [him] of the hopelessness of the future in our country" (5). Although the narrator specifies that there is no hope in Haiti, his phrasing, and efforts to escape imply that he believes there may have been a hopeful future beyond the borders of the nation.

Children often symbolize "the perpetual horizon of every acknowledged politics, the fantasmic beneficiary of every political intervention" as Lee Edelman argues critically in *No Future* (3). The material contexts of Black refugees fleeing Haiti for the U.S. in its complicity in Haiti's instability means that childbirth and futurity in "Children of the Sea" implicate anti-Blackness and anti-Haitian sentiment and policy in the impossibility of a future for people of Haitian descent—there is no Black émigré fantasmic beneficiary of contemporary or future policies, because, as Dorothy Roberts reminds us in *Killing the Black Body: Race, Reproduction, and the*

Meaning of Liberty, "Black reproduction . . . is treated as a form of *degen-eracy*" and "Black children are born guilty" within a white supremacist, eugenicist framework that seeks to exclusively reproduce whiteness. The U.S. has used sterilization of Black women and immigrants of all races to construct and protect whiteness, and to limit the imagined perpetuation of a "bio-underclass."[25] With her attention to reproduction, Danticat invokes these legacies of child-as-future, and the state-sanctioned inhibition of Black futures. Célianne's baby, a girl, is stillborn and the young mother decides to throw her overboard. The narrator recounts, "it fell in a splash, floated for a while, and then sank. And quickly after that [Célianne] jumped in too. And just as the baby's head sank, so did hers" (26). If Danticat casts the baby as a symbol for the future of Haitian people outside of the nation's borders (specifically in Miami), her death, as well as that of her mother, a child herself, suggests the impossibility of a future for the people on the boat.

Célianne's and her child's deaths emphasize the political dependence on reproduction and harken back to tropes of violence and resistance during the transatlantic slave trade. This inclusion thus situates seafaring immigration from Haiti as part of a never-ending Middle Passage that perpetually entraps people of African descent in the Americas. As Jenny Sharpe observes in "The Middle Passages of Black Migration":

> Behind the drowning of Célianne and her baby flit the ghosts of African women who were victims of rape and who drowned themselves or their mixed-race babies. But Célianne's situation both is and is not the same as that of raped slave women, for her body was violated in her homeland at the hands of fellow Haitians. The story alludes to the middle passage to acknowledge Haitian soldiers' engagement in a violence that repeats the criminal acts of European slave traders. (104)[26]

The specters of enslavement and colonization reverberate through Céli-anne's brief, tragic representation within the story to contextualize the present enactment of harm and uses of rape-as-state-control by Haitian soldiers. Sharpe places (some) culpability on European colonization and the perpetual pillaging of Haiti by the U.S. to analyze Danticat's illustration of the neocolonial compounding of machines in/between Haiti and the U.S. Elizabeth DeLoughrey relatedly suggests in her analysis of "Children of the Sea" that "the middle passage must be 'charted' by contemporary migrants, but without a recognition of the ways in which state sanctioned violence (either in European slaving or Haitian autocracy) is repeated, Caribbean peoples are destined to reproduce the same violent diaspora."[27]

Danticat implicates Haitian (male) soldiers in the permanency of the Middle Passage, by suggesting that soldiers replicate European slave-owners' violence against Black Haitian women. Danticat's work represents this dynamic, emphasizing Black female vulnerability and Black patriarchy through her characterization of the story's protagonists.

The sea in Danticat's short story functions as both a spatial and temporal interstice that holds the passengers' recollections (and re-enactments) of racialized, gendered violence and tragedy from the historical Middle Passage and contemporary Haiti. To pass the time and to "appease the vomiting," those on the boat begin to tell stories, often recounting the terror of Haiti (9). Célianne describes being raped and witnessing the soldiers force her brother "to lie down and become intimate with [their] mother" and subsequently "[cutting] her face with a razor so that no one would know who she was" (Danticat 23–24). Célianne's recollection of this state-sanctioned assault on her family demonstrates the reverberating impacts of violence within Haiti's autocracy—Célianne carries these impacts on the scars on the face she tried to disappear. Another man on the boat similarly describes state-sanctioned violence, asserting, "he had a broken leg" after being pursued by the police in Haiti (Danticat 23; 8). Célianne and the unnamed man's physical reminders (her scarred face and his broken leg) operate as embodied traces of political repression in Haiti that they would have carried with them to Miami.

Beyond the specter of the transatlantic slave trade echoing in the experiences of the unnamed couple and the other characters in "Children of the Sea," Danticat describes U.S. complicity in upholding legacies of murderous white supremacy in the context of Afro-Caribbean migration. The man with the broken leg explains that this is his second attempt to take refuge in Miami, and his initial repatriation further details the political efforts and strategies used to repel Haitian refugees from the U.S. The distance between Haiti and Miami is not only physical but also, as the man's story suggests, political. After noting that the faces of those on the boat "are showing their first charcoal layer of sunburn," the man bemoans that "now we will never be mistaken for Cubans . . . Even though some of the Cubans are black, too" (8). His description reflects the comparative treatment of Haitians and Cubans that he links to skin color. Doing so reveals the tendency to code Cubans as white and Haitians as Black, which I explore in the next chapter of this book through my analysis of Carlos Moore's and Carlos Eire's autobiographies. This taxonomy flattens racial differences among Cubans and upholds a reductive binary between Black Haitians and Cubans that informs the U.S.'s process of screening Caribbean refugees' fitness for citizenship.[28]

Beyond the racialized differences that inform the man's treatment by the U.S. Coast Guard, his repatriation exemplifies how U.S. policy differently constitutes the subjectivity of Cuban and Haitian refugees that influences their access to Miami. The man expounds on his comment about passing for Cuban, explaining that:

> He was once on a boat with a group of Cubans. His boat had stopped to pick up the Cubans on an island off the Bahamas. When the Coast Guard came for them, they took the Cubans to Miami and sent him back to Haiti. Now he was back on the boat with some papers and documents to show that the police in Haiti were after him. (Danticat 8)

The man's mention of the documentation signals a need to prove persecution in Haiti that was, and is, simply assumed of those fleeing Communism in Cuba. Alex Stepick outlines the disparate treatment of Cuban and Haitian refugees by drawing attention to the U.S.'s perception and treatment of Communism compared to right-wing authoritarian regimes:

> Historically, [the U.S.'s] practice has been to grant a blanket presumption of persecution to those fleeing Communist states while maintaining a far stricter standard for those fleeing rightist authoritarian regimes. This dichotomous policy and the inherent tension between the policy and the general humanitarian principles of the UN Protocol is one of the underlying issues in the controversy involving the Haitian boat people.[29]

Stepick observes that the pervasive U.S. anti-Communist sentiment played a key role in setting up immigration policies throughout the twentieth century. Recently in his analysis of U.S. management of Haitian immigration as foundational to the contemporary detention/imprisonment schema, Carl Lindskoog explains that "the U.S. government implemented a policy of blanket denial of asylum for Haitians. Fewer than 100 of the approximately 50,000 petitions for asylum that Haitians filed from 1972 to 1980 were granted."[30] The federal interventions on Haitian immigration were joined by local concerns—Christopher Mitchell specifically examines

South Florida's cultural climate: "poor black migrants [entered] a U.S. southern city less than twenty years after the advent of the Civil Rights movement" and grappled with the compounding effects of xenophobic anti-Blackness.[31] Stacking the discriminatory odds against Haitians, Alex Stepick explains that a recent tuberculosis scare in South Florida cast Haitians as "disease-ridden . . . but also uneducated, unskilled peasants who could only prove [to be] a burden to the community." Stepick continues:

As a result, local political groups goaded national authorities into an unparalleled campaign to repress the flow of Haitians into Miami and to deport those Haitians already in Florida. Members of South Florida's political elite—including Democratic party members, elected officials and some Cubans—believed that the boat people were a disruptive force, destroying the community and draining resources.[32]

Miami is an attainable destination for Cubans who then are in turn empowered to dictate border policy enforcement that perpetually rejects Haitians. It follows that potential life in the U.S. for Cubans corresponds with harm, and even death, for repatriated Haitians. Jenny Sharpe explains, "Children of the Sea" is set during "an era when the US government distinguished Haitian from Cuban boat people by defining the former as economic rather than political refugees, a distinction that allowed the Coast Guard to return Haitians to the civil war they were escaping" (Sharpe 104). The categorization and assessment of political persecution as compared to economic strife details how the U.S. constructs varying subjectivities during emigration crises. The distinction between political and economic migrants is tenuous at best, as political instability in Haiti contributed to the economic trouble the nation's inhabitants experienced. As Representative Shirley Chisholm argued:

The poor economic conditions in countries like Haiti provide an easy excuse for labeling Haitians as "economic refugees." This characterization, of course, ignores the political conditions in the home country and encourages the presumption that nationals from Haiti are fleeing to the United States solely for economic reasons.[33]

Danticat demonstrates the relationship between political persecution and economic strife through the young woman's letters. The young woman's father discovers that the soldiers were "going to come get [her] . . . [and] peg her as a member of the youth federation and then take [her] away" (24). In response, her father "went to the post and paid them money, all the money he had. [their] house in port-au-prince [*sic*] and all the land his father had left him, he gave it all away to save [her] life" (24). The military overthrow results in bankruptcy, leaving the family with no economic resources or home in Haiti. Danticat describes a causal relationship between limited economic resources and political turmoil and corruption. Danticat's representation of the lived experiences of terror and violence reveal the U.S.'s policy of accepting political refugees while rejecting economic refugees as a semantic distinction used to weed out those considered undesirable, preventing them from taking up space in the U.S.

The Black Immigrant in Public Space: Mapping Krome Detention Center in *Brother, I'm Dying*

Edwidge Danticat's later work, *Brother, I'm Dying* (2007), continues an analysis of the inhibited access to Miami through her depiction of her uncle's detention and eventual death while seeking asylum in the U.S. Unlike the young male protagonist in "Children of the Sea," Joseph Danticat flies to Miami, but upon arrival immigration authorities take him from the airport to the detention center, and to the hospital. Joseph Danticat's movements chart a terrain of publicly sanctioned violence against Haitian refugees and reveals publicly operated spaces as sites where the stratification of access to particular social spheres is constructed. Put differently, the memoir challenges delineations between public and private space through its depiction of Haitian refugees' limited access.[34]

Danticat depicts the airport as a site where immigrant/refugee subjectivity is determined and categorized, initiating the process of separating desirable visitors from undesirable threats. Joseph Danticat leaves Haiti on October 29, 2004, by plane after increasing political unrest and violence in the aftermath of Jean-Bertrand Aristide's second ousting.[35] When his plane lands at Miami International Airport, the Customs and Border Patrol Officer (CBP) at Miami International Airport asks him and his son, Maxo, how long they intend to stay in the United States. Joseph Danticat, "not understanding the full implication of that choice, said that he wanted to apply for temporary asylum" (215). Danticat foreshadows her uncle's eventual death, and simultaneously highlights the role language plays in interactions with border patrol officers in the U.S., an especially unfair barometer for émigrés who do not speak English. Because of those two words ("temporary asylum"), He and Maxo are immediately "taken aside and placed in a customs waiting area" (215). The movement of father and son away from the "large groups of visitors [and] long Customs and Border Protection lines" is a microcosmic foreshadowing of the efforts to spatially separate undesirable visitors (long-term) from acceptable or tolerable visitors (short-term). The former group is taken deeper into the airport and thus further away from access to the less regulated spaces of the city, while the latter is moved closer. Indeed, despite their valid passports and tourist visas (which would have allowed them to stay in the U.S. for no more than thirty days), the verbal indication of a desire for asylum immediately results in Joseph Danticat's re-categorization as "alien 27041999," signaling his dehumanization in the interest of bureaucratic operations (214).

Joseph Danticat's intake interview evinces the continual dehumanization of Haitian refugees. He explains that he has entered the US because a "group that is causing trouble in Haiti wants to kill [him]" (217). When asked more specifically why he left his "home country of residence," Danticat replies, "because I fear for my life in Haiti. And they burned down my church" (219). Danticat notes that the transcripts of the interview indicate that the intake officer did not request further explanation or details to confirm that the violence Danticat experienced was the result of political upheaval; such a confirmation would have expedited asylum procedures. Instead, when Edwidge Danticat arrives at the airport to pick up her uncle and cousin, an airport employee informs her that the men are going to Krome Detention Center, initiating a frantic effort to have the two men released. When asked by Franck Danticat, Joseph's brother, why Maxo and Joseph have been detained since they have valid travel documents, the CBP officer explains that an earlier medical procedure performed on Joseph Danticat in New York resulted in the creation of "an immigration 'alien' file . . . [that Joseph] was never aware of" (Danticat 220). The officer cites the file as the main cause for the determination of his inadmissibility: "the central index system revealed that the subject had an existing number which revealed negative results to him being a resident" (220). Although the officer provides this formal rationalization, Danticat expresses suspicion and instead attributes the treatment of her uncle to anti-Haitian policies:

Still, I suspect that my uncle was treated according to a biased immigration policy dating back from the early 1980s when Haitians began arriving in Florida in large numbers by boat. In Florida, where Cuban refugees are, as long as they're able to step foot on dry land, immediately processed and released to their families, Haitian asylum seekers are disproportionately detained, then deported. . . . Was my uncle

going to jail because he was Haitian? . . . Was he going to jail because
he was black? If he were white, Cuban, anything other than Haitian,
would he have been going to Krome? (222–223)

As in "Children of the Sea," Danticat pinpoints the comparative treatment
of refugee groups in Florida by reiterating how refugees' nation of origin
and race influence the construction of immigrant subjectivity, and it follows, the varying degrees of admissibility into the U.S. sphere. Danticat
explicitly cites the 1995 revision to the Cuban Adjustment Act (initially
enacted in 1966), informally known as the "wet-foot, dry-foot" policy. In
actuality, the policy had made it more challenging for Cubans seeking asylum in the U.S. as compared to initial policies that would intercept Cuban
people at sea and bring them to the U.S. for asylum procedures.[36] Despite
the recent tightening of access to asylum for Cuban refugees, Danticat recalls that Haitians have never been the beneficiaries of U.S. immigration
policies.

Danticat's serialized questions about her uncle's race and nation of origin
emphasize the extremity of Haitian oppression in US immigration policy;
although Cuban refugees who made it to Miami or other places in the U.S.
were granted asylum, Joseph Danticat was sent to the infamously violent
and inhumane Krome Detention Center.[37] After a contentious debate over
how to address emigration from the Caribbean into the U.S., "in June 1980,
the Carter administration opened Krome as a refugee processing center
for Cubans and Haitians." Krome was formerly a nuclear missile site, in an-
ticipation of threats during the Cold War. Jana K. Lipman has analyzed the
conversion and repurposing of Krome as a notice of how the U.S. polices
and manages threats.[38]

Danticat describes Krome's isolated location, highlighting the center's
distance from the metropole, and it follows, the constructed and vigilantly
maintained distance between detained Haitian refugees and the city proper.
As she outlines, "a series of gray concrete buildings and trailers, Krome was
in what seemed like the middle of nowhere, in southwest Miami" (211). In
fact, as figure 5 demonstrates, Krome is located on the edge of the Florida
Everglades National Park (grey space on the left), about twenty-three miles
from downtown Miami.

The proximity to the Everglades, a "subtropical wilderness," highlights
the detention center's intentional distance from other developed parts of
South Florida.[39] The image also illustrates the center's proximity to the
Everglades Correctional Institution. The presence of both institutions re-

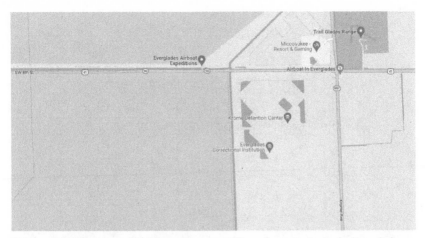

Figure 5. Map demonstrating Krome Detention Center's proximity to the Everglades, a prison, and the Miccosukee Resort. Generated by Google Maps.

serves the area for undesirable, allegedly threatening people, regardless of nationality or citizenship status, who have been removed from the public and intentionally kept out of sight.

The center's sole entrance from Krome Avenue is unmarked and nearly invisible behind dense foliage. Any time I drive past it, I am reminded that you would not be able to find the center unless you were explicitly looking for it. Krome's eerie isolation is all the more striking given it shares a cross-street (8th Street, as in the famed *Calle Ocho*) with Florida International University, Cafe Versailles, and countless other South Florida landmarks. Nicole Waller suggests this juxtaposition is intentional and reflects the legal interstice the detention center and its detainees occupy. As she writes, the inmates "are . . . disappeared into a void . . . [and] are neither fully charted in national nor in international territory and jurisdiction."[40] The detention center thus functions as a liminal space between nations and as an abject site of rejection that operates as a constitutive "outside," held apart from the inclusive, opportunistic, welcoming U.S. Shown below are detailed instructions for visitors to Krome Detention Center that evince the carceral state and its policing not only of the detained, but also those who might visit friends and family. These instructions are on display just ahead of the entrance to the center; security prevented my sister, who took this photograph, from taking pictures of the center's grounds beyond the gate.

Danticat's description of violence against Haitian refugees suggests that the center's political, legal, and geospatial liminality inform the treatment

Figure 6. The visitation stipulations as on display at the entrance of Krome Detention Center. Photo taken by Karina McInnis.

experienced therein. She expounds on this description by recalling an earlier visit to the center on behalf of the Florida Immigrant Advocacy Center. The men detained at Krome "spoke of other guards who told them they smelled, who taunted them while telling them that unlike the Cuban rafters, who were guaranteed refuge, they would never get asylum, that few Haitians ever get asylum" (212). These experiences reinforce the biased treatment of Cuban refugees as compared to Haitian refugees in the U.S. The men also relay the physical ailments, abuse, and withholding of medical care they experienced—they assert "that rather than nourish them, [the food] punished them, gave them diarrhea and made them vomit" (212). The quality of the food might be read as a metaphor for the men's disillusionment with the U.S.—although they likely left Haiti in search of a better, promise-filled life, they were greeted with state-sanctioned punishment. Beyond the sickening quality of the food, the men described bearing witness to physical beatings, one man "asked us to tell the world the detainees were beaten sometimes. He told of a friend who'd had his back broken by a guard and was deported before he could get medical attention" (212). This earlier encounter with detainees in Krome, and their experience of physical violence and withholding of medical care foreshadows her uncle's death.

When Danticat transitions from discussing the detainees' testimonies about Krome to detailing her uncle's experiences in the detention center preceding his death, she adopts a documentary tone, as opposed to the anecdotal tone used throughout, signaling the institutional language and procedures that lead to her uncle's death. She presents Joseph Danticat's interview as a transcript, where Danticat even notes grammatical errors in the intake officer's line of questioning: "Have you had [sic] applied for political asylum before in the United States or any other country?" (219). The invocation of institutional, sanitized language continues as Danticat traces her uncle's movements while at Krome. She notes that at "7:40p.m., he was given some soda and chips" and notes a phone call to another family member, Franck, at 10:03 p.m. in which Franck was "asked . . . whether Uncle Joseph had filed an application to become a US resident in 1984" (Danticat 220). Danticat's reliance on these transcripts demonstrates the physical distance between herself and her uncle, and it follows, the social separation explicit in Krome's mission.

Danticat's reliance on state documents is most notable in her reconstruction of the medical neglect that caused her uncle's death. In Edwidge Danticat's telling, Joseph Danticat's death is the result of an enactment of state sovereignty, as defined by Achille Mbembe as "the right to kill" or "let die" exercised against those who are perceived as a threat or burden to the state.[41] Mbembe opens the titular chapter of *Necropolitics* with a series of questions that illuminate the circumstances of Joseph Danticat's death: "but under what practical conditions is the power to kill, to let live, or to expose to death exercised? Who is the subject of this right? What does the implementation of such a right tell us about the one who is thus put to death and about the relation of enmity that sets such a person against his murderer?"[42] Danticat's description of her uncle's death makes clear that unauthorized access to the U.S. sphere is a practical condition that, if met, justifies the containment, neglect, and death of Black Haitians. The neglect of Krome's detainees has continued—in August of 2019, Ken Silverstein of *The New Republic* wrote:

As at detention camps elsewhere around the country, Krome's broad medical care is horrendous. In addition to being fed terrible food—high-calorie-and-starch institutional fare with little to no nutritional value—detainees face long waits to see doctors and are rarely provided medicines other than Tylenol or other over-the-counter painkillers.

What's more, Immigration and Customs Enforcement (ICE) officials—and the private contractors who run most of the agency's facilities—have a long record of cost-cutting, avoiding spending that
might eat up budgets and profit margins. Because of that, they sometimes refrain from sending detainees in their charge to outside hospitals until their health has deteriorated to a critical point.[43]

Danticat illustrates her uncle's subjugation, and the ongoing death-dealing
practiced at Krome, by detailing the "numerous and diverse techniques
for achieving the subjugations of bodies and the control of populations"
that ultimately weaponize his physical ailments after his medicine is con-
fiscated.[44] Although the interviewer asks about Joseph's prescription medication during the intake interview, Danticat notes that "the transcript has
neither my uncle nor the interviewer mentioning two rum bottles filled
with herbal medicine . . . as well as the smaller bottles of prescription pills
he was taking for his blood pressure and inflamed prostate" (218). Instead,
the transcriber notes parenthetically that Joseph Danticat took "ibupro-
fen . . . for back and chest pain" (218). Neither Danticat nor the audience
can verify the exchange between the CBP officer and Joseph, but the an-
notations suggest that the officer summarily determined that a common,
over-the-counter drug could comprehensively address Joseph Danticat's
multiple physical ailments. Later, Krome officials confiscate Joseph Danticat's belongings, including money and medicine, after he goes through
the property inventory at Krome Detention Center. In her overview of the
catalog of Joseph's possessions, Danticat remarks, "again there's no mention of the herbal medicine or the pills he was taking for his blood pressure
and inflamed prostate" (226). She then explains that an ICE officer "later
derogatorily [referred] to [Joseph's] traditional medicine as 'a voodoolike
potion'" (226). A simplistic, reductive perception of Haitian spirituality
leads to the dismissal of Joseph's medical needs and the confiscation of his
medicine.[45] By the end of the day, Joseph's "blood pressure was so high that
he was assigned to the Short Stay Unit, a medical facility inside the prison,"
where his condition continually declines (227).

Danticat's description of her uncle's deterioration and the inadequate
quality of medical attention he receives implicates officials at the detention center in disallowing the lives of Haitian refugees. Edwidge Danticat
recalls the record of his death, which states that during a meeting with an
immigration attorney that is supervised by a detention officer at Krome,
Joseph "appeared to be having a seizure. His body stiffened. His legs jerked

forward . . . he began to vomit . . . out of his mouth, his nose, as well as the tracheotomy hole in his neck" (232). Despite the obvious signs of Danticat's illness, when the medic arrives, they assert that they believe "he is faking" (234). This nonsensical assessment demonstrates the medic's callous approach to Danticat's illness and exemplifies the (lack of) medical treatment given to Danticat while at Krome. The immigration attorney explains to the medic "that right before he became sick [Joseph] had told him his medication had been taken away" (233). In response, the medic states that "the medications were indeed taken away," a process that the medic explains was "in accordance with the facility's regulations" (234). The medic goes on to note that Joseph Danticat's medications "were substituted" (234). The medic's routinized citation of institutional policy, even as Joseph Danticat vomited before them, indicates the enforcement of Krome's policies even as they endanger the lives of the detainees.

The medic's skepticism of Joseph Danticat's illness delays his transport to a distant hospital highlighting his limited access to medical care in Miami and Krome's infrastructural capacity to make live and let die. Joseph Danticat's condition continually worsens, and he is transported to Jackson Memorial Hospital "with shackles on his feet" (236). This description demonstrates the criminalization of Haitian refugees: even though Joseph Danticat was violently ill, the medics/detention center guards deem him a flight risk, and the need to keep him away from the public sphere ultimately trumped his urgent need for medical care. Although Jackson Memorial Hospital is located approximately thirty minutes and twenty miles from Krome Detention Center, the medical transport chooses this hospital as opposed to one of the closer medical centers, such as Kendall Regional Medical Center (approximately twenty minutes and nine miles away from Krome). Krome's isolated location was on average about half an hour away from the nearest hospital, illustrating that the very geography of the city enables neglect and/or the intentional postponement of medical care. The fastest route from Krome to Jackson Memorial is the Florida State Road 836 (an expressway), from which Miami International Airport is visible. The trip from the detention center to the hospital, assuming the ambulance took the fastest route, would chart a path between the spaces Joseph occupied during his brief time in Miami.

Danticat provides a time-stamped re-creation of Joseph's time at the hospital that highlights the routinized institutional treatment and neglect. Upon his arrival at the hospital, she details the deplorable care provided to her uncle by outlining chronologically the events that precede his death:

My uncle's medical records indicate that he arrived in the emergency room at Jackson Memorial Hospital around 1:00p.m. with an intravenous drip in progress from Krome. He was evaluated by a nurse practitioner at 1:10p.m. . . . At 3:24p.m., blood and urine samples were taken [and] . . . his CBC, or complete blood count test, displayed a higher than normal number of white blood cells, which hinted a possible infection . . . At 4:00p.m., during a more thorough evaluation by the nurse practitioner, he complained of acute abdominal pain, nausea, and loss of appetite . . . his vital signs were checked again at midnight, then at 1:00a.m. and 7:00a.m. . . . By 11:00am his heart rate had decreased to 102 beats per minute, still distressingly high for an eighty-one-year-old man with his symptoms . . . The records indicate that he was seen for the first time by a physician at 1:00pm, exactly twenty-four hours after he'd been brought to the emergency room. (237–239)

Danticat's necessary reliance on official records signals her uncle's isolation from loved ones during his painful death. She even omits sentimental or empathetic language, relying on sanitized descriptions and her own speculation as to what ailed her uncle. Her focus on the medical procedures and theories as to what may have been ailing her uncle, including a potential infection or his alarming heart rate, calls further attention to the medical neglect; had the medical professionals engaged in similar speculation, perhaps Joseph Danticat would have received appropriate, timely medical care. Even though Joseph Danticat's case is critical, he goes an entire day without seeing a doctor. This fact is more jarring given Danticat's reconstruction of events and detail of her uncle's condition.

Danticat's objective description of his passing exemplifies the spatial separation and neglect that characterized and caused her uncle's death. She notes that an immigration guard reports Joseph's death to medical professionals:

At 7:00p.m., after more than twenty hours of no food and sugarless IV fluids, my uncle was sweating profusely and complained of weakness . . . at 7:55p.m., his heart rate rose again, this time to 110 beats per minute. An electrocardiogram (EKG) was performed at 8:16p.m. The next note on the chart shows that he was found pulseless and unresponsive by an immigration guard at 8:30p.m. (238–239)

With this description, Danticat continuously underscores the neglect of Joseph Danticat's medical needs, including the deprivation of food that likely contributed to his death. As she suggests, the management of the hospital mirrors the management of Krome: "while [the immigration lawyer] pleaded with the higher ups at Krome to let us visit, I pleaded with the nurse to let me speak to my uncle. But neither one of us got anywhere, not even after my uncle died" (241). The presence of the immigration guard further demonstrates the persistent and pervasive violence of the U.S.'s immigration mechanisms against Haitian refugees.

Even in death, questions about Joseph Danticat's ability to occupy space in the U.S. sphere continue. Danticat explains that returning Joseph's body to Haiti was not an option, since "news of [his] detention and death had already spread in Bel Air and the gangs had rejoiced" and declared that they did not "want him back in Haiti . . . neither alive nor dead" (244). However, Joseph's son is reluctant to lay his father to rest in the U.S. and cites the potential paradox of "[burying] his father . . . where he had been so brutally rejected" (244). Danticat does not detail any legal obstruction to burying her uncle in the U.S., suggesting that while Joseph was forbidden admission during his life, it was easily granted to him in death. Rather than refuge, Joseph can only use the U.S. as a cemetery. The family decides on cremation, and although Maxo applies for asylum, he is deported and eventually dies during the 2010 Haitian earthquake.[46] Danticat's address of her cousin's death in her later work implies that had Maxo received asylum, he may have not been in Haiti during the earthquake. Maxo's biography as it appears in Danticat's oeuvre illustrates the ongoing consequences of the U.S.'s refusal to grant asylum to Haitian émigrés.

Danticat's concern for her unborn daughter similarly highlights the enduring effects of her uncle's deadly interaction with U.S. immigration officials. As in "Children of the Sea," the address of reproduction in *Brother, I'm Dying* represents both potential hope for the future and a site of transmission for state-sanctioned violence. Danticat's pregnancy is revealed early in the memoir after she learns of her father's diagnosis with emphysema; she reflects that "[her] father was dying and [she] was pregnant" (14). Although her pregnancy is scarcely mentioned beyond the identification of this painful paradox, Danticat expresses concern that her uncle's death will impact her unborn daughter: "I worried for my daughter . . . How would this stress, my sleeping so little, my lifting and lowering things and stooping in and out of closets in the middle of the night affect her?" (242). Through this description, Danticat suggests that her uncle's death can potentially harm the future generation, signaling a repetitive and cyclical trauma within Haitian families across the diaspora. Danticat had been moving things around to find immigration documents before her uncle's death, and then after he dies, "reorganized the room in which [her] uncle was to have stayed, removing the paintings from the walls and stripping the bed of the sheets he was supposed to have slept on" (242). Joseph Danticat's death results in the reorganization of private space, which Danticat devotes limited attention to throughout the memoir.

Where's Little Haiti? The Cultural Enclave within and beyond *Brother, I'm Dying*

The dearth of private spaces described in Danticat's memoir enhances the work's detail of anti-Haitian mechanisms in public spaces. However, the brief mention of private spaces documents continual economic disenfranchisement among Miami's Haitian communities. Danticat explains in the first pages of the memoir that she left her parents in New York to move to Miami where she and her husband had been "renovating . . . [a house] in the Little Haiti section . . . for the past two years" (5). Though her description of private space is limited to this passing line, Danticat's mention of the lengthy renovation process implies substantial repairs and is indicative of the housing and economic climates in Little Haiti and across South Florida's Haitian communities. Data generated as early as 1999 indicates that "Little Haiti's poverty rate of 45.6 percent [was] significantly higher than Miami's citywide average of 31.2 percent and is roughly four times the rate for Florida as a whole."[47] The case study details corresponding decreased homeownership, and in times of financial crisis, high rates of foreclosure with homes left in disrepair. This data reflects decreased economic opportunities resulting from discriminatory hiring practices that limit access to economic resources. Alex Stepick documents anti-Haitian discrimination in *City on the Edge: The Transformation of Miami* (1993), explaining that the economic opportunity structure in Miami was not welcoming to people of Haitian descent and that even minimum wage jobs remained unavailable to them (56).[48] Recent instances of job discrimination demonstrate that anti-Haitian hiring practices persist in Miami.[49] Demographic information generated by *Social Explorer* reveal that in 2007 (the year the memoir was published), 65 percent of households in Little Haiti had an annual income below $40,000. These conditions have continued in Little Haiti as indicated by the Sant La Haitian Neighborhood Center's "Progress and Unmet Challenges: Sant La's Profile of The Haitian Community of Miami-Dade, 2010–2015." The report reveals that "in 2013 the unemployment rate increased to 10.4% and remained higher than the 7.1% unemployment rate reported for the county" and the median household income, $32,973, is 21 percent lower than the county's. The report outlines the effect of inhabitants' low-income rates on Haitian households:

> Unsurprisingly, given the lower income levels of Haitian households, the 2013 data also shows that Haitian homeowners are significantly cost-burdened. The conventional public policy indicator of housing affordability in the United States is the percentage of income spent on housing. Housing expenditures that exceed 30% of household income have historically been viewed as an indicator of a housing affordability problem . . . There were 11,664 Haitian-occupied housing units with a mortgage in 2013, and 58.5% of households residing in those units paid more than 30% of their income on housing costs.[50]

The high rates of cost-burdened households result in an increased inability to repair and maintain homes and higher rates of foreclosure. Persistent increased rates of unemployment, poverty, and consequential limited access to affordable housing results in the decreased value of Haitian spaces in the city.

Little Haiti, along with other Black-majority neighborhoods, has been made particularly and persistently vulnerable to gentrification because of its economic climate.[51] Danticat explains that this climate influenced the acquisition of her home in the fall of 2002 during "the early onset of the real estate boom where you had a lot of gentrification here, a lot of shifts, a lot of turnovers." Her descriptions of the radical changes in Little Haiti exemplify its vulnerability. Danticat continues, explaining that she and her husband "sort of joked that [they were] part of the gentrification" as they were able to purchase their home well below market value.[52] While Danticat does not provide specific details of the cost of her house, its acquisition below market value highlights the devaluation of Haitian space in Miami.

The gentrification of Little Haiti is still a pressing issue: in July of 2015, Jeffrey Pierre of the *Miami Herald* summarized Little Haiti's current predicament by asserting that "Little Haiti is the next downtown neighborhood in place for a revival—or gentrification, depending on who you ask."[53] Pierre's claim corresponds with recent municipal ordinance Sec. 30A-128, entitled "Creation of the task force on urban economic revitalization" (September

2015). The ordinance established the "Task Force on Urban Economic Re-vitalization . . . [charged with] implementing comprehensive economic development strategies to create jobs, cause an increase in the tax base, and promote business activity in Targeted Urban Areas located in Miami-Dade County" (Sec. 30A-129). The ordinance goes on to list the Black majority areas targeted by this new initiative including "Liberty City, Model City/Brownsville, Carol City, Goulds, Overtown, Little Haiti, [and] Opa-locka."[54] There is no mention of race in the ordinance. This absence highlights the colorblind rhetoric that informs city planning in Miami and is detrimental to disenfranchised populations. Christopher Mele suggests this is a common example of the intersection of neoliberal urban policies and colorblind racial discourse: "The regeneration of inner-city areas achieves wide support when promises of quality-of-life improvements . . . appear socially inclusive and appeal across racial, ethnic, and class boundaries."[55] The impetus of the initiative may seem to be the creation of jobs to enhance economic access to Black communities. The results, however, are often to increase the value of the property (and thus the amount of property taxes) at a rate that does not correspond to the economic opportunities available to working-class, low-income people residing in the areas resulting in their displacement.

The statute groups and targets neighborhoods primarily occupied by Black Americans and Black Haitians. Gemima M. Remy outlines the tendency to homogenize Blackness in the U.S. in "Haitian Immigrants and African-American Relations: Ethnic Dilemmas in a Racially-Stratified Society." Remy explains, "due to the racial stratification inherent in the American society . . . Haitian immigrants are not only categorized as 'blacks,' but they are likely to be subjected to similar discriminatory practices as African Americans and other blacks from the West Indies." The homogenized grouping of Black Americans and people of Haitian descent belies conflicts between Haitian and Black people in the city. Remy notes that despite similar treatment because of state-sanctioned anti-Blackness, Haitian immigrants "cannot easily assimilate into the black American culture due to linguistic and cultural barriers." Remy continues, "many African Americans are apt to view Haitian immigrants as taking away the gains they have accrued in this country, Haitians have been put on the defensive, thus making it harder for African Americans to open up their arms and welcome Haitians into their existing communities.[56] Although the targeted language of ordinance 30A-129 suggests similar treatment of Black Americans and

Haitians in Miami, other legislation highlights the discrete efforts to subject both groups.

Contemporary city mandates reveal South Florida's concurrent yet contradictory investment in preserving Little Haiti as a culturally rich enclave while devaluing and pushing out the area's inhabitants. Read together, these disparate ordinances reveal the enclave as a site of cultural celebration devoid of the preservation of Haitian people and their access to necessary resources. According to the City of Miami Planning Department's "Historic Lemon City/Little Haiti Creole District Design Guidelines" which were promulgated in October 2008, the district "shall include all properties along NE 2nd Avenue between 52nd and 71st Streets." The guidelines go on to state that edifices in the area "shall be designed with the Caribbean climate in mind and [complement] the Caribbean-French Creole designed facades reminiscent of the Haitian culture and community's desired appearance."[57] The image of the Mache Ayisyen (Haitian market) is a classically cited example of the "Caribbean-French Creole" architecture that characterizes the area.

In a recent interview, Danticat explains that the re-creation of aspects of Haiti informed her decision to move to Miami: "it has all this flavor, this charm . . . all these colorful things . . . all my family members when they visit they say 'it's Haiti.'"[58] Reflections of Danticat's descriptions are visible in the area in the bright colors of the Little Haiti Cultural center mural, depicting a Haitian street fair and the storefront of the local gift shop. The aesthetic Caribbeanization of the neighborhood reflects the city planning ordinance to replicate Caribbean climate and culture in Miami, signaling a valuation and celebration of Haitian culture. This valuation is strikingly ironic, given the treatment people of Haitian descent experience in the city as detailed by Danticat's recollection of her uncle's experiences. Glenn Ligon comments on the concurrent marketability of cultural artifacts and the devaluation of their producers: "perhaps it is just a feeling that cultural products are used as substitutes for sustained and meaningful contact between people. It's like, 'Send me something from where you are, but don't come here.'"[59] Joann Milord casts caution toward the superficial preservation and valuation of Haitian culture in Miami as part of her work on behalf of the Northeast Second Avenue Partnership, an organization striving to stop the displacement of Little Haiti's residents. Milord asserts that while revitalizing the area is important, municipal ordinances should work to preserve "authentic Haitian culture, art, and history—*and the people who*

Figure 7. A photograph of the mural on the Little Haiti Cultural Center. Photo taken by Karina McInnis.

Figure 8. A photograph of Mache Ayisyen, or The Haitian Market, in Little Haiti. Photo taken by Karina McInnis.

produce them."[60] Milord's language outlines the overwhelming devaluation of Haitian space, so long as Haitian people make up most of its inhabitants.

South Florida's vulnerability to the consequences of climate change has expedited gentrification in the enclave because "Little Haiti sits at roughly double the elevation of affluent coastal areas like Miami Beach, which on average is 4 feet above sea level." [61] Alex Harris, writing in the *Miami Herald* explains

> Miami's two existential issues—a scarcity of affordable housing and rising sea levels—intersect with climate gentrification. There is no doubt developers are snapping up property and pushing out long-time residents. People living in these targeted areas, bolstered by data analysis from some outside researchers, firmly believe elevation is driving the rush for real estate in their neighborhoods.[62]

In her recent reflection on the "Soul of Little Haiti," Edwidge Danticat also reflected on the compounding impacts of anti-Haitian sentiment and climate change:

> In an era of both extreme xenophobia and extreme weather, or climate change, and when immigrants are constantly being told to go back to where they came from, and when some are actually being forced to, via deportation and ICE raids, the soul of Little Haiti is about survival. The soul of Little Haiti lives in any community where people have been driven out and displaced. The soul of Little Haiti lives within all of us.[63]

The forthcoming "Magic City Innovation District" an imagined "$1 billion complex on 18 acres in Little Haiti" is a prime example of the alarming transformation of the neighborhood because of climate gentrification. The developers behind the project, Plaza Equity Partners, have arranged a deal with the City of Miami wherein they will make multiple payments to the newly formed Little Haiti Revitalization Trust "under an agreement that allows bigger, denser construction in exchange for investment in local businesses and affordable housing." Neil Fairman, a Plaza Equity principal, upon delivering payment to the city explained:

> We are extremely thrilled to provide this $3 million check to the Little Haiti Revitalization Trust, which is the first of many . . . the payment to the Trust is part of our promise to empower this vibrant community—to give back and ensure local residents are provided business

opportunities, to create meaningful jobs, to build economic prosperity for all, and to preserve the thriving culture of Little Haiti.

Local activists and residents are skeptical of the project and the alleged investment in building Haitian economic prosperity and the disappearance of Little Haiti's culture, architecture, and people.[64] Construction on the project began in early 2022; at the time of publication, developers have broken ground on several buildings for the sprawling, eighteen-acre development.

The Destruction of an Enclave: Gentrification, Reproduction, and Space in M. J. Fièvre's "Sinkhole"

M. J. Fièvre thematizes the devaluation and potential disappearance of Little Haiti in the eponymous metaphor of her short story, "Sinkhole." In the story, the earth opens beneath parts of the enclave swallowing buildings and people. The short story addresses the experiences of both affluent and disenfranchised groups in Little Haiti and provides an omen that hyperbolizes the effects of gentrification on the area. Through its focus on a married couple in the wake of a miscarriage, the story thematizes inheritance and reveals that the transfer of space, and maintenance of capital, including property, is contingent on conceptions of reproduction and futurity. Fièvre suggests that reproductive spatialization influences wealthy Black Haitians whose possessions are perpetually threatened by manufactured and natural disasters.

Fièvre's story is part of a collection titled *15 Views of Miami* (2014) which presents a literary cartography of Miami. In her introduction, editor Jaquira Díaz explains that her intention was to provide a "diverse" collection that includes "fifteen different voices" whose stories represent "characters from different . . . neighborhoods" (7).[65] Each story details the lived experiences of a wide swath of Miami's inhabitants across racial, political, and economic spectrums and reveals positionality's influence on how and more significantly, where people in the city live. Set in Little Haiti, "Sinkhole" provides a glimpse of how the devaluation of Haitian space affects the lives of upper-middle-class people of Haitian descent. The story follows Pica and her husband, Jonah, in the events that follow Pica's miscarriage. Both Pica and Jonah had begun affairs with Bruno and Simonise, respectively, to cope with their loss when, unexpectedly, a sinkhole mysteriously opens beneath Pica and Jonah's house in Little Haiti, killing Jonah instantly and obliterating substantial parts of the home. This disaster leaves Pica alone to manage the remainder of Jonah's affairs, which include Jonah's disapproving mother and a child he fathered with Simonise.

The short story immediately demonstrates the prevalent anti-Haitian sentiment that influences the representation and construction of Haitian space in Miami. The narrator describes Jonah as an investor who "loved showing off his young and beautiful wife at banquets and fundraising galas."[66] At one such event, Pica notes that "other investors drank martinis and referred to the neighborhood as Buena Vista, *not* Little Haiti, a name that brought images of dark-skinned boat people" (83). To Pica, the investors conflate "Haitian" with Blackness and poverty, associations the wealthy viewers would rather not see represented in Miami's geospatial configuration or acknowledged in the language they use to describe and name parts of the city.

This erasure-by-renaming indexes contemporary debates about the naming of Little Haiti. A 2013 *Miami Herald* article, "Where's Little Haiti? It's a Big Question," reports the ongoing debates to name Little Haiti that have "sparked a backlash and reignited old ethnic tensions and cultural divisions." Marleine Bastien, a local Haitian American activist, explains, "every day you hear of a new group encroaching into what we know as Little Haiti." Bastien is likely responding to local Miami real estate investors like Peter Ehrlich who in the same article stresses that the area "is not Little Haiti, but historic Lemon City." Ehrlich continues, explaining that officially naming the neighborhood "Little Haiti" "will endanger the character of neighborhoods encompassed by the area known as Little Haiti . . . and could make the area less attractive to potential investors."[67] Like the fictional investors and developers in "Sinkhole" who refuse to acknowledge "Little Haiti," Miami's real estate marketers work to make Haitians invisible in the city—the "Magic City Innovation District" signals a concerted effort to erase Little Haiti. Green implicitly links any association to Haiti to a devaluation of the area and a related deterrent to investors.

"Sinkhole" suggests that wealth affords individuals, especially men, the power to manipulate and control space. Jonah has "money in trust funds— lots of it" that enables his interaction with investors who have deemed the reminders of a Haitian presence in Miami unprofitable (83). Pica, on the other hand, explains that "while she'd considered leaving [Jonah] . . . quite frankly [she] enjoyed being kept . . . and didn't want to go back to waitressing at Le Bébé, the Haitian diner" (83). Pica does not have access to wealth and the corresponding spatial control afforded to Jonah and would be dependent on a service job to generate income. Beyond Jonah's unspecified role in shaping Haitian space in the city, his large, privately owned house reflects his power in manipulating space in the neighborhood. As Pica notes, Jonah had "built her [the house that] used to tower above palm trees and bougainvillea and hibiscus trees" (89). Wealth therefore corresponds with an ability to own and manipulate large properties that surpass the natural ecological features that surround the home. Inversely, the destruction of the home in an unforeseeable natural disaster metaphorizes Jonah's vulnerability—despite his wealth, he is of Haitian descent within a social hierarchy that seeks to eradicate Haitian space and people.

Given his prominent role in Little Haiti, Jonah's death in the sinkhole becomes symbolic of the disappearance and destruction of Haitian space chronicled in the *Miami Herald* stories about gentrification and real estate marketing. In her initial description of her husband, Pica imagines him as a "man of immovable solidity . . . solid granite," suggesting permanence that juxtaposes his death in a freak accident (85). Fièvre represents Jonah as a permanent foundation of Little Haiti—fictional reporters from the *Miami Herald* and the *Sun Sentinel* also refer to Jonah as "the Little Haiti man" connecting him to the space of the neighborhood (85). The detailed description of Jonah's luxurious possessions suggests that Jonah's death reads as a commentary on the spatial organization of Little Haiti. Returning to her bedroom to find the aftermath of the sinkhole, Pica recounts that "she'd returned home just in time to hear the deafening noise and find Jonah's room gone—his king-sized bed, his mahogany dresser, his wide-screen TV" (84). The catalogue of the luxurious objects foreground Jonah's material wealth and his capacity to contribute to the Haitian neighborhood. In this way, Jonah's death is an expansion on the figurative subsumption described earlier in the story as a valuable and value-filled Haitian American space is obliterated. Read alongside Joseph Danticat's death in *Brother, I'm Dying*, Jonah's death personifies the perpetual elimination of Haitian Americans in Miami, whether they are downtrodden, or wealthy. Jonah's collusion with white investors who seek to re-name, or un-name, the land that swallows Jonah whole suggests that neither class nor intentions spare folks of Haitian descent a deadly fate in South Florida.

The story's concurrent address of miscarriage and the destruction of space link marriage and childbearing to the transmission of cultural capital and the maintenance of value within Little Haiti. Pica recalls that "even though she hadn't wanted it," after the miscarriage, she "become[s] cold and distant, toxic even. When she didn't withdraw completely, she screamed, *banged doors shut,* threw things" (87; my emphasis). Pica's mourning over the loss of her child manifests spatially, as she takes out her grief on the house itself, foreshadowing its swift destruction in the sinkhole. I will return here to my earlier examinations of children, (or as Edelman stylizes, the Child) as beneficiaries of all political, economic, and social decisions. I suggest that Jonah and Pica's miscarriage may be read both as a refusal to fulfill the mandate of the Child and an inability to do so, which makes visible the restrictive social order that privileges reproductive heterosex and informs the transfer of resources in the story. The specters of abuses and manipulations of Black reproduction within a white supremacist social order haunt Pica's experience.[68]

The sinkhole is both a literal representation of the devaluation of Haitian space and a disruption of the inheritance process that would perpetuate Haitian property in the area. As the story notes, the sinkhole takes place on a Thursday afternoon and "by Monday afternoon, all the walls of the house were gone" and Pica is reluctantly taken in by her disapproving mother-in-law, Philomena, who accuses her of being a "bruja" (witch), exclaiming to Pica: "you don't want a baby—and the baby dies. You don't want my son—and the earth swallows him whole" (84). Philomena shames Pica for not desiring a child, and perceives her initial resistance to childbearing, the culmination of heteronormative marriage, as reflective of Pica's supposed supernatural, malicious powers. The loss of her child haunts Pica, who she imagines as a son, cementing traditional conceptions of the transfer of wealth between males.

In Pica's grief, she begins hearing a baby's cry that is only audible to her. In the first instance, Pica recalls while in her mother-in-law's home, "a baby was crying somewhere, and Pica thought about the soft lavender color they'd planned to paint their baby's room. She imagined the baby lying asleep on his bed, one fist clenched and raised over his head" (85). Although it is made clear that Pica has "no idea whether it was a boy or a girl," the use of masculine pronouns suggests that the disrupted transmission of wealth was contingent on having a son and further elucidates the delineation of commerce to the masculine sphere. Jonah, having fathered a son with Simonise in an extramarital affair stops her from "getting rid of it . . . [begging] her not to" (89). Simonise ultimately explains that Jonah "said he would bring his son home once [Pica] [was] ready" (89). The son's arrival within the house would have potentially reinforced the inheritance process, even though the child was conceived out of wedlock in an unhappy marriage.

Throughout the story, descriptions of Bruno, Pica's lover, including his lifestyle, income/class status, and housing situation in an impoverished area are juxtaposed with Jonah's wealth. Bruno is cast as Pica's respite from the pressure to conform to a heteronormative lifestyle imposed on Pica by her mother-in-law's verbal assaults. Bruno's rented apartment is a "bare, little flat" with "uneven wooden floor[s] . . . on 59th Terrace." Pica also notes that she never showers at Bruno's apartment because "the water was brown no matter how long you ran it" (84). This depiction suggests a smaller, worn-down apartment that corresponds with Bruno's limited budget as a local artist, reflecting the valuation of cultural products but not their producers.

While the publication of the story precedes Haitian artist Joseph Wilfrid Daleus' death, Bruno's fictionalized characterization represents the material circumstances of artists of Haitian descent in Little Haiti. Daleus had moved his studio from "North Miami to Little Haiti to take advantage of a rejuvenating neighborhood . . . But the art collectors and the reservoir of tourists never came." Before his untimely death in 2017, Daleus explained "They tried to push me out of this area . . . The price goes up every month, and I don't have the support to stay. . . . But I don't want to go. I want to stay." Local activists described his death, and the degradation of his efforts to promote Haitian culture and art, "as the first victim of gentrification of Little Haiti."[69]

The description of Bruno's apartment, and the surrounding areas, symbolize the divestment in Haitian art and those who produce it, and come to stand in for the general devaluation of Haitian people. Pica describes illicit activities near Bruno's apartment—while mourning the death of her husband and finding Bruno unsupportive, Pica departs angrily and is "swallowed by the Miami shadows, invisible to the Little Haiti hookers, the unshaven men making drug deals beside a dumpster" (89). The focus on sex work and drug dealing suggests a predominance of alternate economies because of widespread socioeconomic disenfranchisement recorded by organizations like Sant La Neighborhood Center and The Haitian American Community Development Corporation.

Fièvre's descriptions of cultural centers near Bruno's apartment in Little Haiti anchor the geography of the story and characterize the setting as a distinctly Haitian space. Beyond Chez Le Bébé, a prominent Haitian restaurant in Little Haiti, Pica explains that Bruno lives "behind the Little

Haiti Cultural Center," now called the Little Haiti Cultural Complex. The complex defines its mission as "[providing] a space that brings together people and ideas to promote, showcase, and support Afro-Caribbean culture in South Florida."[70] The center is thus committed to disseminating and supporting iterations of Afro-Caribbean culture across ages, educational levels, and provides a space for the creation, discussion, and transmission of Haitian culture in Miami. The complex and restaurant are approximately half a mile apart, each located off Northeast 2nd Avenue.

Upon leaving Bruno's apartment, Pica "stop[s] by Simonise's apartment," intending to inform her about his death. Simonise lives "not too far from the Libreri Mapou bookstore" which the *Miami New Times* describes as the center of Haitian literary culture in Miami since 1986" (87). The owners make a conscious effort to collect "newspapers from Port-au-Prince, Paris, Miami, and New York City to keep readers up to date on the latest news from the island and across the Haitian diaspora."[71] By mentioning the bookstore, Fièvre places Pica's walk within a transnational context of Haitian Diaspora. Pica's movements throughout the neighborhood move across a wide range of class experiences, from her mother-in-law's well-adorned house to Bruno's dodgy apartment. Epicenters of Haitian culture in Miami punctuate her walk. Read with the stories introductory reference to the gentrification of Little Haiti in mind, the description of Creole business names, street numbers, and cultural centers intensifies the gravity of real estate investors' efforts to erase the city, both fictively and materially.

The open-ended conclusion of the story signals Pica's potential inheritance of a child while reflecting on the destruction of her home. During a later visit to Bruno, where she accuses him of not being supportive in the wake of her loss, Pica continuously hears a baby crying which ultimately, and inexplicably, leads her back to her destroyed home, where she finds Simonise, holding the crying baby and "looking at the hole in the ground" (89). Though impossible, it seems that Pica heard Jonah's child crying and was drawn back to her ruined home. Simonise then offers the child to Pica, saying that it is either "[her] or the firehouse" and that the child is "[Pica's] responsibility now." The story concludes with Pica reflecting that "she was a mother now . . . her heart pumping a passion that caused both pleasure and pain" (90). The unusual exchange, wherein Pica acquires her husband's child, born to another woman, occurs in front of the destroyed, sunken-in house. The site of this gift highlights the disruption of inheritance demonstrated by Pica's adoption of a child and her inability to transfer the valuable house to the child in the wake of its destruction. While the story concludes by inspiring questions, rather than providing answers, the image of Pica left with a new child in front of her destroyed house calls attention to the perpetual plight of even the most privileged portion of Miami's Haitian communities.

Conclusion

I have structured this chapter by separately analyzing three distinct, yet related, methods used to control and disappear Haitian people and space. While Edwidge Danticat's "Children of the Sea" reveals the political quagmire that inhibits access to South Florida for Haitian refugees escaping political unrest and violence, *Brother, I'm Dying*, details the construction of liminal spaces (and resulting liminal subjectivities) within U.S. territory to enact violence and kill Haitian refugees by withholding medical care. M. J. Fièvre suggests that economic assimilation does not protect people of Haitian descent nor the spaces they make and claim from anti-Haitian policies. Her short story hyperbolizes the destruction of Haitian space denoted by state-sanctioned gentrification. This examination reveals the distinct levels of oppression, both extreme and explicit like the detention center, and insidious, like the colorblind language evidenced in municipal ordinances that seeks to "rejuvenate" by targeting Black American and Black immigrant-majority areas in Miami.

While the structure of the chapter enhances its legibility and denotes the evolution of strategies used to repel, entrap, and kill people of Haitian descent in the U.S., these systems and experiences are cumulative, repetitive, and compounding, rather than discrete parts that can be easily placed in a chronological narrative. As recently as 2002, a boat full of approximately 200 Haitian refugees ran aground on Biscayne Bay and one contemporary article described the men, women, and children "swarming the highway leading into Miami."[72] Reporter Mark Potter describes Haitian refugees as an infestation that must be contained. As a later article reporting on the same event note, "the refugees were put on buses and taken to detention centers," including Krome.[73] Krome Detention Center continually publicizes its purpose in detaining Haitian nationals. After Akima, a private corporation, secured a ten-year contract to control the facility in 2014, it released an overview of the facility that explains: "Since 2009, the majority of Krome detainees are Haitians, followed by large numbers of Mexican, Guatemalan . . . and El Salvadoran nationals."[74] This catalog suggests a hyper-focus on Haitian detainees, a target population for both immigration policies and citywide ordinances. These issues are concurrent with recent efforts to gentrify Little Haiti and persistent economic disenfranchisement that reflects discriminatory hiring practices, prevalent low-income rates, and the devaluation of Haitian-owned properties in the city.

The landscape of the city reflects anti-Haitian national and international policies that challenge conceptions of inclusivity in even the most diverse areas of the U.S. These sentiments are more visible given the large population of people of Haitian descent in South Florida, but can be extrapolated and modified to explore the experiences of Haitians in New York, which houses the second largest Haitian population in the U.S., and other Haitian communities.[75] The metaphor of the hydra with which I began and structured the chapter might provide a pessimistic outlook on the cumulative and continuing history of discriminatory treatment of Haitian refugees in the U.S. that Edwidge Danticat, M. J. Fièvre, and local community advocates make visible in their work. However, these works pinpoint policies, tendencies, and sentiments, including contemporary immigration policies, urban renewal ordinances, and operations of local detention centers, which shape the experiences of people of Haitian descent in Miami. They therefore provide points of entry to potentially, and hopefully, make and remake space that celebrates, protects, and values Haitian lives.

3

Becoming Whiteness, Rejecting Blackness

Genre, Castro, and Transnational Identity in Carlos Moore's
Pichón and Carlos Eire's *Learning to Die in Miami*

The influence of Cuban emigration on South Florida and cultural production about and from the region cannot be overstated. As the authors of
This Land Is Our Land: Immigrants and Power in Miami note: "Cubans
have a power seldom achieved by first-generation immigrants. By the early
1990s . . . they controlled the most important local political machinery and
they had deeply penetrated the most important economic arenas."[1] However, the Cuban influence is not unilateral and Black Cubans have navigated the compounding experiences of anti-Blackness and xenophobia,
both in Cuba and the United States, and the specific racial stratification
of South Florida where white Cubans have had significant impact on the
cultural terrain.[2]

Former president of the Miami-Dade Chapter of the Black Democratic
Caucus Henry Crespo's reflections remarkably emblematizes Black Cubans'
navigations of South Florida:

Entonces los negros que vinieron aquí a los Estados Unidos en esa
epoca, (so black Cubans who arrived here in the U.S. in that period
[exilic waves]), they come into a transition of what? The Civil rights
movement, you know voting rights, Adam Clayton Powell, all these
kinds of people fighting for this stuff. But where do we go as Black
Cubans? We couldn't go to la pequeña Habana que era todo Blanco
(Little Havana, which was all white) until the white Cuban came in
and kind of dominated the thing and then they left. Then the white
boys left, they went to Broward, you know they started going more
North, all the way down South to Pinecrest or wherever they was
going, you know what I mean? And that's what happened, they said,
"We don't want to be around these Hispanics."[3]

Transcribed in Alan Aja's important investigation of Black Cuban experience, *Miami's Forgotten Cubans*, Crespo describes Cuban emigration, and a series of what Alex Stepick has called "in-migrations" as white people, Cuban or otherwise, move away from Latinx people generally, and Black Cubans especially.[4] In outlining the Civil Rights Movement, Crespo suggests that what awaited Black Cubans moving to the U.S. was a reminder not only of resistance and innovation, but also of inequity and degradation, rather than other more optimistic welcomes for white Cubans. Even Little Havana, the cultural enclave, was not exempt from the practices of Black exclusion that so characterized the United States during the late 1950s and early 1960s.

This chapter joins recent work on the intersections of race, class, and gender within Cuban émigré communities in South Florida. Through a comparative analysis of two contemporary self-representations, I analyze various, contradictory facets of the Cuban émigré experience in and beyond Miami: Carlos Moore's *Pichón: Race and Revolution in Castro's Cuba* (2008) and Carlos Eire's *Learning to Die in Miami: Confessions of a Refugee Boy* (2010). Each text is set from the authors' departure from Cuba in the late 1950s/early 1960s to the early 2000s and they enable a longitudinal examination of how race shapes immigration during global political upheaval.

The authors occupy different subject positions, and analyses of their experiences yield imperative insight into the racial stratification of South Florida and how Cuban émigrés navigate these hierarchies: Carlos Moore, a sociologist, anthropologist, and anti-racist activist was born in 1942 in Camagüey, Cuba, to Afro-Jamaican immigrants. Carlos Eire is currently a professor of history at Yale University where he studies early modern Europe. He was born in 1950 in Havana, Cuba, to an upper-middle-class white family. He emigrated to the U.S. during Operation Pedro (or Peter) Pan in 1962.

By comparatively examining *Pichón* and *Learning to Die in Miami*, I argue that Moore's and Eire's memoirs illustrate that racialization as Cuban émigrés influences both what the authors write about their traversal of geopolitical borders, and *how* they write. The distinct forms of each memoir enable a consideration of how these authors fashion themselves and their narratives to reflect non-assimilation and passing because of language barriers, racial oppression, and class stratification during a national revolution. The formal and generic differences of the texts also enhance the authors' respective representations of rigid racial stratifications as they manifest within and between Cuba and the U.S. Eire and Moore problematize conceptions of Miami as an illustrative site of Cuban enterprise by outlining racialized obstacles to success and present Miami as a site of differentiation for Cuban American assimilation. While I undertake an overall comparison and analysis of the memoirs as my attention to form suggests, I contrast the authors' starkly different descriptions of their time in Miami, which expose how their embodiments inform how they are treated in the city.

Moore's and Eire's memoirs contribute to and reference an already robust Cuban American literary history.[5] Scholars have explored the thematization of colonization, liberation, and exile in Cuban American literature, with many analyzing the Cuban influence in South Florida. South Floridian Cuban literary production represents a nostalgic exile experience and grapples with the consequences of arriving as exiles who imagined returning to Cuba after Castro's never-was overthrow and now remain in the U.S.[6] While both Eire and Moore's works "internalize crucial moments in [recent Cuban history, including] dictatorship, exile, and multiple migratory waves," read together, their works reveal fissures and deep-seated conflicts within Cuban American communities across racial, cultural, socioeconomic, and political lines.[7] Notably, and an example I'll unpack in more detail throughout the chapter, Eire's and Moore's positionalities influence their descriptions of Fidel Castro and the revolution.

By focusing on form, I suggest that the comparative analysis of these works reveals that one's racial subject position influences their engagement with generic conventions of literature and illuminates broader sociopolitical and cultural phenomena. With Moore's memoir, I consider how it emblematizes Moore's precarious navigation of Afro-Diasporic subjectivity in and between different contexts and categorize Moore's memoir as a neo-slave narrative that situates his experiences on a continuum stemming from the enslavement of Afro-descended people in the Western hemisphere. Moore's memoir features an authenticating preface, a depiction of northward movement that corresponds with a shift in political subjectivity, the symbolic representation of space to illuminate racial hierarchies, and an emphasis on literacy. His engagement with these tropes relates his experiences of immigration as an Afro-Cuban to legacies of racialized violence in and beyond his temporary host-nation. By utilizing this form to describe experiences of both the U.S. and Cuba, Moore highlights legacies of transnational racialized oppression.

Eire's postmodern memoir thematizes hyphenated existence and fragmentation in an achronological narrative that exemplifies the disorienting experience of exile. Eire provides insight into how he, as a white man, is racialized. As part of this process of becoming white American, he uses metaphors of racial oppression to describe his experiences of assimilation. Gustavo Pérez Firmat's *Life on the Hyphen: The Cuban American Way* is perhaps the most popularized discussion of hyphenated experience in the Cuban American community and his examination aligns with how Eire describes adjusting to life in the U.S. Firmat writes:

> The 1.5 individual [a person born in Cuba but who leaves before adulthood] is unique in that, unlike younger and older compatriots, he or she may actually find it possible to circulate within and through both the old and the new cultures. While one-and-a-halfers may never feel entirely at ease in either one, they are capable of availing themselves of the resources—linguistic, artistic, commercial—that both cultures have to offer. (4)[8]

Firmat's attention to circulation and resources, access to which is circumscribed by the collusion of capitalism and anti-Blackness for Afro-Cuban émigrés, reveals a notable blind spot in Firmat's formulation of the 1.5 Cuban émigré as one who benefits from cross-cultural interaction. The resourceful fluidity Firmat describes is typified in the structure of *Learning to Die in Miami* and reflects the privilege afforded to Eire in both the U.S. and Cuba, where racial hierarchies privilege white people.[9] I read Eire's frequent deployment of metaphors of slavery to illustrate the gravity of life in Communist Cuba and concurrent disregard for racial/economic stratification among Cuban émigré populations as a series of colorblind gestures that reflect Eire's privilege.

Context

Eire leaves Cuba at age eleven during Operation Pedro Pan (1960–1962), the coordinated removal of approximately 15,000 Cuban children from Communist Cuba; the operation began almost immediately after Fidel Castro rose to power.[10] Eire lived in Miami until the mid-/late 1960s, at which point he moved to Chicago to live with extended family before moving to New Haven to undertake work for his PhD in history at Yale University. Like Eire, Moore spends most of his early youth in Cuba, but during political unrest with the dismantlement of Fulgencio Batista's regime, he and his family moved from Camagüey, Cuba, to Harlem, New York, in 1957. Moore eventually returns to Cuba before living in parts of Europe, returning to the U.S. to live in Miami for a spell, and settling in Bahia, Brazil. He documents his life and his various movements with specific attention to the racial politics in each location.

In *Pichón*, Moore describes his birth and childhood in Central Lugareño, a town in Camagüey, Cuba, as highly segregated by race and class. His family, Black immigrants from Jamaica, lived in a "working class area, with dirt-floor, thatch-roofed houses" while the white elite lived "in a neighborhood of tall, shady trees, asphalt streets, and elegant concrete homes" (1). This opening description immediately introduces the prevalent themes of racialized segregation that Moore analyzes both in Cuba and in the U.S. Moore's memoir covers a vast period, beginning with his birth and childhood in 1942 and his departure from Cuba during the political upheaval in 1957.[11]

In *Learning to Die in Miami*, Carlos Eire explains that he was born in Havana, Cuba, in 1950 to a white upper-middle-class family. The memoir is set primarily in Miami after Eire arrives in 1962 during the controversial Pedro Pan Operation wherein U.S. officials and sects of the Catholic Church evacuated thousands of Cuban children from the perceived threat of a Communist government. This operation took place in collaboration with local and national governments in the U.S., as Yvonne Conde writes outlining provisions of the Pedro Pan plan:

> The Federal Children's Bureau negotiated a contract with the state of Florida's Department of Public Welfare on March 1, 1961, and signed an agreement to provide temporary aid for Cuban refugees, including care and protection of unaccompanied children. This agreement provided for federal funds to carry out the plan. At that time, reimbursement rates were $5.50 a day in individual homes or $6.50 a day in group settings (five dollars and fifty cents in 1961 equals $29.72 a day, or $891.60 a month in 1997. Six dollars and fifty cents equals $35.13 or $1,054 a month). This reimbursement was allotted for food, shelter, and clothing.[12]

As Conde's detailed description suggests, local institutions directed resources toward the children of the operation, facilitating their assimilation into U.S. culture. Eire describes being fostered by a Jewish couple, Louis and Norma Chait, whom Eire describes as "Chosen People, eternal exiles," and thus anticipates a particular kinship with his host family based on their religious persecution—though there is no description of their persecution in the memoir (26).

Entering the U.S. Canon: Moore and the Form of the U.S. Slave Narrative

Moore thematizes persecution and oppression by adopting features of the U.S. slave narrative, including an authenticating preface, northward movement that corresponds with a shift in political subjectivity, and the role of literacy in political participation and self-advancement. Moore's neo-slave narrative relates his experiences as an Afro-Cuban in the U.S. to legacies of racialized violence in his temporary host-nation, and the site of publication for his memoir. By utilizing this form, Moore spotlights and writes himself into legacies of racialized oppression transnationally.

Neo-slave narratives constitute an established genre from which Moore has heretofore been excluded, even as the parameters of the genre have expanded.[13] Focusing on texts like Gayl Jones's *Corregidora* (1975), Ishmael Reed's *Flight to Canada* (1976), Octavia Butler's *Kindred* (1979), Toni Morrison's *Beloved* (1987), and M. NourbeSe Philip's *ZONG!* (2011), scholars like Ashraf Rushdy have analyzed the implications of more contemporary works that "assume the form, adopt the conventions, and take on the first-person voice of the antebellum slave narrative."[14] More recently, in Joy James' *The New Abolitionists: (Neo)Slave Narratives and Contemporary Prison Writings* she close reads the thirteenth amendment's loophole to permit enslavement as punishment for a crime to advocate for the inclusion of writing from and about the experience of incarceration as neo-slave narratives.

In borrowing from and contributing to the neo-slave narrative genre, Moore ensures that his experiences are legible in broader Afro-Diasporic legacies of displacement. The specters of the transatlantic slave trade can be traced in Moore's restless movements across the world as he tirelessly seeks a space wherein Black people are safe. He writes about his disillusionment with movements that allegedly challenge white supremacy, drawing on a long legacy of borrowing from the past to reflect on the present in his neo-slave narrative.

Pichón features a foreword by Maya Angelou that repurposes the authenticating preface to inaugurate Moore into a Black literary tradition for a U.S. audience. Angelou's prominence, along with her oeuvre's attention to race and gender, frames Moore's prominent contributions to Black literature.[15] Moore and Angelou met in Harlem during the 1960s, and he explains that after meeting her he "sensed that this imposing woman was not about to vanish from [his] life . . . Indeed, she was to change it" (108). In her foreword, Angelou writes, "Moore has written an astounding book about revolution, resistance, passion, and compassion. The plot could have been set in Ireland, in China, in Mississippi, or in Algeria. It is an irresistibly human tale" (ix). Beyond the praise of Moore's writing, her suggestion of the universal legibility of the memoir in a variety of contexts validates its Diasporic scope. Further, the specific reference to Mississippi implicitly invokes Southern legacies of racialized violence that form the backbone of Moore's memoir.

Given Angelou's prominence, both in Moore's life, and as an internationally renowned poet, memoirist, and activist, her forward operates as an introduction to a U.S. audience and exemplifies the complex stratification of Afro-Diasporic peoples by symbolically affording Angelou more power to validate Moore's voice. In his groundbreaking work on the U.S. slave narrative, Robert Stepto provides a bit more insight into the purpose of the authenticating preface, explaining that "their primary function is, of course, to authenticate the former slave's account . . . they are at least partially responsible for the narrative's acceptance as historical evidence" (Stepto 3). Moore's memoir repurposes this feature to reach U.S. literary circles and provide testimony to a seldom told global Black Cuban experience.

Angelou's authenticating preface is paired with an image of the National Memorial African Bookstore, a critical locale in Moore's narrative and another modification of a prominent trope in the U.S. slave narrative: literacy. Rather than focusing on learning to read, an integral feature of the slave narrative that scholars have treated as a critical step in the movement toward freedom, Moore discusses his development of political literacy that motivates him to participate in social justice movements.[16] The inclusion of the image of the bookstore on the same page as Angelou's authenticating foreword makes obvious the memoir's invocation of prominent tropes of narratives of enslavement from the outset.

In the body of the memoir, Moore describes the importance of the bookstore in his understanding of global racial discrimination. He asserts that reading books about the U.S.'s and Cuba's histories, and Congo's history of Belgium domination "eroded my boyhood illusions about the United States. The civil rights movement had been brought to my attention, and I followed the situation in the Southern states as eagerly as I did events in Cuba and the Congo. Those three realities became enmeshed in my consciousness as the entangled roots of a tree" (131).[17] Like other authors from Cuba who have explored how "relations between these two nations have influenced and at times defined the histories of both the United States and Cuba," the geopolitical entanglements Moore awakens to in the bookstore come to shape his reflections of the world moving forward.[18] Moore's work to connect the U.S., Cuba, Belgium, and the Congo echoes "cultural pluralism . . . [as] a marker of Cuban and Cuban-American identity," and his reflections connect his perusing in the bookstore to global stakes of colonialism and liberation struggles.[19]

After educating himself on global geopolitics at the Memorial Bookstore, Moore determinedly protests the U.S.'s treatment of Cuba, and becomes intimately acquainted with methods of political repression in the U.S. Through books, Moore learns a difficult series of lessons about how "for resident Afro-Cubans, the contours of a racially bifurcated migration into the USA would continue to rear its disparate head, at the same time that deep-seated anti-black prejudices would reemerge in racially discriminatory forms."[20] The bookstore, and Moore's development of political literacy, enables his resistance to these oppressive structures, while simultaneously increasing his understanding of those structures. By metaphorizing the realities of Cuba, the Southern U.S., and parts of Africa as the roots of a tree, Moore highlights the interconnected realities of white supremacy in a variety of contexts. Further, he suggests that knowing about these events enhances his personal growth and sparks his commitment to anti-racist activism.

Beyond the introductory reference to these tropes of the slave narrative, the linear chronology of the memoir corresponds with Moore's northward movement and acquisition of political agency, though he ultimately complicates this movement by refining his critique of the U.S. Explaining this trope, Stepto writes: "the classic ascent narrative launches an 'enslaved' and semi-literate figure on a ritualized journey . . . charted [through] . . . systems of signs that the questing figure must read in order to be both increasingly literate and increasingly free."[21] Moore opens his memoir with an outline of cultural and racial diversity and corresponding social hierarchies in Cuba to foreground his ascent to perceived liberation both in the U.S. and in a revolutionized Cuba post-Castro. He promptly dispels misconceptions of homogeneity among Cubans to situate himself in Cuba's racial hierarchy. He writes that among Cuba's demographic, "*guajiros*," or "white cane cutters" were "particularly despised" (2). He continues: "*Criollos*, native Cuban whites were at the top of the racial pecking order alongside the Americans and the Spanish born *Gallegos.*" Moore immediately characterizes Cuba's racial landscape by highlighting white supremacy and histories of colonialism and ongoing imperialism by the U.S.

He continues, describing his position in the pecking order as the son of Jamaican immigrants: "Last in descending order, came native Cuban blacks, known as *Negroes,* headed by the fair-skinned *Mulattoes,* then West Indians with Haitians closing the pack" (2). Moore thus outlines what Edward E. Telles describes as a pigmentocratic social organization, wherein skin tone determines social status, and asserts that foreign-born Black people occupy the lowest rung of society.[22] He continues: "Whites grumbled, 'these foreign Negroes are taking jobs away from true Cubans!'" (2). Moore highlights the perception of Afro-Cubans and the disparaging reputation of Black immigrants in Cuba, situating Cuba as a site of arrival for Diasporic people that has shifted Cuba's racial and cultural demographic for centuries.

The title of Moore's memoir encapsulates the dehumanizing treatment of Black Cubans and immigrants of Black descent in Cuba. Moore recalls bullies calling him "pichón," a term that Moore explains means "a bald-headed, curved-beaked, carrion-eating buzzard . . . vicious, repulsive birds" as a form of epistemic violence (9). As Moore contextualizes this insult within the white supremacist Cuban racial hierarchy, he links this insult to broader legacies of anti-Blackness. As Thomas C. Holt argues, "the everyday acts of name calling and petty exclusions are minor links in a larger historical chain of events, structures, and transformations anchored in slavery and the slave trade."[23] Moore explains that white teachers "inculcated [disdain] in black kids against [their] own color," he had grown accustomed to "being called *negrito bizco,* cross-eyed nigger . . . [and] *negrito de mierda*" (6). By outlining the violence of the classroom, Moore connects the systemic anti-Blackness with hate speech, segregation, and the institutionalization of racist ideologies in Cuba's educational system during the 1940s and 1950s.

Moore contrasts these experiences in Cuba with his initial interpretation of the U.S., and specifically the opportunities afforded to Black Americans in alignment with his belief that moving North would enhance his life outcomes. He writes: "My image of black Americans conformed to my overblown view of America: they were the richest, handsomest, most powerful blacks on the planet!" (70). Moore implicitly links the power of Black Americans to the opportunistic qualities of the U.S. as a whole: "everything I had heard seemed true: America was a veritable land of opportunity. No one could have made me think otherwise" (73). Through this description, Moore suggests that new opportunities for self-advancement unavailable to him in Cuba were now available in the U.S.

Moore's description of moving to the U.S. marks a shift in his self-perception and nationalistic affinity as he adopts an "American" identity. After exploring his new apartment with his family and imagining the opportunities available to him in the U.S., Moore asserts that:

> I did not feel the blind commitment to my homeland expected of someone brought up in the ultra-nationalistic Cuban school system. I was not sure I was even Cuban. I no longer cared. Henceforth, I would do everything to be an *American*. I was through with my wretched native island and anxious to put my painful childhood memories behind me. (72)

Moore divests from his Cuban heritage, a temporary gesture that is no doubt precipitated by the treatment he experienced because he is Black, and his parents were born in Jamaica. His declared indifference to his de-raced Cuban identity, and determination to become American signals an effort to shift his economic, political, and social positionality based on what he believes to be true about opportunities for Black people in the U.S. Moore's comparative assessment of Cuba and the U.S. constructs the U.S. as a "mythic North." In this, Moore once again references a trope of the U.S. slave narrative by conveying "the idea that a landscape becomes symbolic in literature when it is a region in time and space offering spatial expressions of social structures."[24] He ultimately complicates this symbolism after becoming more intimately acquainted with the political and cultural landscapes of the U.S., which is best exemplified through his comparison of New York City and Miami.

Race and Revolution in Carlos Moore's Cuban America

After his arrival in the U.S. in 1958, Moore provides contrasting descriptions of Harlem, New York City, and Miami, Florida, suggesting that delineations in the Cuban émigré communities influence the experiences of each locale. Moore's comparative descriptions of a bustling Northern and a burgeoning Southern city reveal Harlem as a site that enables political protest and involvement with left-leaning efforts—this includes Moore's interaction with Castro and his entourage—while Miami disables such involvement and becomes a site of persistent persecution.

The year 1960 was a critical, coalescent year for Moore. He writes: "in that summer of 1960 . . . many things converged: the situation in the Congo, the Revolution in Cuba, the fire-and-brimstone speeches of Malcolm X, and Marxism" (138). Moore describes prominent social and political events that addressed racial and class-based violence globally. He notes that these social phenomena seemed to cohere during Fidel Castro's visit to New York "to address the United Nations General Assembly," an event that Moore explains "would completely change the course of [his] life" (139). Castro's arrival thrusts him into the local pro-Castro movements and onto watch lists of prominent U.S. organizations.

In contrast to revolution in Harlem, Moore declares that Miami became a right-wing stronghold for white Cubans. In September of 1960, at seventeen years old, Moore had become invested enough in Fidel Castro's Revolution to be asked to "work the crowds" when Castro visited New York. Moore explains that he "spoke to the crowds about those Cubans who were running to Miami to flee the Revolution" and describes the Cubans in Miami as "the most corrupt, racist white people of Cuba" (144). Moore is referring to the first major wave of emigration from Cuba, often colloquially referred to as the Golden Exiles who arrived in Miami roughly between 1959 and 1965. Maria Cristina Garcia provides an explanation for this moniker: "Cubans of the upper class were the first to leave."[25] While "golden" is linked to economic status, it may also be an implicit commentary on the racial makeup of this group who were "disproportionately white" and generally held rigid anti-Communist views. For some, these exiles were "exemplary" in multiple categories.[26] In this, Moore suggests that the revolution revealed the asymmetrical class system that disproportionately benefitted white people who sought to maintain their wealth in Miami. He continues, explaining that "Once they arrived in Miami, whites were saying that communism had taken over Cuba and that the Revolution was red and black. That convinced me that the Revolution was *our* thing . . . All blacks with any self-respect must support the Revolution" (my emphasis; 144). Moore takes ownership of the revolution, suggesting that Castro and his supporters enacted the Revolution specifically to benefit Afro-Cubans. Moore continuously contrasts New York, his current inhabitance with Miami, and presents the latter city as a barricade to the transmission of revolutionary information. He focuses on Miami's proximal location to Cuba, and the fact that, as a port city, the region is integral to filtering what enters the U.S. from the Caribbean. As Moore explains, the FBI seized documents confirming his involvement in revolutionary activity in New York in Miami (164).

Moore's derision of Miami continues, as he characterizes the city as a hotbed for counterrevolutionary activities and links white Cubans in Miami to white supremacist organizations in the U.S. South. Shortly after resolving to return to Cuba in early 1961, Moore learns of the Bay of Pigs invasion, a U.S.-based effort to overthrow Castro, from a headline in an unnamed newspaper: "'CUBA INVADED BY MIAMI-BASED CUBAN EXILES.'" Moore explains that "the headlines on April 17, 1961 were like thunderbolts. CIA-trained white Cubans supported by President John F. Kennedy had invaded Cuba . . . The same white Cubans who had helped Fidel Castro take power over two years before were now doing everything possible to topple the Revolution he had created against their narrow interests and racist whims" (158). In his articulation, white Cuban counterrevolutionary efforts are a struggle to re-establish white supremacy and the "pecking order" Moore outlines in the beginning of his memoir.

U.S. officials and media prominently described The Bay of Pigs invasion as a political attack on Communism, widely represented as an affront to personal liberties. Contemporary U.S. President John F. Kennedy Jr. frequently contrasted Communism with an elusive "freedom" throughout his short tenure as president. For example, during his presidential campaign he spoke at the Democratic Dinner in Cincinnati, Ohio, on October 6, 1960, and declared that efforts "to halt the advance of Latin communism" would help to "create a Latin America where freedom can flourish."[27] Kennedy's language, which presents the U.S. as an actor in halting or creating political systems in passive Latin America exemplifies U.S. paternalism and Kennedy's implicit disregard for Latin American sovereignty. He goes on to assert that Castro had "transformed the island of Cuba into a hostile and militant Communist satellite—a base from which to carry Communist infiltration and subversion throughout the Americas." Many, Kennedy included, considered Cuba's proximity to the U.S. (and especially South Florida) dangerous as it enabled "Communist penetration;" Kennedy concluded: "This is a critical situation—to find so dangerous an enemy on our very doorstep." Moore, critical of the U.S. paternalism demonstrated by John F. Kennedy Jr.'s speech, and convinced that anti-Communist strategies were white supremacist, continued his leftist activism in New York.

During a mass demonstration in front of the United Nations building on the first day of the Bay of Pigs Invasion (April 17, 1961), Moore "[rallies] people in Harlem" (158). During the rally, Moore shouts "The Revolution that brought dignity to black people is endangered by the 'Ku-Klux-Kubans' in Miami, the lynchers of Mississippi, and the white imperialists in Washington who murdered [Patrice] Lumumba" (159). With this assertion, Moore alliteratively links Southern legacies of anti-Blackness and global imperialism to white Cuban émigrés and their effort to thwart Castro's revolution. The role of white Cubans in Miami becomes metonymic for national efforts to destroy Castro's administration, and international efforts to thwart anti-racist resistance best exemplified by Moore's reference to Congolese leader Patrice Lumumba's assassination. Lumumba played a formative role in Congolese independence from Belgian imperialism and advocated for pan-African solidarity but was suspected to hold pro-Communist views. Belgian and U.S. agents colluded in his assassination, resulting in protests across the world.[28] Moore's inclusion of Lumumba reiterates his investment in connecting his analysis of Cuban politics to the global stage by focusing on white supremacist and colonial systems.

Moore's representation of Cuban Miami builds on other analyses that assert that white Cuban émigrés have, to varying degrees of success, replicated Cuba in South Florida. Richard Ortiz reiterates this inverted assimilation wherein Cuban émigrés changed South Florida, rather than changing themselves to assimilate:

> Miami Cubans can, in part, quite legitimately, claim a closer connection to Cuba's traditions, less because of their geographic proximity to the island and more because of their success in having transplanted so much of the culture to their adopted extraterritorial home.[29]

Implicit in "Ku Klux Kuban" is that the racial hierarchies that resulted in Moore being made into a "pichón" were replicated in South Florida, to the detriment of Moore's freedom-fighting work.

After the Bay of Pigs invasion fails, Moore problematizes his earlier assessment of the U.S. as the mythic, liberatory North to bolster his criticism of U.S. imperialism. As he writes:

> "ANTI-CASTRO FORCES ROUTED!," read the headlines. The Miami forces had been crushed . . . Fidel had come out on top in his clash with El Monstruo del Norte—the Monster of the North. But we feared the failure of the Miami exiles would lead to a full-scale retaliation. (164)

"Monstrous North" is abstract and can apply to anti-Castro supporters in the U.S., especially in South Florida, which is thus geographically recast in Moore's cartography as he emphasizes the role white Cubans from Miami had in actively opposing Castro's rule. The moniker also refers to the U.S. as a political body that sanctioned and financially supported the Bay of Pigs invasion. Moore directly counters his earlier idealization of the U.S. as a site that enabled advancement for people of Afro-descent. Once again, international debate is linked to Miami, which is represented as a base for anti-Castro strategy and anti-Black politics.

His adamant support for Castro inspires him to return to Cuba in August of 1961. He writes: "my love for Fidel Castro was genuine, profound. The Revolution he ushered into Cuba was changing the face of our country. In a flicker of a second, I'd decided on my next big step in life: I would return to my country" (146). Moore's memoir deviates from a common trope within Cuban American literature wherein authors (sometimes nostalgically) engage in an exilic reconstitution of Cuba, a place to which many have never returned. As Virgil Suarez and Delia Poey write:

> For many Cuban-Americans, particularly those who left the island as children and those born in the United States, Cuba has become a creation of the imagination, a fictional space pieced together from recollections, fading photographs and family anecdotes. Cuba is always el alla, the elsewhere.[30]

On the contrary, Moore returns to Cuba as it exists with hopes that it is different than how he remembers it. His writing makes clear that the nostalgia thematically explored by other Cuban American authors is not a privilege Moore is afforded by virtue of his Afro-Jamaican background and impoverishment while in Cuba.

Moore discovers that anti-Blackness had persisted during Castro's foment of power and determines that these harmful practices of Black degradation undergird both Communism in Cuba and capitalism in the U.S. When observing the entourage traveling with him to New York, Moore asks: "why had no blacks come from Cuba with Castro or the other Cuban delegations? Why were all Cuba's UN diplomats white? Why were all government ministers white?" (148).[31] Moore still maintains his faith in Castro's Revolution, but his suspicions are confirmed after discussing race in Cuba with prominent Afro-Cuban intellectuals. When Moore meets with Black Marxist historian Walterio Carbonell, he makes unambiguous claims "that the Revolution not only had not eradicated racism, but that the regime was scuttling the issue under the rug" (176). Carbonell had a reputation for what has been described as an "overzealous insistence on race-specific issues as the key to comprehending and countering Cuba's neocolonial condition," and was exiled partly because his book, *Cómo surgió la cultura nacional* (*How National Culture Emerged*) argued that popular Cuban histories elevated white bourgeoisie to the detriment of Black and mixed-race people. His work was antithetical to the colorblind objectives of Castro's Revolution.[32]

Moore witnesses further evidence of discrimination in Cuba, including the disproportionate imprisonment of Afro-Cuban men and women. Confronting an authority figure in Castro's administration, Moore asks: "What do you intend to do about the disproportionate number of black men and women in Cuban prisons? Why are 85 percent of prisoners black? Why do so many blacks live in ghettos?" (286). Through this interrogation, Moore highlights the use of imprisonment as a form of racialized population control and ongoing segregation of Cuba's population. Beyond the evidence of systemic anti-Blackness Moore identifies in this confrontation, Alejandro de la Fuente outlines subtle ways Castro's campaign sought to suppress Black dissent:

> The prime minister called on Afro-Cubans to be more "respectful" than ever before, asked them not to give any excuses to those who opposed the revolution's integrationist goals, and argued that racist attitudes would be changed through education and persuasion. Indeed, he remained opposed to passing antidiscrimination legislation and fighting racism through legal means.[33]

The call for respectful behavior evokes Evelyn Brooks Higginbotham's definition of "politics of respectability," which she categorizes as a strategy of assimilation through which Black women mobilized their class privileges to "[condemn] what they perceived to be negative practices and attitudes among their own people." Constructing, demanding, and/or internalizing narrow parameters of acceptable behavior suggests that the onus of freedom struggles lies in the behavior of those subjected to white supremacist systems of oppression. In de la Fuente's citation of Castro, he outlines Castro's non-interventionist approach to anti-racism and misplaced faith that good behavior will advance the fair and equal treatment of Black Cubans.

Moore's initial optimism in Castro's ambitious anti-racist goals for Cuba is likely the result of his strategic use of the press. In Castro's communications (primarily his speeches and impressive skills as an orator), he relied on tropes of unity to galvanize Cubans against predecessor Fulgencio Batista in support of his ascent to power. In the process, as Lillian Guerra argues, Cubans surrendered many of their own rights:

> By creating a common history of struggle against Batista that elided rivalries among the armed opposition and diminished popular complicity, the media became a critical factor in consolidating the legitimacy of Fidel's leadership . . . Belief in the unique morality of Fidel's vision of "humanism" inspired most Cubans to grant him ever greater shares of control over the state and the political arena without concern that doing so implied an erosion of their own freedom.[34]

Despite Castro's expert manipulation of the press and ability to unite suppressed Cubans against Batista as a common enemy, support for his agenda was divided across racial and class lines. As Antonio López asserts:

> Over the twentieth century, Cuban racial injustice continued despite (indeed, because of) postracial and mestizaje nationalisms, which, while providing room for Afro-Cuban mobility, often failed to alter the nation's de facto white privilege, a social legacy the 1959 revolution inherited and revised as raceless.[35]

Pinpointing the rhetorical, but not systemic, erasure of anti-Blackness in revolutionary and post-revolutionary Cuba, López suggests that this erasure bred a renewed Cuban nationalism that was, and is, detrimental to Afro-Cubans.[36]

Moore's criticisms are grounded in statistics about Cuban prison populations, and anecdotal experiences of under- or misrepresentation of Black Cubans, but as López outlines, Castro's post-racial ideologies did reap some benefits for Black Cubans. Alejandro de la Fuente expounds on this idea:

> Most blacks and mulattoes benefited materially from the national redistribution of income and resources implemented by the revolution. Perhaps equally important, for the first time they were, together with other disadvantaged groups, at the center of government attention and given the opportunity to participate substantially in areas that had been closed to them.[37]

However, the public stance against racism and limited benefits of government attention did not entirely resolve the systemic white supremacy that so informed Moore's upbringing. While still in Cuba, Moore witnesses

Castro's associates drive another prominent Afro-Cuban representative into exile after he advocated for racial justice and Moore decides to leave and study sociology and anthropology, fields of study no longer permitted in Cuba.

After earning his PhD from the University of Paris, Moore explores the academic job market and finds his reputation of supporting the Revolution follows him despite his recent rejection of Castro's methods. His applications for teaching positions at American universities "were turned down," until 1986 when he received "an offer from Miami, of all places, stronghold of the rabidly right-wing Cuban exiles" (301). Moore receives an offer for a visiting position in the joint Sociology and Anthropology Department at Florida International University (FIU). According to the contemporary department Chair, Lisandro Peres, he recruited Moore to FIU as a visiting professor to provide a challenging perspective to the majority white/white-Cuban department. As Peres asserts, "I knew Carlos would bring in a refreshing and different point of view on Cuban history . . . He represented a challenge to the traditional perspective of Cuba."[38] By focusing on Cuba's Black histories, Moore challenged the white-dominated Cuban history that characterized the department until his arrival. Unfortunately, members of the Cuban community in Miami ultimately persecuted Moore for doing precisely what Peres hired him to do.

After accepting the position at Florida International University, Moore asserts that his courses were:

denounced [by] . . . the local Spanish-speaking radio stations . . . as Communist propaganda. I could only be a Communist provocateur and a Castro undercover agent since I talked about the racial oppression and segregation that prevailed in Cuba well before Castro took power. Apparently I had come to Miami to sow racial antagonism within the ranks of the exile community . . . The conflict with the anti-Castro Cubans became so fevered that *The Miami Herald* later devoted three pages to the controversy. Examining the content of my university courses, the newspaper concluded that the charges against me were baseless. Simply put, I clashed with a segment of the white Cuban community whose entrenched pre-Castro racism I had exposed. These people paraded as democratic freedom fighters and I had unmasked them as disgruntled racial oppressors in search of a comeback. My courses delegitimized them politically. (301)

Moore argues that even teaching about racialized oppression was an affront to the white Cuban communities in Miami. Despite his disillusionment with Castro, he reiterates trying to overthrow Castro's administration was in alignment with white supremacist objectives. In the *Herald* piece for which Moore was interviewed, he describes a culture of surveillance that led to WAQI-Radio Mambí directly quoting his lectures. Radio Mambí is broadcast from South Florida and prominently features anti-Castro, anti-Communist discourse. The channel reaches Havana, though it is unclear if Cubans on the island can access the station.[39] Moore soon realized "the daughter of one of the station owners was secretly taping his lectures." In these lectures, Moore explained that:

José Martí . . . [and] Carlos Manuel de Cespedes . . . were racists or slave owners who exploited Black Nationalism for political or economic purposes and to ensure that blacks never took power. Further, traditional histories of the island deliberately overlook the contribution of such significant black leaders as Antonio Maceo—an independence war leader—or Jose Antonio Aponte—a pioneer of the anti-slavery struggle.

Moore's course disrupted whitewashed narratives of Cuban history and made Moore a target for university officials and local community members. When interviewed by *Miami Herald* journalist Alfonso Chardy, José Rodríguez, one of the owners of Radio Mambí asserted that he "believe[s] [Moore] is an individual who is resentful of whites."[40] Rodríguez interprets Moore's efforts to expand prevalent (mis)understandings of Cuban history resentfully, and he assumes that Moore is attempting to stir up and fabricate racial antagonisms.

Beyond the amateur espionage in Moore's classroom, university records indicate that Moore experienced acts of racist violence while living on campus, an arrangement that was typical for visiting professors during the 1980s at FIU. On January 26, 1987, Moore filed a campus police report:

At 8:17 am, 26 January 1987, Dr. Carlos Moore, Professor in the Sociology and Anthropology Dept. responded to the Public Safety Tower to report a disturbance. According to Dr. Moore, on 25 January 1987 at 10:30 pm he returned to his residence and heard loud and excessive noise and the sound of chairs being thrown around in Dorm "J" room 209. His wife stated the noise had been going on for a long period of time. Dr. Moore responded to room 209 and asked the occupants to lower the noise. One of the occupants, Mr. Tony Mallek, stated to the victim, "we have the right to make noise and if you don't like it go get the police; we don't give a fuck." Dr. Moore, the victim, stated, "I don't have to take this abusive language. I will contact the police." As Dr. Moore was leaving the area, one of the occupants shouted "That God damn nigger." The victim contacted the Head Resident, Mr. Robert Barragan, and FIU Public Safety.[41]

To protect the students' anonymity, records do not indicate the consequences of Mr. Mallek's actions, but the exchange provides insight into a culture of racialized violence that included and extended beyond the FIU campus. Another record of the incident describes the perspective of the officer who reported to the scene, Officer E. J. Nichols. Nichols admits that although he encouraged Mr. Mallek to avoid using hate speech, he accused Moore of causing an additional disturbance to that which Moore originally intended to report. Although Nichols apologized to Moore, the incident as it is re-created in the police records suggest that Moore was criminalized for "causing a scene" after experiencing a verbal assault, much like his childhood days of being called "pichón." This interaction exposes both the officer's indifference to the trauma Moore experienced, and victim-blaming that both diminishes Moore's experience and makes light of racial violence on FIU's campus.

Despite these challenges on campus, Moore contributed immensely to the intellectual life at FIU and made evident Miami's position as an Afro-Diasporic hub by organizing the 1987 "Negritude, Ethnicity, and Afro Cultures in the Americas" Conference. The conference featured lectures from Léopold Senghor, Alex Haley, and Aimé Césaire, among others, and showcased Moore's commitment to investigating and teaching about Blackness in the Caribbean. The conference was widely reported in U.S. national media as a momentous occasion. In the *New York Times,* Jon Nordheimer reported that "a 22-year-old state school" was hosting/sponsoring "the largest international meeting on negritude since a conference was held in Rome in 1959."[42] FIU's sponsorship of the event, and Moore's description of FIU as a site of racist persecution, reveals the at-times tenuous, and contradictory ground of support and violence within neoliberal institutions.

Perhaps the most unsettling description of Moore's experiences comes from the contemporary President of FIU, Modesto A. Maidique. In discussing Moore's involvement in the convening of the conference to potential donor, Commissioner of Miami, Miller J. Dawkins, Maidique writes:

> The University is fortunate to have Dr. Carlos Moore, a Visiting Professor in the Department of Sociology and Anthropology. Dr. Moore, as you know, is the conference convener. He captures the essence of this conference and its significance for our community; he is an Afro-Cuban with an Anglo name and a French education. He brings together the best of many cultural and ethnic heritages. We hope that the City of Miami and Dade County will help the university to do the same.[43]

While Maidique's factual descriptions are celebratory of Moore's diasporic experiences, when considered alongside both Maidique's and other officials' investments in putting Florida International University "on the map," these descriptions seem exploitative and afford Moore symbolic status in institutional affairs, especially when considering Moore's vexed interactions at FIU. In other correspondence between the conference organizers and potential donors, organizers noted that Florida International University must play "an increasingly larger role . . . in [Miami's] community" and that the conference would "help the University to become recognized as a key player in the cross-cultural, multi-racial, and multi-ethnic process that we are evolving in South Florida."[44] While these interactions celebrate Miami's cultural climate, Moore addresses the tension between celebrating diversity and standing racialized hierarchies in Miami:

> Miami is a place that is multiracial and multiethnic, but the relations between the groups are not satisfying . . . People need to understand that what is different is not threatening . . . There is friction among the white Cuban exiles who dominate Miami and black Cubans, with non-Latin whites, or Anglos, with blacks, and with Haitian exiles. Miami's black community, torn by violent racial disturbances in 1980 and 1982, is likely to benefit from the conference because of the collection of prestigious black thinkers.[45]

Moore outlines racial hierarchies in Miami that favor white Cubans and suggests that these hierarchies pervade even multiethnic and multiracial societies. He focuses on Arthur McDuffie's murder by police and the responding riots in Overtown and Liberty City, Black-majority neighborhoods in South Florida. I investigate the riots and the legacies of these neighborhoods more deeply in chapters 1 and 5. Optimistically, however, Moore describes Miami as a location that now enables connections between different Afro-Diasporic communities, perhaps even because of the pervasive tensions that constitute Miami's cultural landscape. While the conference was a tremendous success, Moore ultimately decides to leave FIU, citing the persistent persecution he experienced. Moore recalls that "FIU expressed interest in [him] staying, but [he] felt [he] couldn't stay and teach in the university in those conditions . . . [and] wanted to leave as soon as possible."[46] After Moore's departure from Miami, he travels across South America, settling in Brazil to research Brazilian culture.

Moore has remained an outspoken critic of anti-Blackness globally, and especially as it manifests in Cuba. In 2008, for example, Moore published an open letter to Raúl Castro in *The Miami Herald,* targeting the Miami Cuban community as an audience. Writing from Bahia, Brazil, Moore declares that he "will not beat around the bush to express my strong conviction that racism is our country's most serious and tenacious problem." He goes on to explicitly critique the 1959 Cuban Revolution and the resulting regime:

> Notwithstanding the grandiose but vacuous speeches, or bombastic but no less deceitful declarations on the alleged elimination of racism and racial discrimination, wherever we look in socialist Cuba our eyes are confronted with a cobweb of social and racial inequities and racial hatred against black people. No doubt, these issues were bequeathed to us through centuries of oppression. The Revolution that empowered itself in 1959 merely inherited them . . . Rather than destroy the legacy of white supremacy and its concomitant racism, the Revolutionary government contributed to the solidification and expansion of it. It did so when it declared the nonexistence of racism, the eradication of racial discrimination, and the advent of a "post-racial" socialist democracy in Cuba.[47]

Moore's scathing criticism of post-Castro Cuba's failure to rectify systemic racism, which he metaphorizes as a complex, sticky cobweb, foils the grandiosity of Fidel and Raúl Castro's speeches with the even larger problem of racism's expansion in post-revolutionary Cuba.

Other Black Cubans have cosigned the harmful impacts of declaring discrimination solved. In 1967, Elizabeth Sutherland Martinez conducted an interview with a young Black person about racism in Cuba where they explained: "the problem is that there is a taboo on talking about racism, because officially it does not exist anymore."[48] The year before, Castro himself had declared that "discrimination disappeared when class privileges disappeared, and it has not cost the Revolution much effort to resolve that problem."[49] Of course, as outlined earlier, there were some tangible changes made in fulfillment of the Revolution's anti-racist objectives, but these efforts also had detrimental impacts on Black Cuban communities. De la Fuente writes:

> The revolutionary government dismantled the old structures of segregation and discrimination (private clubs, recreation facilities, and schools). The socialization of the previously segregated spaces was not achieved without resistance, and eventually black clubs and societies were dismantled as well. It could not be otherwise: the very existence of these clubs defied the revolution's vision of a color-blind society and symbolized the survival of the past. Not only were Afro-Cuban organizations eliminated, however; some Afro-Cuban religious ceremonies were temporarily banned, and race itself was erased from public discourse.[50]

Rather than addressing anti-Blackness and preserving cultural pluralism and the value of Black cultural practices in Cuba, the erasures de la Fuente outlines index an effort to eradicate cultural markers with assumptions that systemic issues would follow suit. Moore elsewhere declared that Castro only made concerted efforts to tackle anti-Blackness systemically to avoid a civil war, noting that Black members of the Rebel Army experienced discrimination and were variously denied accommodation and service in hotels, leading to "violent incidents across the island."[51]

Moore continued to critique suppression of Black dissent in Cuba. In 2009, he collaboratively composed and signed the public "Declaration of African American Support for the Civil Rights Struggle in Cuba." Notably, Moore casts himself as an African American, recalling his youthful aspirations of being in the U.S. With this more recent gesture, he appeals to Afro-Diasporic solidarity across the Americas. The Declaration advocated for the release of Dr. Darsi Ferrer who the authors of the declaration claimed was unjustly imprisoned for criticizing racism in Cuba. The signatories called on President Raúl Castro to "stop the unwarranted and brutal harassment of black citizens in Cuba who are defending their civil rights."[52] Moore's public condemnations of racism in Cuba counter narratives of Cuban racial equality.

Moore's longitudinal examinations of Blackness in Cuba, especially as he has moved across the world, expose how race shapes his experiences in a variety of locations. He draws from a prominent genre within Black American literary traditions to link contemporary racial violence to historical legacies of enslavement across the Americas. His comparative descriptions of New York City and Miami reveal regional fractures within Cuban American communities and demonstrate how immigrant populations transform their host-nations, and even, as Moore's experiences in Miami illustrate, how immigrant populations can make a region inhospitable to other immigrants. His descriptions of white Cubans' discrimination, surveillance, and violence across national borders provide some insight into how the acquisition of economic, political, and cultural power, or "becoming white," manifests in ways that many Cuban American authors, like Carlos Eire, explore in their work.

Ni de Aquí, Ni de Allá: The Luxury of Postmodern Play in *Learning to Die in Miami*

Carlos Eire, a professor of religion at Yale University, has written two memoirs about his experiences of leaving Cuba for the United States during Operation Pedro Pan, including *Waiting for Snow in Havana: Confessions of a Cuban Boy* (2003), and the second anchor text of this chapter, *Learning to Die in Miami: Confessions of a Refugee Boy* (2010). Eire has explained that the latter memoir is meant not just to illustrate his experiences, but also to educate non-Cuban readers of Castro's rise to power and its discontents: "[he] was writing for non-Cubans. To explain pre-Castro Cuba and what happened." Both memoirs detail Eire's time in Miami, which Eire describes as the place he experienced the most discrimination because of his Cuban background. As he notes in an NPR interview:

> I've never really, ever since I moved out of Miami, experienced any kind of discrimination. It was only there, and I think it's because so many of us had come at once and changed the city so completely that there was a lot of resentment on the part of the natives.[53]

In Eire's recollection of his experience, Miami's cultural climate introduces him to ethnic discrimination, and forces him to both acknowledge and deny his privilege to assimilate into the upper echelons of U.S. society. Though looming large in his situational experience of discrimination in South Florida, Eire's whiteness goes unnamed in his outline of how he has avoided discriminatory experiences.[54]

To explore the tenuous relationship between marginalization and privilege, Eire relies on narrative techniques characteristic of postmodern literature, including fragmentation, troubling of the narrative voice, and achronological storytelling. Chapters in Eire's memoir operate as self-contained episodes punctuated by disorienting shifts in time and location. At one point, Eire transitions from a description of a Christmas dinner, his first away from home in Cuba, then writes, "fade to black again. It's springtime . . ." He later indicates to the reader that he is "[flashing] forward a few months" (172; 173). When discussing the form of the memoir in an interview with Silvana Paternostro for *BOMB magazine*, Eire acknowledges and explains the unique, and at times convoluted structure of the memoir, asserting, "I wrote this book from some other part of my brain, a part I've never used before." He continues, contrasting *Learning to Die in Miami* with other works, including his scholarship, which he describes as "very logical, very linear, very well planned." On the contrary, Eire notes that when writing his latest memoir,

The images drove my writing. In a purely intuitive sense, I picked details that I thought would get across the universal nature of childhood and therefore also something about the universal nature of being human. I realized later that if there is anything human beings can relate to across cultural differences, it's childhood. It's a period of life that has certain set qualities regardless of culture. And it's a special time in life that we all in very important ways still relate to. It's who we are.[55]

Eire's emphasis on universal humanism ironically aligns with Fidel Castro's rhetoric in advancing his ascent to power and finding "common ground" to unite Cubans. He mentions "cultural differences," and grounds the universal in childhood experiences. Eire's emphasis on learning who we are in childhood evokes Moore's explanation of understanding racial hierarchies from a young age, and both authors grapple with how their embodiment differently impacts their life outcomes troubling the very universality Eire purports in his statement.

Eire's memoir illustrates the fragmented but reconcilable experience of exile. He metaphorizes the fluidity of hyphenated experience via postmodernism but communicates his privilege as a white Cuban man with the luxury to float between worlds. His whiteness is thrown into relief via his deployment of metaphors of slavery and simultaneous neglect of histories of enslavement in the Americas. He relies on a simultaneous invocation of and distancing from legacies of violence that are integral to Eire's process of assimilation.

While Maya Angelou's foreword frames Moore's memoir, Eire includes two epigraphs: "Time and Eternity" by Emily Dickinson, and his own poetic "Preamble." These poems introduce the major themes of his memoir: death, rebirth, Operation Peter Pan, Communism as slavery, and freedom. Throughout the memoir, as its title suggests, Eire equates exile as a complex negotiation with death as thematized in Dickinson's poem, wherein she writes:

Death is a dialogue between
The spirit and the dust
"Dissolve," says Death. The Spirit, "Sir,
I have another trust."

Death doubts it, argues from the ground.
The spirit turns away,
Just laying off, for evidence,
An overcoat of clay.[56]

Eire not only discusses his isolation and involuntary alienation from Cuba after his parents sent him to the U.S., but also addresses ways in which he voluntarily distanced himself from Cuban culture to more easily, and more quickly, assimilate into U.S. culture.[57] Eire continues this metaphor in the first lines of the memoir proper, writing, "Having just died, I shouldn't be starting my afterlife with a chicken sandwich, no matter what, especially one served up by nuns" (1). In exile, Eire continuously describes the death of his former Cuban self and subsequent rebirth as an American. He suggests this process consistently repeats itself as he adapts to life in the U.S. The replication of this process contrasts with Moore's irreversible disillusionment with the U.S.; while whiteness enables Eire's adaptability and repeated redefinition, Moore is fixed and inhibited by systemic anti-Blackness.

However, Eire, like Moore, works to distance himself from his Cuban heritage through the written word. He "loved to write because there was no accent on the page . . . [he] also practiced like hell to get rid of [his] accent." When interviewer Terry Gross says that she cannot hear any accent, Eire replies: "I can hear it . . . It's funny, especially now, I'm wearing headphones: Boy, do I hear my accent."[58] Eire's persistent distancing from Cuban culture was apparent to a *BOMB* magazine interviewer, who refers to Eire as "the only non-Cuban Cuban in the world, in the most non-Cuban setting possible: the graduate studies center of Yale University, where he teaches religion and history."[59] Eire revisits this comment in another interview, noting that the description did not insult him:

> I know what she means. At some levels regarding certain things, I am Cuban, but concerning others, I am not . . . I like many things about Cuban culture, but I like many other things too. And whatever is good from anywhere in the world is good, so . . . [60]

In his self-exile from his Cuban background, then, Eire embraces a cultural versatility enabled by his subject position. Eire adopts an almost cosmopolitan relationship to his own Cuban heritage, choosing to dabble and enjoy parts of it as he would any other "goods" linked to other cultural backgrounds, while divesting from other attachments to "Cubanness."

Dickinson's poem precedes Eire's "Preamble," a titular gesture that self-authenticates by drawing from the nation-building language constitutions. Eire in turn reclaims the genre that had become so emblematic of political shifts in Cuba and transforms it to address his experiences in exile. His "preamble" marks his transnational movement and the ambiguous state of exile. Eire also began his earlier memoir *Waiting for Snow in Havana: Confessions of a Cuban Boy* (2004) with a "Preámbulo" (Spanish for preamble). His continuous use of this introductory mechanism derives from Cuban and U.S. founding documents, and indexes Cuban political upheaval. In 1952, Fulgencio Batista had suspended parts of the Constitution of 1940 when he gained control of Cuba during a coup d'état.[61] In 1953, during a four-hour speech titled "La Historia Me Absolverá," or "History Will Absolve Me," Castro vowed to reinstate the Constitution, but did not do so until 1976. The Constitution was modified to declare Cuba as a one-party (Communist) state, replacing the position of Prime Minister with that of President, a role filled by Castro. Eire's preamble renders his memoir his own founding document, contrasted with the management of Cuban documents and the tumultuous codification of national policy.

The content of the poem reinforces Eire's criticism of instability in Cuba and the instantiation of Communism, which he compares to slavery. Beginning with the bold first lines:

> Fearing that we'd be enslaved
> Our parents sent us away, so many of us,
> to a land across the turquoise sea

Eire equates Communism to enslavement, reinforcing this metaphor by (perhaps unintentionally) invoking the Middle Passage and oppression of Afro-descended people with the description of traveling "across the turquoise sea." While comparing the institution of slavery to Communism is an ultimately fruitless undertaking for me as a critic, Eire's use of this comparison given his position as a middle-class, white male imply the gravity with which he viewed Castro's ascent to power, even from a young age. Eire's consistent, decontextualized, and dehistoricized deployment of slavery as a metaphor demonstrates that the enslavement of Africans is the barometer by which he measures political repression as a de-raced phenomenon.

Eire continues his metaphorization of slavery, describing himself and other children as "willing, clueless fugitives." This characterization emphasizes Castro's criminalization of exiles and legacies of formerly enslaved people/maroons fleeing enslavement. Providing a bit more context about the Pedro Pan Operation, Eire writes:

> Fourteen thousand of us, boys and girls
> —A children's crusade—
> Exiled, orphaned, for what?
> Freedom
> For us who flew away, our families, and our captive brethren
> Freedom is no abstraction
> It's as real as the marrow in our bones
> Or the words on this page

Eire suggests that in the U.S. the children émigrés will enjoy freedom—a concept that is singularly emphasized. Yet, as the poem foretells, while Eire is insistent on the reality of freedom, he does not provide detail of what this freedom entails, rendering the concept the abstracted idea he refutes. The poem is an example of many rhetorical contradictions that punctuate the text and emblematize Eire's negotiation of his identity with the privilege of a white man, and the vulnerabilities of an émigré.

Slavery, Segregation, and White Cubanidad in Eire's Miami

Through the memoir, Eire travels through time to the capitalist Cuba that preceded Castro and searches for (and finds) this imaginary locale in South Florida. Eire initially staunchly refuses to return to Cuba, explaining: "I, for one, would have rather killed myself than gone back. I'd even have jumped into a sea full of sharks in a feeding frenzy before I'd set foot again in Cuba"

(116). Through this violent, graphic description, Eire once again emphasizes his disdain for the contemporary political situation in Cuba. However,
just a few pages before, Eire marveled at finding a place in Miami that
reminded him of home:

> We're in Coral Gables, the only part of Miami that reminds me of
> Havana. I'm staring at the giant trees on the median strip of this wide
> boulevard. Their branches reach over the roadway, making a natural
> canopy so thick that the sun is denied entrance. Their trunks are a
> tangled sinewy mass, a jumble of hundreds of smaller trunks all wo-
> ven together, each shouting out its age, boasting of superior longevity,
> laughing at me and every other human being. Each and every one of
> those trees is a mirror image of those ancient ones in the park that
> was four blocks from my house in Havana. (113)

The canopy denying entrance to the sun mirrors Eire's challenges in adjusting to the U.S., and like Moore, Eire uses trees to help readers visualize a
Cuban-U.S. embeddedness. In Eire's description, Miami becomes a rep-
lica of Havana in the 1950s. By comparing Coral Gables, one of the oldest,
wealthiest, and whitest cities in Miami-Dade County to Havana, Eire implicitly comments on his upbringing in Cuba. Eire's comparison provides
insight into his position in the Cuban middle class during the Revolution,
which largely informs his descriptions of Miami.

While Moore interweaves his telling of pre- and postrevolutionary Cuba
with legacies of racialized violence and resulting, or related, socioeconomic
stratification, Carlos Eire adopts an entirely different position throughout
his memoir. He declares:

> If you've ever thought that all Cuban exiles were rich or middle class,
> forget about it. The Cuban exodus was not driven by class tension,
> but by political repression, and all of the unresolved class issues went
> into exile too, along with all of us who left . . . Poor Cubans could
> hate Fidel as much as rich Cubans, and often did. No one liked to be
> told what to think, or to be permanently gagged, or to be promised
> nothing but poverty and struggle forever. No one does, save for those
> who are out for revenge against perceived oppressors, or those who
> think they can switch roles with the so-called oppressors and take all
> of their stuff from them. (178)

While Eire's charges of political repression in Cuba are well-founded, he
refuses to link political repression to social hierarchies and effectively shuts

down any possibility of racial or comprehensive class analysis that high-lights the asymmetrical distribution of resources and power. He overlooks the well-studied differences between Cuban waves of emigration, ranging from white and wealthy in the late 1950s to 1960s to Black, mixed-race, impoverished and criminalized in 1980.[62] He mocks the concept of "op-pressors" and leaves principles and vexed histories of property ownership unquestioned, suggesting instead that Castro and his followers sought to steal.

Despite this explicit refusal to explore other causes for the revolution, Eire relies on class delineations to describe his experiences in Cuba as they compare to those in Miami. As was typical for most unaccompanied mi-nors rescued from Communist Cuba during the Pedro Pan Operation, foster parents in Miami temporarily adopt Eire. During his time with the Chaits, he observes both similarities and differences between the U.S.'s and Cuba's class structures. When learning that he is responsible for taking out the trash, Eire reflects:

> Back where I came from, only servants handled the trash. The fact that I was being asked to sink to the level of a servant was shocking at first, even though I knew that the Chaits had no maids, nannies, or gardeners . . . The Chaits didn't have any servants of any kind. They were a middle-class American family, and in this respect, they were very different from their Cuban counterparts. In Cuba, even lower-middle class families often had servants . . . at least until Fidel came along. I caught on to that right away and chalked it all up as yet one more indication that this was a more advanced country. Everyone must do their own work. (52)

Eire describes a rigid class structure, where tasks, such as managing trash, are specifically designated. He further compares the middle class in Cuba to what he experiences in the U.S., reaffirming individualized labor for self-benefit, the opposite of the communal structure of Communism. How-ever, in another contradiction, radical autonomy does not align with his memory of Havana, and thus problematizes his earlier nostalgia for his home city. Later in the text, he provides specific criticisms of Communism, describing the nation's adaptation of the one-party system as transforming "the entire island . . . into a slave plantation" (144). He imagines the poten-tial consequences if he and his brother had remained in Cuba:

Had we stayed in Cuba, where everyone works for the government and everyone gets paid exactly the same salary regardless of what kind of work they do or how well or poorly they do their job, Tony and I would be nothing more than glorified slaves. (197)

While it seems safe to assume Eire would have objected to universal income, his comparison of equal compensation and enslavement overlooks the histories of coercive, brutal, unpaid, and nation-building labor across the Americas. Eire does not mention that enslavement was a pervasive institution in Cuba until its formal eradication in 1886. This silence in Eire's memoir belies the racial elements of slavery in Cuba that continually inform how Afro-Cubans experience the island—and the world. He does not at any point address Black Cubans or racial hierarchies in Cuba. The liberal deployment of "Communism as slavery" with the neglect of Black experiences reflects Eire's willingness to co-opt racialized oppression as a metaphor through which he interprets his own experience.

Though Eire references legacies of slavery as a point of comparison, these references are detached from the experiences of Afro-Cubans and Black Americans. Eire celebrates his whiteness, while simultaneously denying that it affords him any privilege:

It was 1962 . . . and we were in South Florida. Racial segregation was still legal. And we Cubans tended to be viewed by the locals as non-white intruders, even if we had blond hair and blue eyes. The lower you were on the social scale, the stronger the biases against us tended to be, but prejudices against Hispanics permeated the entire culture, from top to bottom, in a much more open way than nowadays. (17)

Eire specifically names light features as a reason he should not be treated as an intruder and suggests that his appearance even confounded people in the U.S.: "My blond hair fooled most Americans, though, confusing the hell out of them" (34). This "confusion" reflects Eire's ability to assimilate into the racial hierarchies, and he inadvertently addresses his ability to "pass" while walking the reader through his experience in public schools: "Prejudice dogs me, everywhere I go. It's inescapable. There aren't any Negro kids to pick on at this school. It's 1962, and Florida schools are still segregated. Why we Cubans weren't sent to the Negro schools still puzzles me to this day. After all, we weren't considered white then, same as now" (100). Eire disavows whiteness, even as it benefits him by funneling him, and other white Cubans into white schools in segregated Miami. He suggests that the presence of Black students would somehow ease his experiences of prejudice, inadvertently detailing the social hierarchy that Moore explores explicitly in his memoir. Further, despite his acknowledgement of how his appearance enables assimilation, he does not acknowledge how racialized segregation reveals his proximity to whiteness.[63]

Eire further details how segregation impacted his other social interactions. During a fishing trip to a local canal, two Black men join him, his brother, and other presumably white amateur fishers. Eire explains that "they've obviously come from some other part of town, for this is 1963 and Miami is still segregated. As the local elites would say, there's nothing but spics and poor white trash in our neighborhood" (199). Eire provides a simplistic overview of Black displacement in South Florida, and further implies that Latinx people cannot also be Black. He has elsewhere expounded on his interpretation of the South Floridian cultural terrain:

> There were two cultures in Miami that I experienced. There was a large Jewish presence and there was the South American culture. There was very little in between: Cubans, and of course the invisible people, the African Americans, who had no place in the schools. I never encountered them in the schools, which were still segregated. Coming as a Cuban to Miami at a time when the city was being flooded by Cubans and transformed on a day-to-day basis was very different from my experience as soon as I moved to central Illinois.[64]

Eire's description notably excludes intra-ethnic diversity but suggests that African Americans were "invisible." This descriptor belies the use of segregation, zoning, and pricing out to disappear Black people from neighborhoods in South Florida, despite the Black labor that was foundational to the region's contemporary economic and cultural prominence. Again, his recollection of segregation is strangely disconnected, or disembodied, and does not consider how his complexion and hair color facilitated his assimilation, even as he elsewhere explicitly names his desire to pass as white.

Eire undertakes a near-obsessive focus on learning English, which he explicitly links to the acquisition of more economic and sociopolitical power in Miami. He began to focus on perfecting English after an experience of discrimination on a public bus. Eire explains that the bus driver attempted to "send [Eire and his brother] to the back of the bus when he hears us speaking Spanish" (74). While this experience is in line with documented anti-Cuban sentiments in Miami, Eire's assessment reveals phenotypical similarities between himself and white Americans that later afford him notable privilege once he learns English:

> There's no better way of keeping Hispanics down in the United States than to tell them that they don't have to learn English. No better way of creating an underclass. No better way of making everyone else think that Hispanics are too dumb to learn another language, or maybe even the dumbest people of earth . . . I'm especially struck by the way in which English gives so much more agency to the self, so much more choice and responsibility. (55;57)

Eire thus links the acquisition of English to assessments of intelligence and agency in the U.S. Eire is of course not alone in associating mastery of English and denigration of Spanish-speaking with successful assimilation. Infamously, in *Hunger of Memory*, Richard Rodriguez implies that losing Spanish contributed to his academic success and has written negatively about bilingual education and affirmative action.[65] Eire echoes Rodriguez, suggesting proficiency in English can be conflated with responsibility and self-control.

His mastery of English, and perception of his strong accent (like Terry Gross, I cannot detect it) keep Eire from the full benefits of whiteness in his estimation. He ponders: "Do I look different than any other white American? No. Have I ever been branded on the forehead like a slave? No. But I'm branded on the tongue. I still speak with an accent" (160). Eire's articulation explicitly illustrates that his proximity to whiteness, and distance from racialized legacies of slavery, is contingent on the eradication of his accented English. His rhetorical questions suggest a regression of violence, in which he situates his experiences of accented English on the same continuum of practices of branding the enslaved people's flesh.

Eire, like Moore, also emphasizes the role of literacy in his assimilation to the U.S. However, while Moore links political literacy to his enhanced understanding of global anti-Blackness, Eire suggests the public library enables his escape:

> The next thing you know we're in [the Miami Public Library] just about every single evening during the week, right after we're done with our kitchen chores . . . Our library cards become our new passports and replace our useless Cuban ones. Mine actually works as a passport to the past and the future, and eventually it gains me admittance to my chosen profession . . . the world that opens up to me in

that library has no boundaries whatsoever. It's infinite and eternal. (150)

Eire juxtaposes the boundlessness of the library to travel restrictions in Cuba to condemn the latter in its inhibition of his intellectual growth. His metaphorical invocation of library cards as passports, however, rather than, for example, a visa, or green card, connotes leisurely travel and implies grounded and comfortable citizenship in his host-nation. He further links the library, a public space in Miami to his own private, capitalistic gain in its enablement of his academically elite professorial position at Yale. In this, Eire additionally slights Cuban politics through emphasizing his success in a capitalistic society.

Eire also links his racial signification to spaces in Miami. In contrast to his description of Coral Gables, Eire describes Overtown, a predominantly lower-income, Black neighborhood I discussed in chapter 1, as "very, very bad" and continues: "we're just a few blocks away from the Orange Bowl . . . The sun beats down on us as it does only in bad neighborhoods, in a foul mood" (113). The former Orange Bowl was in Eastern Little Havana, approximately six blocks away from Overtown's informal borders. Describing the Black majority area as "very bad," before living there reveals the racialized frames through which Eire interprets Miami's cultural landscape. Eire continuously describes the relationship between Cuban emigres and "bad neighborhoods":

We become intimately acquainted with seediness and many of the down-and-out non-Cuban residents of Miami. We Cuban exiles had nothing and we filled up these crummy neighborhoods because all we could afford was at the absolute bottom of the heap. But these neighborhoods hadn't been built with us in mind, and they had become slums long before we showed up, penniless. Before we came, these neighborhoods were full of American bottom-dwellers, men and women who had flocked down here to the absolute south from somewhere up North. (195)

Eire without explicitly naming racial differences, references Black migration from more northern parts of the South into Miami and works to distance himself from these populations, using dehumanizing language, like "bottom-dwellers," to describe the neighborhood's inhabitants. He also suggests that he and other Cuban émigrés arrived penniless and are not responsible for the condition of the neighborhoods. Eire implicitly identifies anti-immigrant rhetoric and displaces "blame" for the condition of these "slums" onto a more vulnerable population: Black Americans.

Although Eire cursorily addresses anti-Blackness in his memoir, in an interview with Robert Birnbaum of *The Morning News,* Eire provides a much more critical and comprehensive analysis of race relations in Cuba:

> In a Caribbean country like Cuba where they had slavery until 1888, I realized that the really old, black people I had seen as a child were probably born as slaves . . . the so-called Revolution has made it worse rather than better for African Cubans. As a matter of fact, most of the soldiers who were sent to Angola and Ethiopia were poor black people. Sadly, there was a long tradition in Cuba before independence of freed slaves who had a fair degree of social standing—they had property. Some were very well off and actually some of the leaders of the fight against Spain were blacks. But then this huge wave of immigration came in and the island became very white. And the most twisted irony in all this for Cuba is that Cuban culture is very African—the food, the music. What people call Cuban music, take away the African element and there is no such thing. Even the way Cubans talk, the Cuban Spanish accent has an African component to it. It is the sloppiest of all Spanish accents and it has a kind of African lilt to it. I hear African languages especially from West Africa and I don't understand what is being said. But it sounds very familiar to me—the cadence and the way things are pronounced. And yet these are the people who are excluded from rulership and ownership even to this day—that's the saddest thing.[66]

Eire's overview of Cuban history recalls Moore's disillusionment with the revolution and its effect, or non-effect, on systemic anti-Blackness in Cuba and in this, he is in alignment with Moore and much recent scholarship that has investigated the impacts of the revolution on Black Cubans. He notes how waves of immigration into Cuba have disproportionately displaced Afro-Cubans as exemplary property owners and citizens in high social standing. This emphasis reveals Eire's assumption that some successful Afro-Cubans challenge the ever-presence of anti-Blackness in Cuban history. While he positions himself as a sympathetic and celebratory ally to Afro-Cubans and of Afro-Cuban culture, food, and music through his use of sentimental language to bemoan systemic oppression, Eire devalues these influences by suggesting that African influence makes Cuban Spanish sloppy. Read alongside his obsessive mastery of English and hyper-focus on his barely-there accent, Eire's commentary devalues Black influences on how Spanish-speaking Cubans communicate.

Conclusion

In his conversation with Birnbaum, Eire recalls a conversation with Carlos Moore, who he describes as a "black Cuban with Jamaican parents [who] was part of the early years of the Revolution, very much in favor of it. He was very dark skinned." Eire's description of Moore's skin immediately after describing his support for the revolution reveals an implicit conflation of the revolution with Afro-Cubans. Eire continues to describe his conversation with Moore, focusing primarily on anti-Blackness in Cuba and the U.S.:

> [Moore] detailed to me how in Cuba as in Louisiana and other places in the South, the darker you were, the farther down in your social class—and he, being the son of Jamaican parents, was at the absolute bottom.... I asked him, just in general, "Do you think there will ever be an end to racism—will the human race ever be able to overcome this?" He said, "No." And then we hugged.

Moore's explanation reiterates the racial hierarchies he explicates on the first page of his memoir. While Moore has never reflected on his interaction with Eire, at least not in any preserved medium, Eire's recollection of this interaction encapsulates the major ideas this chapter has tackled through its engagement with *Pichón* and *Learning to Die in Miami*. It contrasts Moore's certain understanding of anti-Blackness as a series of evolutionary structures in and beyond Cuba, and Eire's privilege that enables a question about racism's perpetuity as a system that only positively affects his life. His description of racism as a system that humans can overcome, rather than one that humans actively maintain to continuously benefit lighter-complected people worldwide rhetorically absolves him as a beneficiary of anti-Blackness and white supremacy. Both his unifying appeal to the "human race" and conclusory description of the hug symbolizes an imagined racial reconciliation; while, to Eire, their interaction surpasses the racial antagonism Moore outlines, Moore remains steadfast in his belief that such reconciliation is impossible, and I hesitantly imagine that Moore's recollection of his time with Eire would be described quite differently.

4

Who Speaks for Miami?

The White Lens in the Tropical Metropole

The most popular, recognizable representations of Miami are the white-authored, white-produced, and white-starring spectacles of immigration, the drug trade, and related crime in the city during the 1980s. In *Scarface* (1983) and *Miami Vice* (1984–1989), I identify tropes that position these productions as realistic documentations of Miami's cultural topography, seemingly used to justify the baroque fantasies of Miami's vices.[1] In what follows, I both expand upon and challenge the implied, aspirational documentary status in these productions. Through an examination of *Scarface* and *Miami Vice* and a consideration of cultural events that preceded and informed their production, I argue that Miami media's hyperbolic representation of drug use/dealing, violence, and illicit economic ascent alongside representations of immigration codified Miami as an Anglo-American nightmare—a result of its perceived vulnerability to unrest, crime, and Communism in the Caribbean. I examine how these media present Miami as a permeable site of cultural transmission that allegedly threatened a white supremacist cultural order through either their depictions of an émigré's illicit wealth (*Scarface*), or the corruption of white police officers because of their proximity to criminalized émigrés (*Miami Vice*). Paradoxically then, while these productions are often structured around émigré, non-white American protagonists, they reveal more about the white-dominated U.S. contexts that frame them than the populations they purport themselves to be representing.

I posit that these films utilize a strategic Browning, that represents anxieties around the Mariel Boatlift's Black and mixed-race demographic without depicting Blackness. The Boatlift's darkening of the Cuban population of South Florida is simultaneously on full display, and invisibilized, through the strategic use of white actors, Brownface, and exaggerated accents. This chapter foils the remainder of the project, and illustrates how white showrunners, writers, directors, and so on, cautiously navigated anxieties around Blackness, queerness, and crime to produce enticing, dangerous representations of South Florida while centering whiteness. These creators utilize what Antonio López has described as a "spicsploitative Brownface" that was dangerous, yet attractive and exciting to white audiences. This exploitation posed an overt threat to white Cuban claims to the possessive investment in whiteness in the United States.[2] At stake in identifications with a "certain kind of Cubanness" and disidentifications with Blackness, queerness, and crime are the geopolitical debates of Cuban America during a rare encouragement of massive emigration.

I focus on *Scarface* and *Miami Vice* as two prominent representations of Miami released almost immediately after the infamous Mariel Boatlift, a significant moment in Miami's history as a primary destination for Cuban émigrés. The Boatlift displayed Fidel Castro's temporary willingness to open the harbor for ex-patriates leaving the island. However, this temporary "benevolence" barely obfuscated Castro's manipulation of the Boatlift population, which included formerly incarcerated people and people who had been previously held in mental asylums.[3] The racial demographic of the Boatlift population deviated radically from earlier waves of emigration from Cuba; the "Marielitos," as they were pejoratively named, included a large percentage of Afro- and mixed-race Cubans unlike the white-majority waves that preceded the Boatlift. Given the criminalization of queerness in Cuba, the formerly imprisoned included a disproportionate number of LGBTQIA Cubans. I treat Castro's manipulation of the Boatlift demographic as integral to interpreting the reception of the Mariel émigrés because it illuminates anti-Black and anti-LGBTQIA sentiment and policy in Cuba and the U.S.[4]

This chapter thus investigates Cuban histories of Afro-Cuban and/or LGBTQIA repression transnationally through a focus on representations of Miami. I situate this investigation with a concurrent consideration of the U.S.'s sociopolitical moment, namely the War on Drugs, which disproportionately impacted Black communities.[5] Through this transnational, intersectional examination, I detail how demonizing narratives of queerness, Blackness, non-Americanness, and drug use multiply entrapped the Mariel émigrés and dominated the U.S. imagination for decades after the Boatlift. Both *Miami Vice* and *Scarface* throw these stereotypes into relief, and my analysis illustrates that these mass media representations compounded non-white, LGBTQIA, and "criminal" identities, rendering Mariel émigrés, and ultimately, as *Miami Vice* shows, immigrants more generally, a threat to "imperialist white supremacist capitalist patriarchy."[6]

Scarface and *Miami Vice* expose the violence and greed inherent in U.S. capitalism and the inaccessibility of the normative "American Dream" for immigrants who do not, or because of their racial, gender, and/or sexual signification cannot, abide by the rules of assimilation. I read this failure to abide in the representations of excess through the illicit acquisition of lavish luxuries, explosive tempers, and exaggerated accents that persistently mark émigré protagonists as socially deviant in these overblown and widespread representations of South Florida during this period. Interviews with directors and producers reveal the intentional exaggeration of these aspects, without concurrent considerations of the complexity of immigration from Cuba to the U.S. (and Miami in particular) during and after the Boatlift.

Mariel Boatlift

The Boatlift began after six Cuban citizens crashed a bus into the Peruvian embassy in Havana, Cuba, on April 1, 1980. The men and women on the bus demanded asylum and vocalized their disapproval of President Fidel Castro's policies. In a matter of days, some 10,000 Cuban citizens joined in, crowding the grounds of the embassy, and requesting political asylum. The sheer number of dissenters and the inability of the Cuban guard to control the situation put immense pressure on Castro. In an unprecedented diplomatic gesture, he announced that those who wished to leave Cuba could do so through the port of Mariel.[7] Castro's announcement spurred many Cuban Americans in Miami to commandeer boats and head to Cuba and pick up friends and relatives and to put political pressure on the Carter administration to address Castro's announcement federally. While there had been no official policy put in place regarding the Boatlift, President Jimmy Carter addressed the situation on May 5, 1980, some two weeks after Castro had opened the port of Mariel, and the first boat of émigrés had docked at Key West, Florida. Carter stated, "we, as a nation, have always had our arms open to receiving refugees in accordance with American law. We'll continue to provide an open heart and open arms to refugees seeking freedom from communist domination and economic deprivation brought about primarily by Fidel Castro and his government."[8] Carter's statement alludes to the U.S.'s ideological imperative to provide safe harbor for those fleeing a Communist government, condemning Castro, and reinscribing U.S. ideals of freedom and democracy.

Carter's condoning of the Boatlift paved the way for a more representative émigré population. Earlier waves of immigration (the Golden Exiles I outline in the preceding chapter) included mostly white Cubans, of European descent, from upper-middle-class backgrounds. The Mariel Boatlift signaled a radical departure from this demographic, with an almost 75 percent increase in mixed-race and Afro-Cubans represented during the Boatlift. The shift in the racial demographic, or a move toward a more holistic representation of Cubans in Miami, corresponded with Castro's political endeavors to defame all who left Cuba as their departures implicitly condemned Castro's administration. Describing the mostly Black and mixed-race group, Castro declared that he had "flushed the toilets of Cuba on the United States." He continued with a phrase that is quoted in the introduction to *Scarface: "no los queremos, no los necesitamos."* (we do not want them, we do not need them). Implicit in this assessment is that ridding the island of political dissidents, or *gusanos* (worms), as they were sometimes called by Castro and his supporters, was a form of racial cleansing of Black Cubans who were equated, literally, with human waste. As outlined in chapter 3, it's clear Castro failed to, and maybe never intended to, deliver on the anti-racist promises of the revolution.

Recently, scholars have investigated the intersections of migrant studies, Caribbean studies, and queer theory, with some devoting specific attention to the perceived threat and corresponding persecution of LGBTQIA communities during the Cuban Revolution and the various waves of emigration therein. Maria Encarnación López asserts that during the Cuban Revolution, "homosexuals were seen as a destabilizing threat to the system, so the government launched an institutionalized homophobic system whose purpose was to keep them under control."[9] These strategies included the disproportionate imprisonment and institutionalization of LGBTQIA individuals; when Castro boasted of emptying the prisons and asylums onto the U.S. during the Boatlift, his claims betrayed the anti-Blackness and virulent homophobic underpinnings of his regime. As Susana Peña asserts:

> The Cuban government developed a selective process to facilitate the exit of people whom the revolution had already identified as undesirable. By prioritizing "undesirables," Cuban officials hoped to eliminate what they defined as problem populations from the country and reinforce the official story that disparaged all those who wanted to

leave. When Cuban Americans arrived in Cuba with empty boats, hopeful that they would be reunited with family members, they were required to transport not only their relatives but also other people the Cuban government had approved for departure, among them, homosexuals, criminals, and the mentally ill.[10]

Peña suggests that a particularly potent thread of Cuban nationalism emerged during the Revolution, and its success was contingent on the abjection, and ultimate ejection, of those who deviated from a prescriptive definition of Cuban citizenship. In this, any non-heteronormative identification and/or performance, or perception of non-heteronormativity, especially among Black and mixed-race people, was immediately conflated with criminality and mental illness.

Given the racial demographic of the Mariel Boatlift, Castro is celebrating the departure of marginalized populations. As Miami news anchor Ralph Renick asserted: "for Fidel Castro, it was tantamount to an act of genocide. With one fell swoop, he rid Cuba of thousands and thousands of undesirables. He emptied his prisons; he cleared the bums off the streets of Havana. Murderers, thieves, perverts, prostitutes, the retarded, crippled, [and] the winos" (WTVJ). Renick uses his public platform to criminalize the entirety of the Boatlift population, relying on dehumanizing, insulting language to characterize the émigrés. He condemns Castro and Cuba's socioeconomic and political climate and guarantees a negative reception of the Mariel émigrés in and beyond South Florida. For Renick, other representatives of local and national media outlets, and likely, their consumers, the arrival of the Mariel immigrants posed a substantial threat to the well-being of the U.S.

The threat was exaggerated and reflected racial, ableist, and xenophobic bias. Maria Cristina Garcia notes that though there was a recorded 66 percent increase in crime in 1980, with "over a third of those convicted of murder [being] Mariel Cubans . . . the troublemakers were a small fraction of the camp population."[11] Regardless, the criminal behavior was emphasized in the media; one New York Times headline, published on May 11, 1980, read: "Retarded People and Criminals are included in Cuban Exodus," making clear that the socially undesirable came to represent the larger group. Those within and beyond members of the Cuban community compared the 1980 émigrés to the earlier arrivals, observing the Mariel émigrés as darker, criminal, less affluent, and less educated.

The 1980 émigrés were also distinct from earlier waves of immigration from Cuba because they were categorized as "entrants" searching for

economic opportunities in the U.S., as opposed to fleeing political persecution. Under the 1980 Refugee Act, the Carter administration asserted
that the 1980 "entrants" could stay in the U.S. temporarily until a more
permanent status was defined.[12] This categorization, in the context of the
group's demographic, and the concurrent rise of drug distribution and violent crime, coded 1980 Cuban émigrés as an external, unwelcome threat to
Miami and the U.S. more broadly. *TIME* magazine devoted the November 2, 1981, cover page to Miami, posing the rhetorical question "Paradise
Lost?" The question addresses both Miami's booming industry as a winter
tourist escape, or paradise, and the potentially cataclysmic blow an assessment of Miami as an unsafe, drug-ridden metropolis could, and did, have
on Florida's economy. The corresponding editorial is quick to point fingers
at the latest wave of immigration into Miami: "Marielitos are believed to
be responsible for half of all violent crime in Miami."[13] Drug circulation,
including cocaine, preceded the Mariel Boatlift, but the 1980 émigrés were
scapegoated, no doubt a consequence of the racial, economic, and reported
criminality of the émigrés.

Dramatic Documentary

In both *Scarface* and *Miami Vice*, Miami's "objective reality" as interpreted
by the media's creators, is foundational to their overblown representation
of Miami's role in the transnational drug trade, cross-cultural collision, and
violence. *Scarface* (1983) begins with a prefatory, contextualizing scroll and
intercut footage of Cubans arriving in Key West from Mariel Harbor during the 1980 Mariel Boatlift. The film focuses on fictional Mariel émigré,
Tony Montana's, evolution from a refugee who murders a Communist in
exchange for quick access to a green card, to a major drug kingpin whose
boundless ambition results in an early, violent murder at the hands of com-
petitors. The introductory scroll provides a brief overview of the Boatlift,
including Fidel Castro's complicity in the exodus and contrasts his apparent
benevolence with his manipulation of the Boatlift to empty Cuban prisons
and mental asylums.[14] The scroll concludes ominously with a vague reference to the high number of émigrés with criminal records to introduce the
film's protagonist Antonio "Tony" Montana's emigration from Cuba and
illicit ascent into Miami's drug world.

The introductory, informative scroll is interspersed with images of the
Boatlift, and Al Pacino's name is presented amidst these images, contextualizing his character's story within history. The filmmakers intentionally

criminalize émigrés omitting that during this period, representatives of the Cuban state used prisons as a mechanism of group-differentiated population control and a tool to suppress political dissent.[15] The introductory framing of the film negates the complex composition of the previously incarcerated demographic and incites fear in the viewer regarding this massive wave of emigration.

Miami Vice includes and goes beyond the Mariel Boatlift émigrés, and uses its primary focus on two police officers to explore crime in Miami within and beyond various immigrant populations; Michael Mann notes that in creating the show, the production team "takes like one-tenth of one percent of the objective reality of Miami and that's what we render."[16] The series followed two Metro-Dade Police Department detectives, Ricardo Tubbs (portrayed by Philip Michael Thomas) and Sonny Crockett (portrayed by Don Johnson) in their undercover investigations and pursuits in Miami, primarily thematizing immigration, the influx of drugs, and various violent and non-violent crimes. The series referenced the Mariel Boatlift in its first episode with a suspected murderer and drug dealer, Trini DeSoto, portrayed by Martin Ferrero. In introducing himself to Crockett and Tubbs, DeSoto reveals that he is a Mariel émigré, and refers to the émigrés as riffraff, or undesirable people, who were detained by U.S. officials. In the remainder of the interaction, however, he works to distance himself from this reputation, stating that unlike other émigrés who watched TV while in detention, he sought to read, and prepare himself for his entry into the U.S. proper: "Not me, man . . . you could be stuck in this place six months, man, waiting for your papers. Use the time, man. Improve your mind." DeSoto's mention and subsequent self-distancing from this reputation indicates his awareness of how it variously entraps him, and limits his access to resources in the U.S.

Scarface and *Miami Vice* Production Histories

Scarface's December 9, 1983, release date, nearly three years after the Mariel Boatlift and a little over a year after Reagan's declaration of a War on Drugs, reflects an impulse in the film's production crew to exploit contemporary events. De Palma's adaptation of the film is thematically true to Howard Hawks' 1932 original, which follows the rise and fall of a gangster. The earlier version of the film addresses Italian immigration in Chicago and similarly criminalizes Italian immigrants through its focus on mafia violence. The film came out after Italians were beginning to identify and be identified as white, a shift historian Andrew G. Vellon traces to the post World War I era. Vellon asserts that Italian Americans began to publicly align themselves with whiteness to assure that they were afforded "viable route[s] toward full inclusion."[17] This alignment worked to challenge anti-Italian discrimination, predicated on the belief Italians were of a "swarthy, inferior race," and corresponding stereotypes that emphasized criminal, socially deviant behavior.[18]

The remake required the arrival of immigrants who would or could be criminalized and transformed into a source of fear that destabilized notions of American opportunity for all. The creators of the 1983 adaptation transpose the themes of "The American Dream," and relatedly, the stakes of inclusion, onto interethnic, interracial, post-Mariel Boatlift Miami. The film introduced Tony Montana as a Mariel émigré who "wanted the American Dream. With a vengeance," emphasizing an illicit pursuit of the money and resources that are otherwise inaccessible to Tony. As Al Pacino notes, the idea of re-creating Scarface had been in the air long before its production: "Martin Scorsese and Robert De Niro had *Scarface* in their repertoire of things they wanted to do [but] it was a difficult thing to do in today's world."[19] From Pacino's commentary, the Boatlift, and the pervasive representations of the majority Black émigré population, provided a prime opportunity to recycle the fear-mongering and tragic immigrant tale.

The film thematizes, but for the most part does not feature, Cuban people, and none of the actors in the film are Black. Only Steven Bauer, who plays Manolo, or Manny, Tony's loyal friend and associate is Cuban American. Born Esteban Ernesto Echevarría Samson, Bauer immigrated to the U.S. from Cuba at the age of four in 1960 and grew up in Miami. Bauer asserts that when interviewing/auditioning for his role in the film with director Brian De Palma, De Palma asked if he was "really Cuban" and whether he spoke Spanish. Bauer's treatment throughout the casting process of the film is reflective of the production team's engagement with Cuban people in Miami—they were interested in the experiences of this population in so much as they would help in the construction of a convincing, marketable film.

The voyeurism that informed Bauer's interactions with the casting crew is evident in the finished product of the film—Manny and Tony are Cuban émigrés, who speak almost exclusively in English with exaggerated accents as they navigate Brown, white, and decidedly not Black worlds. Antonio López and Frances Negrón-Muntaner have outlined the political implications of the construction of "Brownness" in U.S. media. For López, this Brownness places "Afro-Latino[s] . . . in a precarious relation to such 'brownings'"—they are in place and displaced by representations like Al Pacino's Tony Montana.[20] Negrón-Muntaner outlines Brownface, such as that exemplified through Pacino's performance, "as a way to get outside of 'white' skin—although not too far—and into the skin of the other without the risk."[21] The risks for white producers and viewers might include a more authentic representation of Latinx experience, or coming too close to earnest racial anxieties—viewers might be more easily able to enjoy *Scarface* because Pacino is not *really* the Black or Brown Cuban émigré.

The risks for Cubans, however, were high. Organizations like Facts about Cuban Exiles (FACE) boycotted the film because of its negative, essentializing representation of Cubans in Miami.[22] They were partly successful, as producer Martin Bregman, notes: "there was an element of the Cuban community that was convinced that this was a Castro-financed film, which was obviously not true . . . [but] there were a number of threats made and we thought it would be best to move production to California."[23] The accusation of Castro's involvement in the making of the film, as farfetched as Bregman believes it to be, makes the affront of the film to Cubans clear. Such a representation would have served Castro's interests in vilifying the U.S. and Cubans who abandoned their nation of origin for capitalism and democracy.

At stake but unspoken for both FACE and Bregman is the role the Mariel émigrés racial demographic, as contrasted with earlier Cuban émigrés' whiteness, played in community responses to *Scarface*. Montana signified a threat to white Cubans, in Miami and elsewhere, by "troubling their claim to whiteness in the United States" and threatening the economic, political, and cultural gains of white Cubans by potentially associating them with what was widely represented as racially coded deviancy. Earlier Cuban arrivals worried that the pejoratively reputed 1980 Cuban émigrés would jeopardize the high-standing and political sway the established Cuban American community held in Miami and Washington, D.C. Maria Cristina Garcia notes that the earlier émigrés, known as the Golden Exiles, who arrived between 1959 and 1965, were members of the Cuban upper class who were likely familiar with U.S. culture and practices "because of the pervasive American economic and cultural presence in post-revolutionary Cuba." In addition to their familiarity with U.S. culture, the Golden Exiles were "disproportionately white and middle class . . . including doctors, lawyers, and businessmen." The Golden Exiles were thus at an enormous advantage in their assimilation into the U.S. economic, cultural, and political sphere when compared to the newer arrivals who occupied a lower-class position in Cuba and tended to hold positions in unskilled labor.[24] Coupled with the Mariel criminal reputation, the established Cuban community pinpointed the risk of *Scarface*, which would, they argued allow negative stereotypes of the Mariel émigrés to over determine—one might even say blacken—the perception of Cubans in the U.S. overall.

Although the Mariel émigrés were able to move beyond the camp, likely through less violent means than those utilized by Montana, the Mariel émigrés encountered many more difficulties than earlier waves of Cuban emigrants. The national government provided less financial support to the 1980 Cuban émigrés and the latter group provided a challenge to the already-established Cuban American community in Miami. Heike Alberts notes that the Cuban community in Miami was initially enthusiastic about the Boatlift and the opportunity to reunite with members of their families and other social groups, but their "enthusiasm quickly decreased . . . as it became clear that the Marielitos included criminals and mental-health patients . . . [and] because of the United States' attempt to end the preferential treatment of Cubans, it did not make extensive aid programs available to the newcomers, placing a high burden on the Cuban community."[25] Aid programs, which previously facilitated the assimilation of earlier waves of emigration, were not available to the newcomers, likely a result of their widespread notorious reputation. The Mariel émigrés were thus both a financial burden, and potentially, a reputational burden on the Miami Cuban community.

Tubbs and Crockett: "Jamaican" New Yorker and "Southern Cracker"

Unlike *Scarface*, *Miami Vice* featured a racially and ethnically diverse cast, though it also simultaneously challenged and reified the demonization of émigrés.[26] The pilot of *Miami Vice* introduces the show's recurring themes of highlighting and troubling international and regional borders. The contrasting characterizations of and relationship between Detectives James "Sonny" Crockett and Ricardo "Rico" Tubbs reflect both tension and reconciliation across racial and regional lines. While Crockett is from Miami and lives on a houseboat with his pet alligator, Elvis, Tubbs is a Black American native New Yorker, with conceptions of Miami as "slow" and "backward" especially when compared to the fast-paced lifestyle he led in New York ("Heart of Darkness"). Perhaps unsurprisingly, then, the pair butt heads in their initial encounters, but eventually work together in their shared interest in "keeping Miami's streets clean."

Although the show depicts, and exploits, the at-times violent diversity that forms the setting of the show, the central focus is still a white, heterosexual, male police officer who commits to protecting the streets of Miami from an outside threat. The show positions Crockett as a native Southerner against "foreigners" and embodies white American racism, fears, and efforts to resist changes manifested by immigration into the city. Crockett's initial interaction with Tubbs, who is undercover as a Jamaican drug peddler (alias: Teddy Prentiss) in efforts to get closer to international drug dealer Esteban Calderone, reflects assumptions about people who have immigrated to Miami. Hearing Tubbs' fake and exaggerated Jamaican accent and assuming him a drug peddler, Crockett refers to Tubbs as "Mr. Voodoo" in a simplistic conflation of non-Judeo-Christian spiritualities practiced within and beyond the Caribbean.

Tubbs' adoption of a Jamaican accent and his "in-migration" to Miami from New York link his arrival to region's cultural transformation. He occupies a somewhat liminal position as a Black police officer; to Crockett, Tubbs is just another foreign criminal. His performed accent is also a further representation of his ethnic fluidity that allows him to blend in with non-white criminals. R. L. Rutsky notes *Miami Vice* inextricably links ethnic fluidity and criminality: "The international flavor of Miami and the mixing of language and cultures that this involves are major parts of the show's style. And this international circulation is also very strongly connected to the notion of vice."[27] The show links the movement of people and increased contact between different cultures with the threat of crime, particularly the influx of illicit substances. While Tubbs' green eyes, light brown skin, and softly curled hair facilitate his interactions with drug dealers while undercover, they also, as his initial interaction with Crockett suggests, link him with crime and potentially undermine his authority.

The first episode's plot interrogates Tubbs' authority; Crockett's engagement with drug dealers is legitimated in a way Tubbs' violent behavior toward Calderone is not. The audience is not formally introduced to Tubbs until approximately twenty minutes into the second half of the pilot (an hour into the series). Although Tubbs and Crockett first meet earlier in the episode, Tubbs introduces himself (after it is revealed that "Teddy Prentiss" is an undercover identity) using his deceased brother's badge to gain access to the Calderone case. Until Crockett confronts Ricardo Tubbs, having discovered that Rafael Tubbs is dead, the viewer is unclear as to Tubbs' role within the show, while Crockett's role as an authority figure is presented immediately. Though Tubbs ultimately achieves a similar form of authority through his partnership with Crockett, his introduction invites the audience to perceive him as an unreliable and untrustworthy character for the majority of the first two-hour episode.

Tubbs's and Crockett's interactions also draw on Southern stereotypes of anti-Blackness. When Crockett confronts Tubbs, explaining that he knows the latter officer has lied about his identity; Tubbs explains that he is attempting to avenge his brother's death. Pulling out Rafael's badge, Tubbs draws Crockett's attention to the physical resemblance between him and his brother, trying to convince Crockett that he has ties to law enforcement: "I know we all look alike to you Southern crackers but not this much! Look at the picture, man!" In this retort, Tubbs expresses an understanding of Southern stereotypes of Blackness, evoking a history of white supremacy and violence against Black people that he associates with contemporary law enforcement in Miami. In so doing, Tubbs vocalizes his perception of Crockett's racial politics, and reiterates his designation of Miami as a historically Southern city.

Crockett agrees to help Tubbs capture Calderone and the pair's first collaboration, and continued partnership, emblematizes a kind of racial reconciliation to resist international crime. Though the pair arrests Calderone, he escapes and flees on a plane to the Bahamas. Calderone's destination accentuates connections between Miami and the Caribbean, especially in relation to drug trafficking. After Calderone's escape, Crockett, in a conciliatory gesture, asks Tubbs if he has "ever [considered] a career in Southern law enforcement" to which Tubbs replies, "maybe," marking his eventual transfer to the Miami Vice department ("My Brother's Keeper Pt. II"). By agreeing to work together, the conclusion of the pilot suggests that distinctions between white, male, Southern, and Black, male, Northern are dismissible in efforts to address the threat of international crime. Indeed, it is only as a united front that Crockett and Tubbs kill Calderone in the sixth episode of the series ("Calderone's Return").

Of course, their partnership, when not immediately threatened by violent crime in Miami, is not entirely free of conflict and metaphorizes regional differences within the U.S. Tubbs and Crockett frequently banter, contrasting Miami and New York throughout the first season. In the third episode of the series, when Tubbs asks about the delayed receipt of lab results, Crockett replies, "this is Miami, things move a little bit slower here" ("Heart of Darkness"). While both Crockett's and Tubbs' earlier descriptions depict Miami as a slow-paced, overgrown, Southern town, the fast-paced plots of the episodes (centered predominantly on high-speed chases and frequent shoot-outs), the show's incorporation of contemporary music, and its address of immigration and corresponding influx of cocaine and drug money into the city suggest otherwise. The introductory focus on Southernness serves as a contrast to the violently diverse city that characterizes the show throughout the remainder of the series.

Alex Stepick and Guillermo Grenier echo Sonny Crockett's and Ricardo Tubbs' assessment of Miami's former Southernness, specifically calling attention to the city's demographics and corresponding sociopolitical and economic hierarchies:

> Before the 1960s, Miami's population consisted largely of Black and white southern *in-migrants* and their descendants . . . Bahamian immigrants provided the local, unskilled labor, and they outnumbered Black Americans, who came to Miami primarily from northern Florida and Georgia. But neither Bahamian Blacks nor Black Americans had significant political or economic power in early Miami. It was a southern city, one in which Blacks were denied most basic rights: whites, including the police and the Ku Klux Klan, could harass and even kill Blacks with impunity.[28]

Their explication conflates Southernness with the economic and political oppression of Black Americans and other Black people. This description of the treatment of Black Bahamians and Black Americans contrasts with the treatment of recent immigrants to the city between 1959 and 1980: "In Miami, these groups are not powerless in any general sense. Rather, immigrants in Miami exert power over significant aspects of the social structure, including city politics and some sectors of the economy."[29] Through this comparison, Stepick and Grenier describe a complex hierarchy that privileged recent arrivals over disenfranchised Black groups with a longer history in the city.

The show associates immigration, or more aptly, non-white and/or non-English speaking immigrants and "foreignness" with crime. Conversely, the show links whiteness to "Southern law enforcement" through the series' primary focus on Detective Sonny Crockett. As Steve Sanders notes, while the show's plot primarily relies on the interactions between Crockett and Tubbs,

Don Johnson is clearly the center of dramatic interest. This is shown not only in the way the framing consistently privileges Johnson over Philip Michael Thomas and Edward James Olmos, but also in the way the camera movement focuses on Johnson, following him when he enters or leaves a room with the other vice squad members.[30]

Centering its white male protagonist betrays the series' white gaze. *Miami Vice* constructs a tenuous binary between white, law-enforcing Miamians and non-white/non-native law-breaking immigrants that the show troubles through its persistent representation of police corruption—usually presented as an unavoidable consequence of their illicit connections and relationships with immigrants.

The show's original producer, Anthony Yerkovich, outlines the show's objectives of demonstrating a corrupt and corrupting American Dream that ensnares Crockett and implicates South Florida's shifting racial demographics. Steve Sanders writes that Yerkovich was inspired to create the show after learning that "nearly one-third of unreported income in the United States originated in or was funneled through South Florida."[31] Beyond his interest in the amount of money circulating in Miami, especially through illicit channels, he, like the creators of *Scarface*, expresses interest in the corrupt elements of the American Dream: "I wanted a city in which the American dream had been distilled into something perverse . . . I wanted to use the city figuratively and metaphorically. I wanted to place an existential hero in a city based on greed."[32] The show's existential hero, Crockett, is corrupted by his proximity to dramatized Black and Brown crime. As Steve Sanders notes:

> Long a bilingual city, Miami's rapid multiculturalization is due largely to immigration from Cuba, Haiti, and Central America, and so it is woven into the program's storylines . . . Storylines in episodes like the following give but a hint of the show's use of Caribbean, southeast Asian, Chinese, and South American cultural backgrounds: a Haitian crime boss . . . convinces his followers he has returned from the dead ("Tale of the Goat"), a Santerían priestess . . . is consulted to develop evidence of the connection between the ritualistic killings of police officers and drug traffickers ("Whatever Works"), a Chilean police officer . . . buys cluster bombs from an arms dealer referred by a renegade DEA official ("Baseballs of Death"), a Central American poet (Byrne Piven) is sought by assassins ("Free Verse"), a Chinese drug lord (Keye Luke) comes to Miami to taunt Castillo ("Golden

Triangle, Part 2"), an Argentine assassin (Jim Zubiena) has Crockett on his hit list. [33]

As Sanders' brief overview suggests, the serialized nature of the sitcom allowed the producers of the show to tackle a different immigrant group within each episode as well as political strife more globally. The show presents an at-times voyeuristic representation of these groups and reveals anxieties surrounding the possibility of sociopolitical conflicts in South America (and other regions) spilling out onto Miami's streets.

In this list, Sanders affords more documentary status than the sitcom deserves given its hyperbolic representations of South Florida's "multiculturalization." Like *Scarface*, *Miami Vice* intended to exaggerate and exploit the region's reputation while simultaneously capitalizing on Miami's position as "a global city." Sheila L. Croucher links Miami's globality to its diversity, noting that the city's "international commerce . . . and demographic makeup" have resulted in its characterization as a "City of the Future."[34] *Miami Vice* suggests, through its characterization of its white male protagonist, secondary characters, and ephemeral antagonists, that the tension between Southernness and the varying racial, ethnic, and religious groups entering the city during this period informs globalization in Miami. With its sustained engagement with immigration and related police corruption, the show provides an alternate, and indeed more violent and pessimistic, representation of the diversity so often celebrated in Miami.

Although Crockett's curmudgeonly and sometimes rage-filled characterization emblematizes his investment in clean policing, his character ultimately violates many of the ethics he initially espoused. The final season links Crockett's eventual corruption to U.S.-Caribbean crime rings. After the murder of Crockett's second wife, Caitlin, at the hands of a vengeful criminal whom Crockett had encountered and arrested earlier in the series, he uses his skills and resources as a police officer to track down the murderer, Frank Hackman, on Caicos Island and murders him. Crockett commits the murder in the Caribbean, drawing on his police skills in fulfillment of extralegal persecution and execution of criminals. Before Crockett fires the fatal shot, Hackman taunts him referring to Crockett's pride in being a clean cop and his otherwise spotless history. As Hackman explains, "you can't shoot an unarmed man" to which Crockett replies, after killing him, "wrong" ("Deliver Us from Evil"). Hackman's murder marks an important transition point in Crockett's character; before this episode he explained that though "he cut corners," it was always in the interest of "getting the bad guys" and keeping others safe. Murdering Hackman who posed no immediate threat, reflects an interest in vengeance, as opposed to public safety ("Cool Runnin'").

Hackman's murder seems to be a tipping point that foreshadows Crockett's complete immersion into criminal life. Though Crockett returns to undercover work after his wife's death, with the illegal execution of Hackman unacknowledged (and likely unknown) by members of his department, he is notably depressed and encouraged by Tubbs to take some time off ("Mirror Image Part 2"). Later in the same episode, Crockett boards a boat as his alias, Sonny Burnett, to attend a meeting between two notable rival gangs. An unknown person detonates a bomb on the boat and though Crockett survives the blast, he endures head trauma and the resulting amnesia leads him to forget all aspects of his identity, including his position as a police officer. Members of one of the gangs take him to the hospital, and convince him that he is Sonny Burnett, prompting him to adopt his undercover, drug-dealing alias as his full-time identity.

In a complete inversion, Crockett becomes the most pressing threat to the Miami Vice department by aligning himself with a Colombian drug dealer. Throughout his time as Sonny Burnett (a three-episode arc spanning from the end of the fourth season to the beginning of the fifth), Crockett infiltrates the ranks of Miguel Manolo's cocaine cartel and shoots two police officers: a white cop who is working with Manolo (who is killed), and Tubbs (who is saved by his bulletproof vest). Crockett's immersion into street crime, especially when considering the murder of a white police officer, is a hyperbolic reflection of the corruptive capacity of his surroundings. Crockett eventually remembers who he is after Tubbs meets with him one-on-one and poses leading questions to jog his memory: "You from around here, from Florida? You've been married?" ("Hostile Takeover"). Though not immediately convinced, Crockett decides to visit the police department and his memory is sparked while looking at his locker. Crockett's coworkers distrust him upon his return, and interrogate him, which sparks his ultimate departure from the department in the series' final, two-part episode.

Paradise Lost: Crockett and Tubbs Leave the Force

The series finale criminalizes the entirety of the Caribbean through its metonymic construction of a fictional island's dictator and ominously presents corruption within the U.S. national government. Tubbs and Crockett are tracking a major drug figure and violent, dictatorial leader of the fictional Costa Morada, General Manuel Borbon. Tubbs explains that Borbon's "regime is banked by drug dealers" and that he is responsible for "most of the drug flow into Miami" ("Freefall Part 1"). While the show's earlier seasons link the cocaine trade and general political strife to real nations in South America (mostly Colombia) or the Caribbean (mostly Cuba), Costa Morada acts as a flexible symbol, encouraging the audience to project their conceptions of strife in Latin America onto this fictional island that threatens Miami by virtue of its imagined proximity. The island could be Cuba or an intentionally distorted representation of Colombia, but it could also be a composite of the different nations represented in the series' earlier seasons. Given the international stakes of taking down Borbon, Crockett is understandably reluctant, but Tubbs explains that they have many leads to the drug lord. Crockett replies sardonically "for once we can really make a difference," revealing his disillusionment toward the department's ability to keep Miami's streets clean ("Freefall Part 1"). Though they eventually catch Borbon and turn him in to federal agents expecting him to be prosecuted, they discover that "the Feds are protecting Borbon," because he has potentially harmful information on a high-ranking official in the U.S. government who is profiting from international drug trade.

Upon discovering the high-level corruption that has resulted in Borbon's protection, and thus facilitates the influx of drugs into Miami, Crockett and Tubbs continue to track down Borbon, discovering him boarding a plane with several federal agents. As the plane ascends, Tubbs and Crockett shoot at it causing it to explode while in air, presumably killing all passengers. In this dramatic conclusion, the *Miami Vice* officers take a stand against Caribbean drug lords and against corrupt federal agents. Agent Baker, a representative of the federal government, chastises Crockett and Tubbs, asserting that he "will have [their] badges" for interfering with federal affairs and adding that "[their] brand of law and order went out with Wyatt Earp" ("Freefall Part 2"). By asserting that Crockett's and Tubbs' mode of policing is antiquated, the agent suggests that contemporary law enforcement of Miami is characterized by negotiating with and even protecting the criminals Crockett and Tubbs frequently arrested, or, as the Wyatt Earp reference suggests, shot, and killed. By linking Earp's loud and confrontational mode of law enforcement with Crockett and Tubbs' methods, Baker provides a contrast between fighting crime and an allegedly new mode of clandestine policing that protects monetary interests as opposed to public good. Rather than fighting crime, then, this new mode of negotiatory law enforcement is contingent on the redistribution of power, through illicit venues, across and within international borders. In an acknowledgement of burnout and the pervasive corruption within local and national government, Crockett and Tubbs throw their badges on the ground in front of Baker.

Later in the episode, Tubbs arrives at Crockett's houseboat, explaining that he will be returning to the "big bad Bronx," though it is unclear if he intends to continue his career in law enforcement. Crockett explains that he will head "somewhere further south . . . where the water's warm, the drinks are cold and [he] [doesn't] know the names of the players" ("Freefall Part 2). While there is ambiguity about Tubbs' career in law enforcement, Crockett escapes from law enforcement altogether—while he may very well be heading to the Caribbean or South America, the regions frequently attributed to the challenges he experienced as a police officer, he hopes to be ignorant of the perpetrators of violent and/or drug related crime. Crockett then offers Tubbs a ride to the airport and reiterates the question that sparked their partnership: "you ever consider a career in Southern law enforcement?" to which Tubbs replies, laughing, "maybe, maybe" as the pair drives away. The show's introductory and conclusory evocation of Southernness is striking as it suggests, given Tubbs' and Crockett's departure, that Southern law enforcement must now be found (and enacted) elsewhere. Their departure, coming on the tail end of Crockett's complete immersion into crime, suggests that representatives of Southern law enforcement are vulnerable because of their proximity to criminal lifestyles, especially those demonstrated by people who recently immigrated to Miami. While Baker seems to embrace this phenomenon, encouraging transnational arrangements with nonnative drug dealers, Crockett and Tubbs choose to abandon the city that has enabled and encouraged such corruption. With their abandonment of Miami, the finale suggests that corruption, consistently conflated with immigration, has made way for a unique hierarchy in the city in which police like Crockett and Tubbs are now obsolete.

Policing Borders: Law Enforcement in *Miami Vice* and *Scarface*

Despite the latter show's focus on law enforcement and the policing of immigrants, *Scarface*, more explicitly than *Miami Vice*, highlights how the fear of Mariel émigrés manifested in tense clashes between émigrés and law enforcement/border control. Upon arriving in Miami, three white American Immigration and Naturalization Service (INS) officers interrogate Montana. The scene features a series of close-ups of Pacino, in which the scar on his face is prominently displayed and he speaks with a pronounced accent that marks his liminal position in the U.S. During the interrogation, the INS officers are standing over Tony in a physical enactment of their hierarchal power over him and his fate in the U.S. Montana sits, looking up defiantly as the agents surround him, as though concerned that Montana can escape the confined room.

Observing his scar, and even grabbing Montana's chin to tilt his head upward, one of the agents asks, "how'd you get the beauty scar, tough guy? Eating pussy?" Montana points out how unusual this question is ("how am I gonna get a scar like that eating pussy, meng?"), and highlights the invasive nature of the interview that interrogates his sex life. Susana Peña's investigation into the *papi* discourse that circulated in Miami after the Mariel Boatlift helps to contextualize the bizarre conflation of sex and violence as it manifests in the agent's question:

The *papi* discourse draws on racialized assumptions that depict Latino urban male youths as street-tough and somewhat dangerous even as it eroticizes this danger.[35]

The question, and physicality with which it is asked, gesture to this eroticization of Montana's dangerous difference as a Mariel émigré. The agents proceed to ask Montana if he spent any time in jail, before noticing a tattoo on his hand. The agent notes that he has seen many of the same tattoos, asserting, "pitchfork means assassin, or something," before asking if Tony wants "to take a trip to the detention center." Permanent marks on Tony's body metaphorize his marginalization as a Mariel émigré. Within the interrogation, Tony also explains that he learned English in school and that his father "was a Yankee [and] used to take [him] a lot to the movies [where he] watched the guys like Humphrey Bogart" and explains that the films "teach me to talk." His experience of learning English through the dissemination of U.S. popular culture preceding Castro's rise to power is reflective of the cultural permeability that facilitated earlier Cuban émigrés' assimilation. When asked about his family, Tony asserts that both his father and mother are dead, though later in the film we see Tony reuniting with his mother and younger sister, Gina. Given the stakes of the interrogation, which could result in Tony's repatriation to Cuba, his responses to the interrogators can be read as ambiguous at best. Despite his efforts to trick the interrogators, they focus on the physical markings on his body, including the scar on his face and the tattoo on his hand.

Tony finally confesses that he spent time in jail after attempting to purchase U.S. dollars. While the officers drag him away, Tony asks them if they are Communists. He continues, asking how they would enjoy a Communist regime with "People telling you what to think, what to say," and asks the men if they would "want to work eight, ten fucking hours, man, [owning] nothing, [having] nothing?" Here, Tony expresses the appeal to capitalism where work is rewarded with property and wages that allow citizens to assert economic autonomy. He continues, explaining that despite the prejudices of the officers, he is not a criminal: "I'm Tony Montana, a political prisoner from Cuba and I want my fucking human rights, just like Jimmy Carter said." By citing Carter, Montana reiterates the ideological promise the President made to him that entitles him to asylum in the U.S. Despite his brief, yet detailed, explanation of his experiences in Cuba, which included eating octopus three times a day, the interrogators remain unmoved, asserting they "don't believe a word" of Tony's speech. They conclude that "that son of a bitch Castro is shitting all over us." Though the film eventually reveals that Tony has a history of crime in Cuba, consisting primarily of robbing banks and bodegas, his criminality is legible on his body as opposed to any criminal record or his own testimony. Because of his physical markings and pronounced accent, the interrogators immediately deem him as violent, foreign, and dangerous; his tattoos are affirmation of Castro's malice in an exaggerated representation of the immigrant body.

Montana's violent acquisition of a green card that allows him to leave the camp, Freedomtown, further hyperbolizes the ill-reputed arrival of the Cuban émigrés. He and his friend Manny are offered expedited access to green cards in exchange for murdering an alleged Castro informant/collaborator. Tony responds to the proposition, boasting: "I kill a communist for fun, but for a green card, I'm gonna carve him up real nice." By murdering Emilio Rebenga, Montana kills off the vestiges of Cuban Communism and marks his inauguration into U.S. capitalism in which a service is recompensed with a material payoff. Throughout the remainder of the film, Montana refuses to engage any conversations about Communism and his experiences in a Cuban prison—shortly after Tony and Manny begin to work for Frank López, a local drug lord, Tony voices his desire to overtake Frank and have an affair with his wife, Elvira Hancock. Hancock's last name when read with her ultimate possession by Tony (to use his logic) layer the film's metaphor of distorted U.S. assimilation. Manny encourages him to keep his ambition in check: "just remember last year this time we were in a fucking cage in Cuba." Tony quickly replies, "You remember. I'd like to forget that."

By killing Rebenga, a representative of Cuban Communism and refusing to recall his experiences in Cuba, Montana attempts to erase the abuses he endured in Cuba that by his estimation have no bearing on his future in the U.S. His efforts at erasure counter the immediate judgments from the INS officers during the interrogation, which suggest that Tony's past is permanently imprinted on his body. Initially marked as an outsider by the INS officers, Tony achieves a somewhat liminal status with the murderous acquisition of the green card—he is not yet an American citizen despite his insistence that his experiences in Cuba be forgotten, but he is able to move beyond the physically restrictive tent camp and into the broader U.S. sphere.

Other interactions between Tony and law enforcement function to contribute to his racialized alienation from other Cuban émigrés. When local undercover police officers bust Tony for fraudulently converting money he has earned from selling drugs, one of the arresting officers identifies himself as Cuban. After revealing his identity as an officer to Tony, the unnamed man expresses disdain: "Cabrón, you call yourself a real Cuban? You make a real Cuban throw up." In referring to Tony as "cabrón" (a slang term that means coward or cuckold, depending on the context), the officer endeavors to emasculate him, conflating a definition of Cubanness with masculinity. The officer interrogates Tony's Cubanness from his position as a representative of U.S. authority, a heightened form of assimilation that is juxtaposed with Tony's position as a "browned" drug dealer. The interaction with the Cuban police officer reinscribes Tony's exclusion from ideals of Cuban respectability and successful assimilation.

This exclusion even alienates Tony from his own family, interactions with whom continuously reify the intra-communal tensions in post-Mariel Miami. After establishing some financial success working with López, Tony finds his mother and sister, and attempts to retire his mother and support both women financially. Tony asserts, "My kid sister doesn't have to work in no beauty parlor and Mamá don't have to sew in no factory. Your son made it, Mamá." Montana uses language to suggest he has fulfilled the American Dream. In this context, Montana's imagined fulfillment necessitates a corresponding inscription of gendered norms wherein men provide for women financially. Tony's mother is immediately skeptical, asking Tony who he killed to earn the thousand dollars he has presented to confirm his promise of financial support. Tony fictitiously explains that he is an organizer for an anti-Castro group that receives many donations. In offering this story, Montana appeals to the widespread anti-Communist sentiment among Miami's Cuban communities. His mother sees through his facade and accuses him of violently taking the money from someone, asserting, "All we hear about in the papers is animals like you and the killings . . . it's Cubans like you who are giving a bad name to our people, people who come here and work hard and make a good name for themselves. People who send their children to school." Montana's mother reiterates the pervasiveness of negative broadcasting about the Mariel population. She further argues that these "animals," to use her dehumanizing language, both mis- and over-represent hard-working individuals who strive to fulfill middle-class values of good reputation and education. Tony's methods of "making it" are frowned upon by his mother. Before kicking Tony out of her house, she firmly asserts, "I don't need your money. Gracias. I work for my living." Tony's acquisition of money is not the problem, but rather how his mother assumes he earned so much money so quickly. His illicit methodology in achieving an aspect of the American Dream, economic success, is a commentary on the characteristics of the 1980 émigrés that ostracizes him from the remainder of the Cuban community.

Both *Scarface* and *Miami Vice* reference these intra-community tensions among Miami's Cuban/Cuban American populations. They exaggerate these tensions by aligning white, well-to-do Cubans with law enforcement who use their power to arrest, and sometimes kill Mariel émigrés. In a general example, *Miami Vice* represents many white Latinx in positions of power within the show, emblematized by Lieutenant Castillo's role (portrayed by Edward James Olmos) as the head of the department. His position speaks to the shifting economic and sociopolitical hierarchy in Miami that eventually came to favor white Latinxs. In "Heroes of the Revolution," the twenty-fourth episode in *Miami Vice*'s third season, the audience learns that Gina Calabrese, a high-ranking detective within the Miami Vice department portrayed by Saundra Santiago, is a Golden Exile. The episode opens with the detectives of the Miami Vice department pursuing a major drug lord, Orrestes Pedrosa, who murdered Gina's mother in Cuba in the early years of the Revolution. In reviewing the file on Pedrosa, Detective Tubbs asks: "was he a Marielito?" The question was likely inspired by the date of Pedrosa's arrival in Miami in February 1980. Another detective responds, "he grew up in Cuba, but he has a Belizean passport" ("Heroes of the Revolution"). This is neither a yes nor a no response to the question Tubbs posed, and suggests that Cubans, especially those involved in criminal networks, who came to Miami were implicitly linked to the Boatlift. Gina both before and after learning Pedrosa's role in her own life, contributes to the state-sanctioned pursuit and persecution of Pedrosa. Her position as a police officer reflects a hyperbolic form of assimilation, as she has the authority to enforce U.S. laws, oftentimes against people who have recently immigrated to Miami. Her successful assimilation is reflective of the favorable treatment of white Cubans from earlier waves of emigration, especially when compared to the Mariel émigrés.

Scarface makes clear that Gina's successful assimilation was not a trajectory afforded to all émigrés. Montana's illegal moneymaking endeavors demonstrably alienate him from his community, yet earlier parts of the film suggest that he has limited options to help him achieve economic success. For example, the film depicts the inhumane, impromptu housing offered to Mariel émigrés, including Tony, in Freedomtown where they are unable to make their own money and further, unable to leave until INS processes them and gives them their green cards—this process is expedited for both Manny and Tony after Tony kills Rebenga. The real "Freedomtown" did not differ widely from that re-created in the film and further marked Black and Brown Cuban émigrés as separate from the broader U.S. public. The encampment was composed of several large tents behind high, barbed-wire fences and was located under one of the overpasses in downtown Miami. While the fences implied an effort to quarantine the recent arrivals from the broader Miami population, the highly visible placement of the camps (in one of the most populous and frequently traveled areas of Miami) made the émigrés a spectacle, reinforcing sensationalized representation of the Boatlift. Because of the massive amounts of émigrés who lacked sponsorship in Miami, many were processed and housed in churches, recreation centers, hotels, dog kennels, and eventually in "tent cities," the largest of which was close to Little Havana, a predominantly Cuban neighborhood.[36] The management of the arrival of the 1980 Cuban émigrés indicates both a lack of resources to deal with the massive influx and dehumanization of the émigrés evinced by their housing in dog kennels. The film's inclusion of the tent city reiterates the 1980 Cuban émigrés' exclusion from ideals of acceptability and frames the ostracization Montana experiences throughout the film.

Montana's transition from the camp into Miami proper further exemplifies his limited access to well-paying jobs. Unsurprisingly, when Tony and Manny leave the camp, they have limited opportunities for employment and end up working as dishwashers in a food truck. While working, the pair enviously watches wealthy white Americans valeting their cars at a nightclub across the street. Tony complains, hunched over a sink full of dishes, that "[he] did not come to the United States to break [his] fuckin' back," making clear that he expects to make money without engaging in physical and/or minimum wage labor that will not propel him into the world of elite nightclubs. While they are working, Manny informs Tony that he has arranged a meeting with local drug dealers and during a break, the two men negotiate a deal in which they will move two kilos of cocaine for $5,000. The payment is substantially higher than what Tony and Manny combined could make working a minimum wage job as dishwashers, highlighting the appeal of drug dealing for a Mariel émigré with limited "marketable" skills. After they make the deal, Tony throws his apron at the owner of the food truck and declares, "I'm retired!" Quitting the job marks Tony's voluntary departure from a normative and unsubstantial form of employment in lieu of quick, illicit, and bountiful cash. Although getting the green card is enough to move him away from a site that is excluded from broader U.S. society, Tony's legibility as a violent immigrant limits him to forms of employment that are unlikely to lead to speedy economic prosperity. The film's attention to the limited access to stable employment experienced by the 1980 Cuban émigrés is indicative of the production crew's efforts at accurately contextualizing the film.

Miami and the War on Drugs

These intra-ethnic cross-racial tensions and limited avenues for economic uplift are navigated with a backdrop of increased policing of drug dealers and users (especially those who were not white) during the so-called War on Drugs. These representations thus present a dilemma for émigrés who, like Tony Montana, create and rely on alternate, though highly policed, economies. The Nixon administration coined the term "War on Drugs" in 1971, but the announcement proved largely rhetorical, as there were no corresponding alterations in U.S. drug policy apart from the founding of the Drug Enforcement Agency (DEA) in 1973. The administration established the DEA to deal with all aspects of the nation's drug problem.[37] However, eleven years later, the Reagan administration re-launched the War on Drugs with, as many scholars have noted, an almost vengeful attack on drug users. President Reagan declared his War on Drugs on October 14, 1982, and throughout the remainder of his presidency, the Reagan administration exerted immense resources to address what he viewed as a pressing cultural problem. As noted by Bruce Michael Bagley, "to accomplish this urgent 'national security' objective, the federal government rapidly increased expenditures for narcotics control programs . . . reaching $4.3 billion annually in 1988."[38] The administration directed this increased budget toward agencies that would penalize drug use, including sects of the Federal Bureau of Investigations, the Department of Defense, and the Drug Enforcement Administration. Meanwhile, the budget of agencies that were tasked with providing rehabilitative treatment for users was cut dramatically—the budget of the National Institute on Drug Abuse dropped from $274 million in 1981 to $57 million in 1984.[39] It was clear that Reagan's War on Drugs was not a beneficent effort to rehabilitate drug users and dealers, but rather an effort to eradicate drug use through the increased penalization and prosecution of both users and dealers. Though the War on Drugs was considered a national problem, the consequences of the increased policing of drug use in the U.S. affected certain populations substantially more than others. Michelle Alexander asserts that inner-city communities, populated mostly by minorities, saw significant declines in employment throughout the 1980s because of deindustrialization and globalization, and argues that a "decline in legitimate employment opportunities among inner-city residents increased incentives to sell drugs."[40] Tony Montana's brief employ as a dishwasher exemplifies this point, and in the film serves as the catalyst for Montana's work moving cocaine.

The policing of the international drug trade frames anxieties about the spread of drugs and concurrent xenophobic rhetoric surrounding U.S. immigration policies. Namely, both the influx of drugs and immigrants manifested in a fear that the admission of "undesirables" compromised the overall health of the nation; the influx of drugs corresponded with an increase in street crime, and transmission of diseases.[41] While the drug epidemic was and is a domestic issue resulting from fluctuations in employment and manufactured scarcity of rehabilitative services, officials opportunistically projected systemic issues onto outsiders in a xenophobic effort to vindicate the U.S. Given Miami's location within the Caribbean basin and its depressed economy in the 1980s, the corresponding growth in illicit drug sales also affected the incarceration rates of Black men, including recent immigrants.[42] Marvin Dunn outlines the carceral boom in the context of Black Miami, and a largely Black Mariel Boatlift to exemplify the clear biases in the enforcement and punishment of drug use and selling.[43]

The Reagan administration also "[intensified] interdiction efforts along US borders and law enforcement programs in foreign source and transit countries."[44] The consumption and movement of drugs evolved from a national problem into a hemispheric witch hunt; the 1980s saw increased policing of Caribbean, Central, and South American countries, perhaps especially Mexico, Jamaica, Colombia, and Peru. The U.S.'s focus on these nations as major drug producers culminated in the formation of the South Florida Drug Task Force in 1982, which combined agents from the DEA, Customs, the FBI, IRS, U.S. Army, and U.S. Navy in efforts to take down drug traffickers. This coalitional organization served as a model for other regional task forces within the U.S., such as Operation Alliance.[45]

Miami, as a major port city and known site of cocaine smuggling, was an area of especial concern. In *Scarface*, Tony Montana remarks on the corresponding increase of policing of Florida's waters when trying to smuggle cocaine in from Bolivia: "you got the fuckin' Navy; you got frogmen; you got EC-25 with the satellite tracking shit; you got the fuckin' Bell 209 assault choppers up the ass. We're losing one out of every nine loads." Montana's assessment of the increased policing of Miami and nearby waters reflects the contemporary militarized prevention of drug transmission into the U.S.

Tony's interactions with figures of authority metaphorize other contemporary socioeconomic and legal dynamics. Once he has made a name for himself and broken away from other major drug dealers, Mel Bernstein, the Chief Detective of the Miami Narcotics Unit, proposes that Montana pay the department an undisclosed amount of money monthly. In exchange, Bernstein promises that "[they will] tell [Tony] who's moving against [him] and . . . shake down who [Tony] wants shaken down." With this offer, Bernstein affords Montana authoritative power in controlling part of Miami's law enforcement. Bernstein is a metonymic representation of a larger phenomenon of authorities turning a profit on the local importation and distribution of drugs; in 1987, four years after the release of *Scarface*, fifteen Miami Dade County police officers were charged with running a drug distribution business.[46] Although Bernstein's offer makes clear that the local authorities are complicit in the distribution of drugs and violence, they can maintain their authority and legality while Montana's unauthorized, criminal, immigrant status marginalizes him.

Montana voices a related critique against politicians who profit from the drug trade while watching a news broadcast about the potential legalization of illicit drugs to eradicate organized crime: "politicians . . . want coke to be legal so they can tax it and get money and they can get votes." Manny responds that "[politicians have] been around a thousand years, they got all the angles figured out." Once again, the film calls attention to a complicity in the management of drugs that glorifies politicians, depicted in the news clip as predominantly white, and vilifies non-white men who are involved in the same system, though to differing degrees.

Given its central focus on law enforcement, *Miami Vice* more explicitly addresses the collaborative efforts of law enforcement agencies and similarly metaphorizes the hyper-policing of Black and Brown bodies and nations. The show represents these collaborations through the mention of the limited jurisdiction of the Miami Vice police department and resulting collaboration with the FBI (a frequent occurrence in the series, and related crime dramas), and elsewhere through the violation of jurisdictional parameters evinced by Crockett and Tubbs' multiple trips to the Caribbean for police work. In the fifth episode of the first season, Crockett and Tubbs follow international criminal, Esteban Calderone, to the Bahamas, and although they have "absolutely no jurisdiction" in the Bahamas, as their supervisor who discourages "any vigilante stuff" reminds them, they illustrate an undercover operation to get at Calderone by tracking down his daughter. Their interaction with their supervisor details how international travel for police should work, asserting that they are "just there for surveillance" and that they will inform the Bahamian authorities of Calderone's presence and anticipate his extradition. This interaction suggests international collaborations in the pursuit of drug dealers, expanding on Bagley's mention of the South Florida Task Force.

Miami Vice takes several cues from *Scarface*, perhaps especially with its attention to corruption in law enforcement. The show links immigration, or more aptly, non-white and/or non-English speaking immigrants and "foreignness" with crime, and whiteness to "Southern law enforcement." Through these associations, *Miami Vice* constructs a tenuous binary between white, law-enforcing Miamians and non-white/non-native law-breaking immigrants. However, as in *Scarface*, there are several integral moments wherein this binary is troubled by the show's persistent representation of police corruption, particularly the corruption of local, and eventually national, white law enforcement officers through their illicit connections and relationships with immigrants. Because of these illicit collaborations, immigrants yield substantial economic and political power to influence the city. Unlike *Scarface*, however, *Miami Vice* does not offer a sustained engagement with the Mariel Boatlift. Instead, the themes of the show suggest that in a post-Mariel Boatlift cultural moment, all manner of vice, especially that carried out by Caribbean and South American émigrés happens in Miami. The show thus positions the Mariel Boatlift as a watershed moment wherein crime is linked to Caribbean and South American émigrés.

Through its depictions of police corruption, and the nature of these depictions, *Miami Vice* presents the fictionalized department and Miami generally, as a permeable and vulnerable contact zone that challenges and redefines Southern, and thus U.S. authority. As such, beyond the criminality attributed to their involvement in cocaine smuggling, the transgressive infiltration of nonnative drug dealers in the Miami Vice department suggests another more pressing degree of criminality. Indeed, it suggests that non-white immigrants challenge the authority of the police department, the racial/ethnic hierarchy of the city, and signal an imperative to defend borders.

In navigating emerging borders between racial and ethnic communities in South Florida, *Miami Vice* took a unique approach to depicting the social position of Black Americans, both through its casting of a Black American as Tubbs and its depiction of a Black informant, Nugart Neville Lamont, portrayed by Charlie Barnett, a recurring secondary character throughout the first season of the series. These representations position Black Americans in a secondary role to the show's white protagonist, yet afford their characters authority over non-white, non-American antagonists. Though Stepick and Grenier suggest a hierarchy that privileges immigrants and exiles, Lamont's favorable treatment by Crockett and Tubbs reveals *Miami Vice*'s specific interest in vilifying Miami's immigrant population. Lamont's character is debuted in "Cool Runnin'" when Crockett and Tubbs are attempting to arrest a group of Jamaican drug dealers. Lamont, recently arrested by the two officers, finds out about the duo's efforts to bring down the Jamaican crime ring and convincingly lies to Crockett explaining that he is familiar with a prominent Black Jamaican drug dealer, Desmond Maxwell, to avoid jail time. Crockett catches on and ultimately demands that Lamont use his street connections to "set up a drug deal between Desmond and [Crockett and Tubbs]" assuring Lamont that he will be protected by the police ("Cool Runnin'"). The Miami Vice department's utilization of a Black informant with a criminal past to detain a Black immigrant criminal suggests that crimes committed by émigrés are ultimately more threatening offenses.

Lamont's ongoing collaboration with the Miami Vice department suggests an impulse to overlook natives' status as criminals in effort to present a united front or impassable border between the more pressing threat in immigrant criminality and Miami's native population. When Crockett and Tubbs visit Lamont at the hospital after he sustains injuries in a shoot-out with Desmond Maxwell, they offer him chocolates as a token of gratitude for his assistance in the case; he replies angrily, "You know what? You guys are something else. You try to get me bumped [killed] by three crazed Jamaicans and you buy me a box of candy?" Lamont pinpoints his exploitation in this interaction. He continues, explaining that he understands the nature of his relationship with the two police officers: "you use me one time, I'll use you the next time." Tubbs and Crockett laugh off this suggestion, making clear that Lamont is only worth the information he has supplied, and the officers would likely arrest him should he continue committing crime and cease to be helpful in closing their cases. Though Lamont's arrangement with Crockett and Tubbs can hardly be equated to power, the Vice department temporarily protects him, and his engagement with criminals is legitimated in a way Maxwell's is not.

In addition to presenting a hierarchy within Afro-Diasporic communities in Miami, *Miami Vice* suggests that proximity to immigrant communities (of whichever race and/or ethnicity) potentially corrupts white law enforcement officers. In the pilot, while Tubbs and Crockett are undercover to link Trini DeSoto to Calderone, they learn of a leak in the Miami Vice department. When Crockett confronts Detective Leon, the leak, he explains: "all they [DeSoto and Calderone] wanted was information ... and me clearing a lousy thirty [thousand] a year getting shot at by guys who blow that much in a restaurant in a month ..." Leon trails off suggesting he simply could not resist getting involved with Calderone ("My Brother's Keeper"). He suggests that it is unfair that he makes so little money as a police officer while others, involved in illicit activities, make much more. Leon's description of how he became involved with DeSoto and Calderone links the Miami drug scene with immigration, as Leon explains that he was accosted by "a guy [Trini DeSoto] outside a club in Little Havana." In describing DeSoto's initiation of the relationship, Leon renders himself the passive, submissive party, suggesting that DeSoto and Calderone held more power in Miami than a police officer with "fifteen years as a stand-up cop and two medals of valor" ("My Brother's Keeper"). Upon confirming Leon's involvement with Calderone and DeSoto, Crockett attempts to strangle Leon, expressing his rage at his former partner's betrayal and his own investment in working with "clean" cops, especially, given the nature of Leon's trespasses, in the wake of potentially threatening immigration.

Dangerous Bodies: Queerness and the Boatlift

Other identity-markers and negative stereotypes facilitated the threatening representations of the Mariel émigrés. With their respective address of homosexuality and deviation from normative gender roles, *Scarface* and *Miami Vice* gesture toward the perception and corresponding persecution of the Mariel Boatlift's LGBTQIA population. While the representations of non-heteronormativity are given only cursory attention, often in quick flashes either at the beginning of the film or in a sub-plotline of the first episode, these glimpses provide insight into the infamous criminalization of queerness during the Boatlift. These representations, coupled with the raced perceptions of the Mariel Boatlift and the contemporary condemnations of LGBTQIA people in Cuba created a "perfect storm" that variously entrapped Mariel émigrés with overwhelmingly pejorative stereotypes about crime, race, gender identity, sexual orientation, and status as refugees. In *Miami Vice*, Trini DeSoto, the antagonist of the pilot episode collaborates with Esteban Calderone (an antagonist with a recurring role in the series). Once DeSoto learns that Crockett and Tubbs are police officers, he dresses in women's clothing to disguise himself intent on killing Tubbs before the officer has a chance to shut down an extensive drug ring. As a Mariel immigrant dressed in drag while intending to commit a crime, DeSoto becomes an exaggerated representation of the perceptions of the Mariel Boatlift and the anxieties surrounding racial, sexual, and class difference. DeSoto points a gun at Tubbs while wearing a thick, brown-haired wig, large hoop earrings, lipstick, and eyeshadow. In this caricature, DeSoto is a hyperbolic combination of perceived threats of criminality and deviation from cisgender norms, heterosexuality, and whiteness. DeSoto's death, after Crockett runs him over with a car to protect Tubbs, metaphorizes law enforcement's resistance to corruption, a complex phenomenon that, in the world of *Miami Vice*, combines criminal behavior with non-traditional gender identities as a compounded threat.

DeSoto's representation in *Miami Vice*, along with the interrogation scene in *Scarface*, reveals that the persecution of LGBTQIA Cubans persisted in the U.S. This exchange, and the (non)representation of queerness within the film metaphorizes the paradoxical non-/hypervisibility of Black and mixed-race LGBTQIA Mariel émigrés during the Boatlift. During the interrogation, one of the three agents interrogating Tony asks, "You like men? You like to dress up as a woman?" The agent asks these two questions in quick succession, implicitly disallowing Montana's response to them as distinct ideas, and indicating that a positive answer to either question will result in his persecution, perhaps even his deportation to Cuba. The agent's questions dramatizes tendencies to homogenize LGBTQIA communities; the first question attempts to get at Montana's sexual orientation, while the latter interrogates his gender performance/identity. Tony answers defensively, "No, okay? Fuck no." Montana's assertive rejection of non-heteronormativity implicitly models how intersections of immigrant identity and masculinity entrapped Montana in both pejorative, exclusionary assumptions of queerness and the fetishized hypermasculinity of Black and Latinx men. There is no further explicit reference to LGBTQIA Mariel émigrés in *Scarface*.

The fetishized machismo is an integral part of both Tony and Manny's characterizations within the film, perhaps especially through their objectifying, dominating treatment of women. As a specific example, the trajectory of Tony and Elvira's relationship, and his own reflection on their courtship, illustrates how both men viewed women as acquisitions. The pair's views on women are perhaps most apparent during an oft-cited scene, shot near a hotel pool, in which Tony lectures Manny on how to pursue women just after Manny has, after Tony's jestful encouragement, flicked his tongue seductively (he thinks) at a bikini-clad blonde woman. In this scene, Manny leans into the woman's space emphasized in the shot through the excess negative space on the right side of the screen; the camera angle almost traps the woman in the corner of the shot, emphasizing Manny's role as a sexual aggressor. The scene also sharply contrasts Manny's dark, stiffly gelled hair, a stereotypical marker of playboy masculinity, with the woman's loose blonde waves. She looks befuddled, then repulsed, before slapping Manny across the face. Manny turns away to rejoin Tony, declaring that if he were not a nice person, he would strike her in return, and yelling out "Bitch . . . lesbian!" His insulting farewell marks an arrogance in his own appeal; if the woman is not attracted to him, then she must not be attracted to men. Montana lectures Manny: "In this country, you gotta make the money first. Then when you get the money, you get the power. Then when you get the power, then you get the women." Montana's progressive explanation asserts that power and money are prerequisites to women. Further, it suggests that Montana will use money and power to "get," through either coercion or purchase, women, exemplifying a mode of domination and control.

While this exchange between Manny, Tony, and the unnamed woman exemplifies a certain masculine, playboy stereotype, it is necessarily shaped by the men's positions as "foreigners." Peña dismantles this stereotype, focusing specifically on Cuban American masculinity. She writes, "In the United States the macho is a racial inferior whose patriarchal power is criticized. In part, the macho works to deflect attention from how middle-class Anglo patriarchy operates across national and class boundaries" (145). Peña pinpoints how criticisms of Cuban masculinity, inflected in both Tony and Manny's treatment of women, and immigrant masculinity generally, as she emphasizes in a later section of her book, are a projection that distracts from, and disables criticism of, white patriarchy.

In her attention to the intersections of gender identity and performance and race, Peña gestures toward the insidious implications of Pacino's "Brownface" performance. As she implies, the representation of the virile, uncontrolled Latin man is contingent on a certain Brownness, or selective distance from both whiteness and Blackness that enables alienation, but in some ways neutralizes threats of Blackness:

> The danger and allure of the Latin lover are related to stereotypical historical depictions of a hypersexual and uncontrolled temperament characteristic of Latin Americans, especially those of Caribbean descent . . . Latin lovers always phenotypically depicted as brown-skinned, that is, somewhere between black and white. Second, they are portrayed as only slightly dangerous; thus they pose less of a threat than black males.[47]

In this sense, we might assume that an actor of African descent could not have played Tony Montana's character, as this characterization, while more representative of the Mariel demographic, might have made the film too threatening for U.S. audiences. Although the film relies on compounding representations of marginalized communities, Al Pacino's olive skin tone neutralizes a threat that might have detracted from the film's profitability.

Scarface's Grandiosity

The neutralization implicit in the decision not to cast a Black lead to represent a majority Black/mixed-race emigration wave contrasts with the otherwise grandiose representations of Tony. All elements of the film are indicative of the overblown image De Palma wished to construct, especially Tony's boundless ambition; as Tony notes in the film before establishing his footing in the drug game, he wants "the world . . . and everything in it." Tony's ambition is an individual characteristic that inspires his self-motivation and upward mobility, but he is drawn to the United States because it will enable the quick acquisition of private wealth. Tony's danger as an ambitious, manipulative immigrant is dispersed to include a fear of what capitalism encourages and enables. His ambition and greed are observable in his extravagant purchases once he becomes a major player in the drug game: he purchases a large house, equipped with a tiger, a painting of him and his wife, lush red carpets, gold fixings, and a Jacuzzi bathtub. The film frequently shows Montana with wads of cash and amidst mountains of cocaine; these casual scenes normalize the excess Montana seeks and fulfills within U.S. capitalism. His wife, Elvira, is also treated as an acquisition—in his move to overpower Frank López, another drug dealer, Tony woos Elvira by asserting that because he now has more power, Elvira will be safer and better provided for with him. The acquisition of the objectified woman is the culmination of his success within a capitalist landscape; his marriage to Elvira, given his own hypermasculinist framework indexed in his earlier discussions of "money, power, then women," indicates that he has enough money and power to stake a claim in Elvira. Tony's seemingly endless acquisition of material objects and objectified white women is indicative of a more detailed critique of capitalism.

De Palma confirms the film's condemnation of U.S. capitalism while responding to criticisms of the film's hyperbolic violence, profanity, and drug use:

> I've been accused of pandering to the worst aspects of the human character in order to make more and more money . . . now we're all in a capitalistic society and one of the reasons we're able to continue doing what we do is that we make money . . . accusing someone of a profit motive from one sector of society to another is basically nonsense because we're all involved in a profit motive.

De Palma's address of these criticisms mirrors the treatment of Montana throughout the film. Though Tony is, to pull from De Palma, all of us, in a profit-motivated landscape, various audiences scapegoat him for revealing the corruption and greed all U.S. inhabitants are either actively pursuing or complicit in perpetuating. Of course, the stakes of this projection of blame onto Montana are inextricable from his position as a Mariel émigré and stand-in for the racial darkening of the Cuban population in Miami. The film depicts "the American dream gone crazy . . . the capitalist dream gone bizarre and berserk." Within the world of the film, the mania of American capitalism is projected onto a brown faced, criminalized immigrant whose corruption by ruthless capitalism is as exaggerated as Pacino's accent. As De

Palma argues, "because he is honest [about his interests and modes of acquisition] he's the obvious bad guy, but they're all bad guys." Given his earlier outline of capitalistic motives entrapping us all, the deferred "they're" is interesting, as it still displaces accountability for capitalistic greed away from the white director, and perhaps white Americans more generally.

Conclusion

Miami Vice and *Scarface* are likely the most iconographic representations of Miami. Beyond sharing their setting and post–Mariel Boatlift context, these productions reflect white-dominated media's tendency to exploit the Mariel Boatlift and other waves of immigration to Miami and project derogatory myths about various marginalized identities. Public officials have used these myths, especially when compounded within the overblown representations of Miami, to entrap and persecute Mariel émigrés for decades. These myths and the widespread dissemination and preservation of them reflected in the iconoclasts of Miami media reveal how anti-Blackness, homophobia, transphobia, and related persecution of other marginalized identities compounded to represent immigration as a threat to white supremacy; even while white film producers, news broadcasters, and immigration officials were controlling the narrative that spread about the Mariel Boatlift.

Scarface embellishes the violent, alienating, and ultimately tragic greeting that awaited the 1980 Cuban émigrés and capitalizes on the manufactured fear that surrounded their arrival. The film's efforts to capitalize on fear are twofold; it reinforces biased reports that suggested the 1980 émigrés were dangerous, yet also encourages a fear of the urges U.S. capitalism allows Tony to satiate. Though *Scarface* is a sensationalized film, it documents a moment of xenophobia that fundamentally altered the experiences and treatment of the 1980 Cuban émigrés in Miami. Tony's characterization as a 1980 Cuban émigré and a drug lord pinpoints two overlapping discourses that resulted in enormous expenditures and shifts in international policy affecting the nation's permeable borders and the waters that link the contiguous U.S. to the rest of the hemisphere. While the film is an Anglocentric representation of the Boatlift and its consequences, it successfully, if inadvertently, exposes the way government agencies and local communities scapegoated the émigrés in lieu of addressing inherent, preexisting problems within law enforcement and within the structures of U.S. capitalism more broadly.

Miami Vice presents the Mariel Boatlift as a watershed moment that enables violent, often-drug related crime and targets various marginalized groups in its focus on law enforcement. Like *Scarface*, the series pinpoints widespread corruption and the various, illicit temptations enabled by capitalism. Further, the series raises interesting questions about the violence and conflict in the breaching of regional boundaries and encourages an interrogation of the cultural diversity of the city, by simultaneously representing marginalized groups as criminals and as police with various degrees of political and cultural power.

Other television shows and films, such as *CSI: Miami*, *Bad Boys*, and *Bad Boys II*, similarly combine immigration, violence, crime, law enforcement, and corruption and they, too, require closer examination in their indirect address of Fidel Castro's intentional, boastful manipulation of the Boatlift population. Contextualizing analyses of *Scarface* and *Miami Vice* with critical attention to their representation of criminalized Brown, Black, and/or queer people indexes a transnational collusion to uphold repressive anti-Blackness and anti-LGBTQIA practice. With these phenomena at the center of analysis, Miami media, especially its major productions is fertile ground to examine white supremacist anxieties in the tenuous transnational negotiation of difference.

5

Dawg Fight in the Moonlight

Black Masculinity in Miami

I knew you wasn't soft.
—Kevin to Chiron, in *Moonlight* (2016)

After wrestling each other in a playful display of strength and dominance, Kevin, a young boy portrayed by Jared Piner, helps Chiron, the protagonist of *Moonlight* (2016) played in his childhood by Alex R. Hibbert, up from the ground. The young, Black boys began wrestling after Kevin baits him while playing together in a larger group. When the two are alone, Kevin offers "you just gotta show these niggas you ain't soft" as a strategy for self-protection to Chiron. Proving his hardness, or at least, an absence of softness, becomes an almost single-minded pursuit for Chiron throughout the second half of the film. This pursuit radically inhibits his capacity for vulnerability, and self-expression, as notably demonstrated by the character's near silence and limited self-expression throughout the film.

Like *Moonlight*, *Dawg Fight*, a 2015 documentary, thematizes the compounding intersections of Blackness, masculinity, poverty, and the imperative of "hardness" for Black boys and men who endure the consequences of urban blight in South Florida's Black-majority neighborhoods. Generically, however, the films could not be more different. *Dawg Fight* is a low-to-middle budget documentary that has received little, if any, critical or popular attention. *Moonlight* is an Academy Award–winning film that has been lauded for its representation of Black queerness. The latter film is based on Tarell Alvin McCraney's autobiographical play, *In Moonlight Black Boys Look Blue*. The coming-of-age narrative follows Chiron, a Black queer protagonist who grows up in Liberty City and navigates a world that rejects his vulnerability and forcefully imposes upon him a brand of impenetrable masculinity so toxic that he does not experience physical nor emotional intimacy during his young adulthood. The film also depicts drug dealing, abuse, addiction, and a complex reimagining of family that is shaped by Chiron's environment. Chiron's sexuality was a main talking point about the film and this chapter takes on how the cultural terrain of Black poverty imprints upon and renders itself inextricable from Chiron's expression of his sexual orientation.

Dawg Fight more explicitly documents the effects of poverty on expressions of sexuality and gender norms. The film follows a popular underground fighting club in West Perrine, the same neighborhood that sparked Tananarive Due's reflections on Black impoverishment in *Freedom in the Family*. The documentary, to quote one of the fighters, is about how Black men who live in the neighborhood literally "fight to improve their lives." He outlines how capitalism, anti-Blackness, and patriarchy compound and leave Black men with limited options to, as the fighter says, improve their lives.

Dawg Fight was released by Rakontur, a Miami-based film production company founded by Billy Corben, Alfred Spellman, and David Cypkin. The documentary was directed by Billy Corben, a white filmmaker whose work has explored race, class, and crime in South Florida.[1] Images of makeshift boxing rings with a backdrop of urban blight that is characteristic of most Black majority neighborhoods in South Florida set the tone and focus of the documentary. The film centers Dhafir Harris's effort to give back to his community by organizing the fights, publicizing the performances, and ensuring that skilled fighters get picked up for more popular, better paying venues. Throughout the documentary, community members emphasize that Dhafir, or Dada 5000 as he is referred to by fellow fighters, organizes the unsanctioned fights at great legal risk to himself. While he charges admission for guests, he divvies up profits to the fighters, taking almost none for himself. He is represented as a Robin Hood from the Miami hood, and subjects of the film celebrate him for, as one spectator notes, stimulating the economy in a way that former President George Bush could not. Implicit in this comment is a critique that undergirds the documentary; political and socioeconomic structures have, at best, failed and at worst worked actively against Black Americans. In the wake of such failure, the Black inhabitants of blighted, neglected, and overpoliced neighborhoods have developed alternate economies and strategies to survive.

I argue that both films implicitly chart and document segregation, highlighting the effects of unnamed zoning policies, urban blight, and transnational anti-Blackness on Black people, but Black men and their expressions of masculinity specifically. Read together, these films make clear that space is not only raced, but gendered, and classed, all of which come to bear on life opportunities, as well as capacity to express the full range of human emotions. The films make visible the subtle, but ubiquitous ways white supremacy and anti-Blackness have made, unmade, and remade South Florida for Black constituencies. *Moonlight* and *Dawg Fight* rely heavily on their settings to convey the stakes of the narratives presented. Analyses of their respective contexts is integral as it informs the interactions portrayed in the films. I provide this context to avoid a dangerous naturalization of Black blight that might mistakenly designate Black people as the cause of their own misfortunes. Instead, I historicize the neighborhoods that shape, and entrap, the men from West Perrine and the characters represented in *Moonlight's* iteration of Liberty City. One of the fighters in *Dawg Fight* summarizes the interplay of masculinity and poverty and connects it to a profound feeling of entrapment: "a lot of the men want to be providers and they are not allowed that opportunity because of their criminal backgrounds." Implicit in the unnamed man's statement is a conclusion that shapes the trajectory of both films: to fulfill the restrictive, patriarchal, and capitalistic expectations lorded over them, Black men must fight.

Dawg Fight and Moonlight draw attention to white supremacist enactments upon Black people as well as the spaces constructed, and methodologies employed to contain them. These films contrast explosive instances of direct violence (easily observable in the physical attacks experienced or dealt by the main players) with the mundane, every day indirect violence of surveillance, economic depression, and other iterations of societally sanctioned violence. Cursory observations would deem cursing, fighting, and drug dealing as aberrant, immoral behavior if considered without attention to the context within which these actions occur. In segregated, impoverished, and over-policed neighborhoods that make visible the various compounding, systemic mechanisms that further the project of anti-Blackness, *Dawg Fight* and *Moonlight* declare a need for complex, nuanced engagement with media representations of Blackness, and posit masculine aggression as an almost necessary outlet for escape, self-affirmation, and survival in ways that either explicitly or implicitly gesture toward the pervasiveness of white supremacy.

Both films present extralegal violence as a strategy to resist directly/indirectly, or circumvent the unspoken, and invisible, but largely sanctioned violence that besieges Black communities. Underlying the assertion of criminality and morality is a conflict between what being a man ought to be, and what they cannot be because of how various oppressive systems compound to radically limit Black access to resources that could potentially enhance their quality and length of life. In the films, respect from others, and the garnering of clout and reputations of "hardness" are almost as important as material resources, and men disguise their vulnerability, fear, and apprehensions to maintain their reputations and positions within their communities.

To return to the claim of limited opportunity due to criminal records presented in *Dawg Fight*: given that the fights themselves are illegal, the audience witnesses cycles of crime that disproportionately entrap Black people as they attempt to "get on the right track" while fully acknowledging that the game is rigged. In both films, the main players construct and rely on alternative, extralegal economies be that street fighting or selling drugs to sustain themselves and their families. More pressingly, these films present violence and masculinity as inextricable, and suggest that roughness and hardness are the only alternatives for Black men in a world that patently rejects any demonstration of tenderness and vulnerability.

First Shots: Setting the Tone

In sight and sound, *Dawg Fight* and *Moonlight* thematize how race takes place in their opening visuals. *Moonlight*'s opening credits are set to waves crashing, followed by an excerpt of the refrain from Boris Gardiner's "Every Nigger is A Star," that repeats the titular statement multiple times. The refrain itself paradoxically outlines oppression, through its reclamation of a slur used against Black Americans, and uplift. Listened to in full, the song continues this focus with Gardiner singing:

> To be hated and despised (poor nigga)/
> no one to sympathize (poor nigga)/
> but there's one great thing I know/
> you can say "I told you so"/
> they've got a right place in the sun/
> where there's love for everyone.[2]

By combining Gardiner's track with the ambient sounds of waves crashing, the sonic introduction of the film emblematizes the narrative's focus on how these intersections take place in Black Miami. The song, somber in melody, promises a redemptive space for "hated" Black Americans. Extrapolating the struggle-to-triumph narrative in Gardiner's lyrics to Chiron's development throughout the film, the redemptive triumph after experiences of verbal and physical violence, and the precarity of having a lone source of income as a child, is respite in the arms of his friend, and lover, Kevin. The phrase "love for everyone" contextualized in Gardiner's song suggests a racial utopia; recontextualized in *Moonlight,* this phrase takes on an additional meaning with an intersectional attention to the racism and anti-queer/gay sentiment, policy, and action that informs the experiences of and interactions between the characters represented in the film.

With this opening sonic ambiance, *Moonlight'*s creators draw on Afro-Caribbean legacies of cultural production. Jamaican singer, songwriter, and guitarist Boris Gardiner's song was featured on the soundtrack to the 1974 film of the same title, produced in Jamaica by Calvin Lockhart and shot by Black American filmmaker William Greaves. The film "arguably failed to live up to its producer's expectations . . . [and] disappeared shortly after its release" but, as Erica Moiah James notes, "the photography, paintings, and music drawn from its creation not only performed the political and cultural work within diaspora over time . . . but articulated something that refused to be contained within singular, linear histories, discourses, and media."[3] Similarly, *Moonlight'*s scope and disrupted chronology refuse the categories James outlines in her analysis in its capacious address of Black sexuality, poverty, and diasporic experiences.

The opening scene of the film proper places the audience in a Black-majority neighborhood, the setting for the first character exchange that promptly introduces the extralegal economies from which Juan, a primary character in the film and a caretaker to Chiron, benefits. Juan pulls up to a spot, checking in on a dealer that works for him. He is driving a sky blue, polished Cadillac, and a golden crown is visible on the dash, a symbol of his powerful position within his community. He approaches an unnamed dealer, greeting the man while ignoring an addict who begs him for his fix. During the interaction, the camera circles the men multiple times, simultaneously centering their interaction while also providing wide, rotating shots of the setting.

While encircling the men, the camera shows several two-story residential buildings, and a few single-story houses. The street is mostly empty, with Black men occasionally seen walking across the street; only Black people are shown to occupy the neighborhood, visually emblematizing the historical and contemporary segregation that forms Black-majority neighborhoods; although this history is not explicitly discussed in the film, its consequences are visible. I think through potential consequences of this decontextualized visibility in a forthcoming section.

The scene introduces the business of drug dealing that is formative of both Juan's and Chiron's characters, while also putting forth a painful paradox that haunts Juan's conscience; while he cares deeply for members of his community, he is complicit in distributing toxic, and potentially lethal substances to them. The unnamed addict leaves, and Juan asks the dealer if business is good, before telling the man to hold onto money as they will "empty the register on the weekend." Juan then asks how the unnamed dealer's mother is doing and confirms that "she's doing better." In checking in about the dealer's mother's health, Juan emblematizes his contradictory position as one whose profit is contingent on the addiction and overall unhealthiness of Black people. The scene transitions as Juan witnesses a group of Black boys chasing Chiron and calling him a "faggot" as they pursue him. Juan follows and rescues Chiron from a drug den, again calcifying his precarious role as caretaker. The very fact that Chiron can only seek shelter in such a treacherous location highlights the inescapability of his circumstances as a queer, Black boy with a single and unavailable mother in an impoverished neighborhood; he flees the homophobic taunting of other young boys and finds refuge in a physical symbol of drug-ridden impoverishment.

Dawg Fight similarly calls immediate attention to space and the uses of violence in low-income communities in its introductory minutes. The documentary opens with an aerial shot of West Perrine, zooming in closer until the audience can see a large crowd gathered in the backyard of a pale blue house. In voiceover, Dada 5000's voice declares "let me get y'all attention!" While the opening minutes reveal that Dada is speaking to fighters, announcing the rules of engagement, the voiceover serves a second purpose in demanding the attention of the viewer to the neighborhood itself. The indirect violence of segregation and poverty is made direct, and although white supremacy constructs the ring, its explicit mechanisms remain unseen.

The scene transitions, showing Dada gesturing with his hands to a mostly Black crowd (giving the viewer further context as to where we are) as he explains that there are three ways to end a fight: "knockout, referee stoppage, or by you quittin.'" Rather than forfeiting, tapping out, or being disqualified, as it is referred to in professional fighting contexts (whether boxing or mixed-martial arts), "quitting" further highlights the treatment of the sport in West Perrine as an alternate occupation for those whose options are otherwise limited. Dada continues by declaring that "What y'all seeing here is going worldwide," breaking the fourth wall, and emphasizing the need to publicize the fights so fighters will have the opportunity to be picked up by professional leagues. Dada's declaration further highlights the white gaze of the film's producers on Black male bodies and suggests that this gaze is necessary for the fighters' success. Two muscular Black men are shown swinging on each other as Dada highlights the need for publicity, and though they lack the poise and finesse of professionally trained boxers, there is an urgency and desperation in their style that cements the gravity of the circumstances they are trying to escape. The documentary also introduces the physical sacrifices the fighters must make; one man's eye is swollen shut while the second fighter is shown spitting out blood.

The documentary's opening credits are intercut with Dada's training regimen, and a voiceover from an unnamed news broadcaster describing West Perrine, spotlighting the documentary's attention to place. Dada runs through the neighborhood, high-fiving children as he goes by, and then is shown jumping rope, squatting, and pushing a manual steamroller. The camera adopts wide angles, focusing as much on Dada's muscular body and intense training regimen as it does on the background and scenes of uncut grass and fences in states of disrepair. The neighborhood is Dada's gym, which is perhaps especially demonstrated by the punching bag hung on the tree in his front yard next to weight bars—the sport is quite literally integrated with the space of West Perrine, a neighborhood that an unnamed woman, one of a few interviewed for the documentary, explains "was once a haven for nothing but drugs." She continues noting the danger of the neighborhood: "You could come outside, and bullets would be flying all over your head. I can't tell you how many people have lost their lives on that street there," gesturing toward 112th street, the main street of West Perrine.

Not unlike Tananarive Due's reflections (see chapter 1), and the various subjects interviewed for *Dawg Fight*, I grew up with stories about and experiences of West Perrine—for many, West Perrine's reputation preceded any lived experience of the neighborhood. My high school, Coral Reef Senior High, was near West Perrine, and there was frequent tell of armed holdups at the nearby McDonald's and encouragement from parents that students staying after school should not wander too far from campus. I never witnessed anything dangerous or alarming in the neighborhood, and now wonder how grounded the fearful stories I heard about West Perrine were based on the race and class-standing of its inhabitants.

The voiceover that accompanies Dada's trek through the neighborhood echoes and emphasizes the anti-Black myths constructed around West Perrine that shaped my traversal of the surrounding areas of my high school:

Twenty-two miles south of Miami's famous South Beach is West Perrine, Florida . . . a suburban ghetto of sorts with a population of less than 10,000, 63% of which is Black. The unemployment rate is a third higher than the national average. Poverty and crime are rampant. And it is from these mean streets that Kimbo Slice emerged. Videotaped competing in underground backyard fights, he became an internet sensation . . . this is inspiring a new generation to literally fight their way out.

The narrator begins by emphasizing the physical distance between West Perrine and the glitz and glamour of Miami Beach. This chasm is also marked by the demographic differences between the wealthy, tourist haven of South Beach and the Black-majority impoverished, crime-ridden streets of West Perrine. The narrator implicitly links the Black-majority constitution of the neighborhood with the high rates of crime and poverty from which other fighters like Kimbo Slice must escape with their fists. The equation of violence with escape continues beyond the focus on Kimbo Slice, born Kevin Ferguson. Ferguson was born in the Bahamas, grew up in Cutler Ridge (now Cutler Bay), and after participating in documented street fights like those organized by Dada 5000 was dubbed "The King of the Web Brawlers." He signed a contract with EliteXC (a professional mixed-martial arts organization) in 2007 and is held up as a standard for what can happen to, and for, Black men in West Perrine if they demonstrate their skills for the cameras.

Both Kimbo Slice and Dada 5000 share Bahamian heritage, and their experiences demonstrate how anti-Blackness and poverty contribute to challenging, bloody, violent tales of immigration when avenues to success and escaping restrictive Black neighborhoods are limited. Bahamian immigration was central to Miami's emergence—Bahamians comprised more than half of Miami's local Black population at the time of the city's founding.[4] Kimbo Slice's and Dada 5000's experiences index a long history of anti-Bahamian sentiment in South Florida—as Raymond Mohl writes, although "Black immigrants from the Bahamas . . . gave immigration to Miami its special character in the early years of the twentieth century . . . they encountered segregation and white racism. The Miami press routinely denigrated Bahamian newcomers as lazy and shiftless."[5] Today, Bahamians in South Florida constitute the largest Diasporic population outside of the country and are subject to similar wealth disparities as other Black people in the region.[6] These wealth disparities are correlated to high crime rates, drug use, and, as both *Moonlight* and *Dawg Fight* suggest, illicit economies for Black people, perhaps especially for Black émigrés.

Dawg Fight goes further to present both drug dealing and fighting as a double-edged sword. The male fighters posit that their involvement in the matches, and reliance on drug trade, have as much potential to benefit certain members of the community as they do to harm them. The documentary gives insight into the physical consequences of drug abuse and bare-knuckle fighting, and the potential legal ramifications that impact various fighters shown in the film. Treon "Tree" Johnson, who takes on Jimmy during a documented fight, explains: "I couldn't get a job, and I ain't wanna sell no drugs, so I just thought of doin' what I know how to do . . . ain't no fighting for free no more."[7] Tree articulates both dealing drugs and fighting as alternative economies given his inability to opt into more traditional, and legal ways of earning money. Another fighter, Fruity, similarly outlines a sense of opportunity provided by Dada's organization of the fights, explaining:

> A couple of years ago I used to box . . . in the late 80s and early 90s, I had a brush in with the law where I found myself doing an eight-year sentence in prison for armed robbery. I got out of prison and got right back to the streets doing some of the same things and everything. And then the dawn of the backyard brawl started. Man, I thought "I got this shit going on. I got a chance to redeem myself, you know?"

Fruity outlines his prior criminal background, and gestures toward a cycle of criminal recidivism that is nearly unavoidable given limited opportunities in an impoverished neighborhood. Fruity implicitly communicates shame at his earlier actions and approaches fighting with self-discipline in efforts to redeem his past.

Dada 5000 explains this reality in a voiceover as he advertises a fight during a Martin Luther King Jr. parade in West Perrine. Spoken alongside imagery that centers Dr. King, the film juxtaposes a reliance on violence with the legacy of the Civil Rights leader that is inextricable from legacies of non-violent resistance; many explain to Dada that they plan to attend the backyard fight after the parade. As Dada passes out fliers for, and vocally advertises the fight, in voiceover, he explains: "This is where dreams are lost. This is where hope is diminished. This is where individuals find themselves because this is the bottom. There's only one way to go from here and that's up." The film continues to contrast iconoclastic associations with Martin Luther King Jr. (dreams, hopefulness) with the lived experience of the people who currently live in West Perrine. Implied in this contrast is a broader legacy of the oppression of Black people, and an ominous revelation that King's dream of uplift for Black people has not been realized.

Other fighters similarly outline not only an economic benefit of fighting, but also suggest that winning fights comes with community clout, which functions as a commodity; as an unnamed promoter observes "if they love you in the ring, they gon' love you outside the ring." The use of fighting and demonstrations of physical strength as a commodity that Black men can exchange for basic respect is reiterated in Chiron's use of violence in *Moonlight*, wherein he, after years of torment, adopts an offensive posture to confront his bullies. Complicating stereotypes of Black, masculine brutishness, violent posturing is presented in both films as an avenue through which Black men can be viewed and treated with basic respect in a world that is otherwise determined to blot them out.

The film documents many community members, and members of local government, affirming Dada's efforts at organizing the community and celebrating the fighting accomplishments of the fighters. Preceding a fight, B. J. Chiszar, the contemporary chair of the Miami-Dade Democratic Party introduces himself to the crowd, noting:

We've got 600,000 Democrats here in Miami-Dade . . . I'm here to support these hardworking gentlemen and for what they stand for and what they're trying to do. It is very positive in the community to give kids an outlet other than the streets. And I just want to say that the Democratic Party stands behind y'all 100%.

Chiszar holds fighting apart from other nefarious activities one might associate with "the streets," suggesting that Dada serves as a role model and community leader, rather than a threat or advocate of violence. Chiszar's language also categorizes Dada's efforts as hard work, reframing narratives of acceptable labor that might otherwise exclude Dada and the fighters he endorses. Further, Chiszar enacts the power of the U.S. political system to endorse the activities organized by Dada. It is not revealed whether this stamp of approval yields tangible benefits for the fighters, but it symbolically incorporates them into Miami's political sphere, which as earlier chapters outline, have historically excluded and actively oppressed Black people in South Florida.

The fighting's capacity to challenge sociopolitical boundaries is further exemplified in Dada's description of and interactions with the police. Prior to the fight Dada advertised during the Martin Luther King Jr. Day parade, the film builds a sense of suspense by showing the police appearing to surround the event, before it is revealed that they have come to help control the crowd, and not to stop the event, or worse, arrest its participants. Dada shakes hands with the police officers and in voice-over explains:

The police, they love us. We've been doing this for quite some time. They know at least for that day they have almost everybody inside the community right there. So, they know there's not gonna be any problems.

Implicitly, Dada 5000 makes a claim for what is possible when systemically neglected communities have the resources and outlets that render punitive policing obsolete. Perhaps surprisingly, street fighting becomes a communal deterrent from committing other kinds of crime and becomes an assistance to the local authorities.

Despite the localized assistance to patrols in West Perrine, the film incorporates insight from authority figures in boxing to outline the legal risk Dada, and any participant in the fight are taking each time they organize, engage, or even attend the fights. Filmmakers interviewed Thomas Molloy, the Executive Director of the Florida State Boxing Commission, who explains what the "unsanctioned" designation could potentially mean for men in West Perrine. Molloy explains:

It means that you have non-qualified referees, judges, no physicians. Participate in it and you can get a second-degree misdemeanor for it. As a promoter, you can get a third-degree felony charge on it. If somebody gets killed there, there's gonna be two people going to jail, at least, for murder.

Paradoxically, the avenue fighters use to escape a life of crime is criminalized, and Molloy's whiteness stands in stark contrast to what Dada earlier describes as the "dark side"—further exemplifying a tension that delegitimates and criminalizes the same behavior when it is Black-led and organized. Of course, Dada's management of the fights does raise concerns about the safety of the fighters—as he notes, a regulation boxing ring is approximately sixteen feet by sixteen feet, as compared to Dada's ring, measuring about twelve feet by twelve feet. An unnamed man, who helps Dada organize the fights explains that Dada's rings are "specifically designed to eliminate running and to encourage confrontation. So if somebody don't have the skill to be there, we gon' know as soon as they step in." Yet the fighters maintain that Dada's fights become a way to release anger, frustration, and even settle disputes that might otherwise result in death but, because of the controlled environment of the fights, can conclude "without nobody having to leave home in a casket."

While no one dies in the ring in *Dawg Fight*, the documentary presents state-sanctioned violence and death in low-income Black neighborhoods as a mundane reality that merits extraordinarily little comment or expressions of grief. Toward the end of *Dawg Fight*, the film documents Chauncy's shooting by his girlfriend's brother. Chauncy survives the initial shooting but never recovers and is removed from all life preserving equipment; his funeral is intercut with footage of Dada's first professional fight.

Dada emerges victorious, but the film suggests a painful, overwhelming reminder of the life Dada has escaped by entering the professional league—and the possible outcomes for those who cannot escape. Before the credits of *Dawg Fight* roll, the audience also learns that Tree Johnson died in 2014, after being pepper sprayed and tased by Hialeah police. Contrasted with Dada's earlier collaboration with the police, the circumstances of Tree's death operate as a stark reminder of the limited efficacy of the "dawg fights" with a backdrop of systemic onslaughts against Black communities. No details are provided about why the police were pursuing Tree, nor is there any overview of how his death was mourned by the community.

The expected realities of violence and premature death are evinced through Juan, a role model Chiron eventually emulates, and his death in *Moonlight*. The audience learns of his death only through Paula, Chiron's mother, who reports that she has not seen Teresa "since [Juan's] funeral." Tarell McCraney in an interview with *Fresh Air on National Public Radio's* Terry Gross relates Juan's character and ultimate demise to a man named Blue who was influential in his upbringing, explaining:

The drug dealer who was in my life was a man named Blue who was dating my mother at the time and sort of came into my life when I was 5 or 6 years old and was very affectionate to me, very kind to me, very generous to me in a way that I hadn't quite experienced with many male figures, including my own father at the time . . . I remember at some point thinking he treats me like I'm his son regardless of the fact that I don't share any of his blood. And I did know that he was a drug dealer. And I did know that my mom did drugs . . . And I came home, and my mom said, you know, Blue's dead, and he's not coming back anymore . . . He had been shot and killed over the weekend. He had gotten shot and killed by, we assume, rival drug members in the neighborhood—drug dealers in the neighborhood who then later came in and moved into that neighborhood. And I just remember having this kind of feeling of—what's the word? I remember feeling like I need to start counting now. I need to pay attention now because when I go away, things will go away. When I stop looking, when I stop paying attention, the things that I care about, the things that are good to me will disappear. (Public Radio East)

McCraney's experiences are mirrored in *Moonlight*, as he acknowledges that Paula and Juan mirror the paradox of his mother's drug addiction and his surrogate father's drug dealing in their neighborhood. Juan's sudden disappearance is a metaphor for how quickly good, if complicated, things, and people, can disappear for Chiron as a young Black boy in an impoverished neighborhood. McCraney also outlines the kinship presented in the film that develops alongside the alternate economies that characterize the low-income neighborhood of Liberty City. McCraney's precarity is exacerbated by the ominous information that drug members who rivaled Blue are moving into his neighborhood, creating a sense of danger given his proximity to Blue. McCraney's experiences, as noted in the conclusion of his recollection of Blue, imparts a sense of precarity to McCraney's overall experience, as he notes that people living in those circumstances can disappear without warning, much like Juan does in the film. The audience is not provided a cause of death for Juan, but it is implied that his death is in line with his lifestyle that rendered him vulnerable to both street and state-sanctioned violence.

As McCraney's reflections suggest, the conditions of the neighborhood, and the literal space of Liberty City itself entraps, and imposes itself upon the partly autobiographic Chiron in *Moonlight*, as West Perrine as a neighborhood entraps the men depicted in *Dawg Fight*. In examining the sense of entrapment put forth in *Moonlight*, Kannan, Hall, and Hughey note the film's powerful representation of space, explaining:

The all-black characters live in the shadow of a white supremacy that is systemic rather than individually prejudicial. The film is devoid of white racists in pointy hoods (or blue uniforms) to force their will upon a sea of black victims. Rather, *Moonlight* is effective in its portrayal of how the weighty legacy of centuries of intentional white supremacy, how the treatment of black communities with "benign neglect" . . . and how the racial resegregation and government roll-back of civil rights legislation in the 1980s created anything but an equal playing field upon which Little could roughhouse or Juan could sling dope.[8]

I take the observation of disembodied whiteness's representation seriously, especially as it manifests in Black media. An additional concern arises for me while viewing both films when considering that even if the mechanisms of white supremacy were made visible that this would not alter reception of the films. Audiences might opt instead for a painfully common assumption of Black people's complicity in their own oppression.

These assumptions lead to the naturalization of constructed phenomenon, i.e., Black impoverishment, criminality within Black communities, and rates of drug use among Black people. After all, neither film explicitly describe the legislation that segregated and resegregated Liberty City or West Perrine, and while *Dawg Fight* introduces the film with a clear sense of West Perrine's demographic, we are not informed as to why or how West Perrine became majority-Black, nor does the narrator mention the historical disenfranchisement that has contributed to the experiences of Black people who live there. *Moonlight*, beyond setting the scene as I described earlier, provides no context about the formation of Liberty City. With ease, Blackness, poverty, and crime can be linked, without attention to the construction and deconstruction of these neighborhoods, introduced in part in my overview of Overtown and Liberty City as presented in Patricia Stephens Due and Tananarive Due's memoir in the first chapter.

Liberty City and West Perrine: Spatial Legacies of Black Exploitation

The histories of the neighborhoods necessarily come to bear on the representations of the people in the films. As Katherine McKittrick explains:

> While transparent, space is a view, or a perspective . . . governing social desires continually bolster its seemingly self-evident characteristics, particularly local and global mappings, infrastructures, regional boundaries, and transportation routes are examples of how transparent space, seemingly innocent, is materialized in the geographic environment. Prevailing spatial organization gives a coherency and rationality to uneven geographic processes and arrangements: a city plan, for example, can (and often does) reiterate social class distinctions, race, and gender segregation, and (in)accessibility to and from specific districts. (3)

I take McKittrick to mean that just because we cannot necessarily see the processes behind space-making (these processes, however, are arguably more and more evident with the rise of gentrification and its distinct aesthetic) when we walk on a busy commercial street or old residential neighborhood does not mean that these processes are not actively informing our occupation and consumption of space. Necessarily, and inevitably, historical asymmetries in power and resources are reflected in our constructed environments. In analysis of *Moonlight* and *Dawg Fight*, films that rely heavily on their constructed environments to convey the stakes of the narratives presented, context is integral as it informs the interactions portrayed in the film; I provide this context to avoid a dangerous naturalization of Black blight.

West Perrine, the setting of *Dawg Fight*, was informally established in 1939. "Informally," because while Perrine was established in 1939 with the extension of the Florida East Coast Railway to South Dade, the Black laborers were housed away from the formal township, which was later integrated by what can best be described as rezoning. Liberty City, one of the settings of *Moonlight*, was originally Liberty Square, and was founded as one of the first housing projects in the southeast during the Great Depression era. The project was an overflow site for Overtown, a historically Black neighborhood marked by slum conditions until a boom during the 1950s. Liberty City, too, saw a boom during this time period and was populated by middle income Black Americans whose businesses, churches, and community centers lined the streets until, as these things go, an executive decision was made to build I-95 through Liberty City, displacing many Black families and sending the neighborhood into a blighted depression from which it has never recovered.

The legacies of South Florida's Black neighborhoods have always been connected, reflecting the racist logic that informed the space-making of metropolitan areas in the U.S. Liberty City, as it is now called, was formally opened in 1937 as Liberty Square, "one of the two public housing projects built for South Floridians."[9] Specifically, Liberty Square was for Black occupants, unlike an all-white project, Edison Courts; "despite their being mere blocks from each other, Edison Courts and Liberty Square had been deliberately constructed to stand apart and to expand in opposite directions as South Florida's population grew."[10] Developed in a formerly sparse region in northern Miami (within the parameters of the city proper), the Square, and other projects like it, were a strategic effort to address housing crises that arose during the Great Depression. The ultimate construction of I-95 directly through Overtown, then the heart of Black life in Miami, after the Great Depression, fractured the economically diverse community; those with enough resources to move to better neighborhoods did, but "much of the area's low-income, elderly and welfare-dependent citizens migrated to Liberty City."[11]

Liberty Square's construction is a reminder of the disproportionate effects of the Great Depression on the already economically depressed Black demographic; indeed, the expansion of the "square" to the "city" mirrors the higher rates of poverty and need for publicly subsidized housing for Black populations. Further, as the separation of Edison Courts and Liberty Square suggest, these housing projects were marked by the segregationist logic of New Deal politics and what is sometimes put forth as the development of a welfare state; the alleged national benevolence was still formulated on an ideology of racial separation contingent on assumptions of Black inferiority.

N.D.B Connolly concisely asserts that in Liberty Square's development "The project was, in effect, supposed to draw the black population out of Miami's downtown and finally help whiten a region that had been black, Indian, and Caribbean since before the arrival of the Florida East Coast Railway."[12] Shayne Benowitz, writing on behalf of "Greater Miami and Beaches," a prominent tourist website, explains that the impulse to separate white and non-white people also inspired material changes to the landscape: beyond notable white flight from nearby neighborhoods,

> Officials responded by erecting a seven-foot wall in the late 1930s along Northwest 12th Avenue from 62nd Street to 71st Street along Liberty Square separating the newly founded black community from the white neighborhood on its east side. Most of the wall was demolished during the 1950s. However, today remnants of it still remain and can be seen plainly separating Northwest 12th Avenue and Northwest 12th Parkway along Liberty Square. It's a haunting reminder today of the Jim Crow era of the past.[13]

We might refer to McKittrick and her reliance on "haunting" as a metaphor for the past influences on the present. Doing so requires that we push on Benowitz's suggestion that the Jim Crow era has ended. Rather, the continued segregation and legacies of impoverishment, and more ominously, efforts to remove and contain Black people from the "glitz and glamour" of downtown Miami and South Beach provide further evidence that refutes the naturalization of neighborhoods like West Perrine, Overtown—instead we must reckon with how these neighborhoods were constructed by white supremacist logics of separation and exclusion.

Lights, Camera, Violence

Dawg Fight and *Moonlight* emerged alongside public discourse about the utility of representing state sanctioned violence. The public discourse ranged from burgeoning demands for the use of body cameras to address police brutality to "trauma porn," and the limited representations of Black life on screen—the #oscarssowhite discourse began in January 2015.[14] Both films were released in the wake of the executions of Trayvon Martin in February 2012 (killed by neighborhood watch coordinator George Zimmerman, who was acquitted of all charges in 2013) and Michael Brown in Ferguson, Missouri (killed by Ferguson police officer Darren Wilson in 2014; the decision not to indict Wilson was announced in 2015). Beyond reigniting historical discussions about evolutionary anti-Blackness in the U.S., protesters and organizers from Black Lives Matter and other locally based organizations focused on the imperative need to document and publicly release footage of police brutality, advocating for police officers to be equipped with dash cam and body cameras in hopes that allegedly objective evidence would contribute to the likelihood of conviction in police involved shootings—this has unfortunately not held true.[15]

Many may approach footage of encounters with police as having the potential to reveal "what really happened" but as Cheryl Harris and Devon Carbado argue in "Loot or Find: Fact or Frame?" this is an impossible goal given the pervasive cultural frames that associate Blackness with criminality, violence, and perhaps most imperatively, declare that Black people are deserving of punishment. Cultural frames have long suggested that violence is inherent to Black masculinity and as a result, that Black men are deserving of state-sanctioned violence.[16] Myths of Black male brutality have been widely noted within and beyond scholarly discussions of Blackness, especially as they intersect with the alleged vulnerability of white women to the sexual potency and general aggression of Black men. The construction of Black male brutality departed from earlier depictions of Black men as silly, unintelligent, docile, and submissive prior to the U.S. Civil War. As CJ Smiley explains:

Newly freed Blacks began to obtain social, economic, and political rights with the passage of the 13th, 14th, and 15th Amendments to the Constitution . . . This growth in power challenged White supremacy and created White fear of Black mobility. Particularly, wealthy Whites were fearful of political power newly freed Black people could acquire via voting, whereas poor Whites saw Blacks as competition in the labor force . . . this fear was met with a shift from Black people being viewed as compliant and submissive servants to savages and brute monsters. . . . This time, the argument was that Blacks were naturally more prone to violence and other aggressive behaviors. (359)

Smiley's explanation details how historical context informs the construction of frames, of stereotypical schemas that are too easily employed to justify the mistreatment of any group perceived to threaten the racial order that privileges white people. This analysis suggests that the direct violence enacted upon Black men occurs in tandem with the indirect violence of the construction of such cultural frames. They further call attention to the need to historically and geographically contextualize the violence depicted in both *Dawg Fight* and *Moonlight*.

In *Dawg Fight* and *Moonlight*, violence is complicated by the cultural frame that projects self-imposed poverty onto Black people and myths of brutality, superhuman strength, and aggressive violence onto Black men. In *Dawg Fight*, the street fighters' reliance on cameras and deliberate provocation of an external gaze inverts a particularly gripping contemporary issue of documented, and documenting, state-sanctioned violence against Black people. The documentary challenges narratives of Black masculine violence and savagery by boldly documenting and encouraging fighting to monetize and empower members of disenfranchised communities. In so doing, the documentary inverts tropes and stereotypes of Black masculinity that entrap and criminalize Black men. The men in the documentary gaze back defiantly, into the camera, as if to say, "we will strive to turn a profit and monetize the assumptions you have made of our strength and brutality to escape the conditions to which we have been condemned."

Perhaps the most poignant example of individual outbursts against routinized systemic degradation from *Moonlight* comes in Chiron's retaliatory, explosive outburst in his high school science classroom in the second chapter of the film. The poignancy of this moment, and the audience's empathy in justifying Chiron's rage are a result of the effective representation of his persecution throughout the film. Chiron's victimization because of his sexuality is a prevalent motif within *Moonlight*, marking even the audience's first introduction of Chiron as a young boy fleeing from a group, terrifyingly outnumbered. Later in the second chapter of the film, he is violently assaulted while on campus. After a series of threats, including being followed home, he is confronted by a group led by Terrell, a classmate who has recruited Kevin, Chiron's seemingly only friend, to instigate the fight. Terrell approaches Kevin over lunch and asks if he remembers a middle school game of "knock down/stay down," wherein Kevin boasts that he used to be "the king of that shit." Terrell declares that "niggas don't do that shit no more," before looking pointedly at Kevin. In this look, Kevin rightfully detects a threat in Terrell's observation, and shifts his body language—holding Terrell's gaze unwaveringly, no longer eating or chewing, and squaring his shoulders slightly, almost imperceptibly, as Terrell asks: "if I point a nigga out, is you gonna knock his ass down?" Kevin's posture emblematizes the need to perform hardness to avoid vulnerability, and in this case, a physical assault. Unspoken in the exchange is that Kevin's previous "kingship" within the game is being called into question, and he will need to prove his strength and callousness again—or else. While it is unclear if Terrell knows about the romantic relationship that has evolved between Chiron and Kevin, the attack on Chiron and Kevin's complicity in it metaphorizes the obstacles they face in building an intimate and caring relationship, whether sexual or otherwise, that is not dependent on the currency of hardness.

In what appears to be the front of the school after the final bell, Terrell organizes a group of boys, Kevin included, into a semi-circle as they wait for Chiron to approach, at which point he looks at Kevin and says, "hit that nigga . . . hit his faggot ass." Terrell's use of a homophobic slur links his perception of Chiron's sexuality (Chiron never verbalizes his sexuality for himself) with his experience of physical subjugation. The camera centers Chiron's face as he defiantly lifts his chin, and Kevin nervously, and reluctantly replies, punching Chiron twice before pleading with him to "stay down," implying that he will not have to hit him again if he does. Chiron rises twice, before Kevin hits him a third time and he is swarmed by the larger group, who assail him with punches and kicks before the onslaught is interrupted by a security guard.

While Chiron's antagonistic peers endlessly target Chiron because they perceive him to be gay, or at least to not perform an acceptable form of masculinity, for adults and authority figures, Chiron's queerness goes largely unspoken even as it alienates him and leads to his repeated subjugation throughout the film. This is best exemplified when, immediately after the security guard breaks up the fight, Chiron is consulted by the principal who provides a stern warning: "If you don't press charges, I can't stop this from happening," to which Chiron responds, "you don't even know." This is perhaps the most outward expression of Chiron's sense of invisibility and unknowability given the cultural terrain that radically inhibits his self-expression, subjecting him to a kind of half-life. In response, the principal asks sarcastically: "oh I don't? . . . you think all this just started, boy?" Here, there is an acknowledgment of Chiron's endless persecution as the principal pleads with Chiron to engage the state to aid in his protection. To do so, however, would codify Chiron's reputation as weak-willed, an association that is rendered inextricable from his sexual orientation.

The principal appeals to his masculinity, asserting that "if you were a man there'd be four other knuckleheads sittin' right next to you." In her efforts to comfort and protect Chiron, she relies on the very rhetoric that has alienated and harmed him by questioning his masculinity and accusing him of not demonstrating "real manhood." This statement causes Chiron to begin crying harder, as he repeats "you don't even know," implicitly expressing that the principal has failed to see how the false standards of masculinity are the very problem that Chiron is trying to escape, and in appealing to them, the principal has confirmed a seeming inescapability from his circumstances that inspires his violent retaliation against Terrell the following day. The principal seems to acknowledge, however implicitly, Chiron's unique struggle of queerness, "I know it's hard . . . I'm not trying to disrespect your struggle . . ." she begins, as her voice fades into the background. "Struggle" becomes an ambiguous stand-in for Chiron's sexuality, and the scene emphasizes Chiron's erasure, both through the attempt to physically blot him out, and the subtle, yet painful refusal to recognize the full extent of his experience which leads to Chiron's tears, indicating a psychic injury that even the punitive suspension or expulsion of his bullies would not begin to heal. As the principal's consolatory words fade out, the message of the scene is clear—consolation is impossible, the damage is done, and Chiron is on his own.

The film brilliantly demonstrates Chiron's tragic resolve and acceptance of how his life will and will not work as a queer Black man, and an acknowledgement of who he will have to be, or rather what he will have to perform to spare himself the rejection he has experienced for most of his life. After his tense, and fruitless interaction with the principal, Chiron is shown dipping his swollen and injured face in a sink full of ice water before observing himself in the mirror, moving his face slightly as if studying his wounds, a fierce determination in his eyes. The following day, he walks purposefully into school, pushing doors open before entering his science class, picking up a chair, and slamming it across Terrell's back. The camera pans to Chiron's teacher's shocked expression, before he and a group of male students intervene. Terrell lies on the ground motionless, and Chiron is shown being taken away by police, Kevin appears at the front of the school, and watches as he is taken away. There is a striking contrast in the treatment of Terrell's violence against Chiron as compared to the latter's retaliation against the former. Although there are witnesses to Chiron's assault, including a security guard, the principal suggests that she requires Chiron to name his attackers to protect him. Within Chiron's attack itself, Chiron is automatically restrained and subjected to punishment; it is later revealed he ends up in Atlanta, which makes literal the alienation and isolation he experiences while still in Liberty City. While this is likely a consequence of the attack taking place within the classroom as opposed to the courtyard, the contrast metaphorizes Chiron's compounding oppression as it compares to those of his prototypically masculine and heterosexual peers.

Moonlight's representation of violence goes beyond direct physical contact to include the injury inflicted by Black people upon other Black people because of limited economic opportunities. Juan's drug dealing, and Chiron's ultimate emulation of Juan, exemplify the consequential intracommunal violence that results from systemic disenfranchisement. This intracommunal violence falls along gendered lines, portraying the complex fallout of the systemic failures that entrap each character represented within the film. Juan is confronted twice in ways that implicate his own failure of his community: once by Paula, Chiron's mother, and once by Chiron himself. In the latter confrontation, which takes place in the first chapter of the film, Chiron deduces that Juan is complicit in his mother's descent into drug addiction, right after a poignant scene in which Juan fields questions about Chiron's sexuality. The scene begins with a desperate knock on Juan's door, the sound shown from inside his house, as he approaches the door with a gun in his hand. Juan puts the gun away upon realizing that Chiron is at the door, but the armed, cautious approach conveys the paranoia that marks Juan's dangerous lifestyle, and ultimately foreshadows his shocking, yet unsurprising, death.

Chiron seems to inherit Juan's paranoia and the older man becomes a model for Chiron of masculinity, survival, and success as Black men. When

Chiron enters the house and sits at the dining table, Juan corrects his positioning and encourages the young boy not to sit down with his back to the door. Juan asks, "how you gon' know if someone creepin' up on you?" Juan models a defensive, protective posture that we see Chiron emulate, moving obediently to the head of the table so he can see the whole room. Taking up a position of power associated with the head of the household, Juan directs Chiron in his fulfillment of masculinity and the ensuing conversation provides an example of Juan's ongoing mentorship of his surrogate son. The conversation moves through a series of questions from Chiron, who declares that he hates his mother moments before asking Juan and Teresa, "what's a faggot?" The series of questions, moving from Chiron's hatred of his mother to slurs launched against him because of his sexuality, suggests a link between his experience of familial alienation and his sexuality. Jared Sexton, in outlining Chiron's compounding experiences of persecution because of his sexual orientation, explains that:

> The frictions arising between [Chiron] and the other boys in the neighborhood . . . seem to represent a generalization of the cruelty he first experiences at home. Little, we learn, hates his mother, as Juan hated his mother before him. The wrinkle introduced by Juan's affirmation of this intergenerational hatred is his realization, after her death, that he was also bonded with her and loved her within that hatred, that he misses that strange brew of feelings as an aspect of her absent presence . . . Little's hatred of his mother, like Juan's, may very well be an inverted expression of her introjected hatred of him. (177)[17]

For Sexton, the parallels between Chiron and Juan extend to their shared alienation from their mothers that he characterizes as an absent presence; Juan's mother is present only in his recollection of his hatred for her, while Paula's absent presence provides a painful, hostile domestic environment that drives him to the weighty conversation with Juan about his sexuality in the context of being repeatedly called a homophobic slur. Juan pauses, a pained expression on his face, "a faggot is a word used to make gay people feel bad." Chiron considers this answer, then asks, "am I a faggot?" Quickly, Juan shakes his head, "You can be gay, but you ain't gotta let nobody call you a faggot." With this statement, Juan provides the only verbal affirmation of Chiron's identity, providing permission for Chiron to be who he is, or what he speculates he might be as detached from the degrading slurs and otherwise dehumanizing treatment he has received within his community throughout the film.

Although Juan's acceptance stands apart from the overwhelming alienation and abuse Chiron experiences throughout the film, his line of questioning reflects his awareness of the systemic failures that have informed the desperate knocking that preceded his search for comfort in the surrogate family Juan and Teresa have constructed for him. He follows Juan's explanation of the distinction between "gay" and "faggot" with "how do I know?" to which Juan responds, "you just do. I think," and Teresa expounds, "you'll know when you know," before Juan reassures Chiron: "you ain't gotta know right now, all right?" Juan and Teresa encourage Chiron to trust his intuition, fostering self-determination, even as Chiron emulates Juan's behavior. Chiron follows this advice, perhaps too closely for Juan's preference, and changes topics, asking Juan directly: "Do you sell drugs?" Juan hesitates before confirming that he does, to which Chiron questions: "And my mama, she do drugs, right?" When Juan confirms, Chiron promptly rises and leaves, indicating his understanding and outrage at Juan's involvement in his home circumstances, and indeed, in contributing to his need to seek shelter and comfort beyond his mother's home. As Jared Sexton formulates:

> That arithmetical equation prompts a break in the relation upon which the break is dependent in the first place: Paula uses drugs and Juan sells the drugs she uses; therefore, Juan contributes directly to the cause of Paula's permanent disarray and Little's prolonged ordeal. Little exits stage left after the "clarifying" exchange and Juan dies, somehow, in the interregnum. Little continues to receive Teresa's moral and material support through the end of the second act. (178)

Far from simplifying Paula's role as a catalyst to Chiron's experience, *Moonlight* presents Paula's formative experiences, implicating men, their care, and their harm alongside her own narrative arc.

The film provides only infrequent scenes of Paula, almost exclusively in interactions with her son, and the decline in her patience and compassion for him as she develops an addiction to crack that she purchases from Juan's dealers. Paula points out the tragic circumstance of her addiction, and Juan's complicity during a confrontation. Juan approaches Paula while she lights up near a drug spot, an act that is discouraged in the earlier part of the film as it attracts unwanted attention to illicit activities. Juan is outraged to see Paula abusing drugs, perhaps especially in the behavior's implication of Chiron's neglect. Juan adopts a moral high ground, forcefully removing

Paula from the car while saying "bitch get the fuck out of here . . . what's wrong with you?" Juan's antagonism functions not as a misogynistic condemnation of drug use, but of Paula's motherhood, which she immediately recognizes, and retorts: "what, so you gon' raise my son now?" Paula mocks his impromptu parenthood of Chiron by implicating him in the loss of his mother and further notes his failure and/or unwillingness to take responsibility for his role in the ravages of addiction within their community.

Paula's mockery implicates the paternal, mentoring relationship Juan adopts with Chiron, evidenced both with his responsiveness to Chiron's questions about his sexual orientation, but also his understanding of race. This mentorship is best evidenced when Juan takes Chiron to the ocean, teaching him how to float and explaining, while holding him up in the water, "I got you. I promise you, I'm not gon' let you go." Juan's reassurance and literal support can be extrapolated to metaphorize the overall care he demonstrates for Chiron. After teaching Chiron to float, and swim, the pair sit on the beach, and Juan explains "there are Black people everywhere. Remember that, okay? . . . We's the first on this planet." The setting of this conversation, read in tandem with its content, invokes a symbolic reminder of the Middle Passage, the terrain African-descended folks coercively travailed to be all over the planet.

The gripping scene takes on another cadence when considering where it was filmed—Virginia Key, a beach that was formerly a "colored only" beach, the result of protests and advocacy. Virginia Key's history makes Juan's gentle lesson revolutionary, mapping Black paternal care and intimacy on a backdrop of Black sea. As Gregory W. Bush writes in his examination of Virginia Key and its reflection of contemporary and ongoing dynamics of racist space-making in South Florida, "recreational spaces were subsumed under broader patterns of urban planning that were pervasively racialized."[18] Virginia Key or Bears Cut, as it was known in the early twentieth century, was a "rougher" beach, rocky, and was initially only accessible via boat; urban planners chose the "deserted and forlorn place [because it] was not of interest to white real estate developers and would not jeopardize white tourism."[19] Despite the lesser accommodations in the nation's winter playground, Bush asserts that "Black identified spaces such as Virginia Key Beach enabled black Americans to forge the solidarity that eventually empowered them to overcome, in many cases move beyond, segregation itself."[20] No longer segregated, Juan's willful decision to teach Chiron to swim, an activity that remains widely inaccessible to Black people, at Virginia Key contributes to the film's investment in Black geographies.

The symbolism of the sea, especially the Atlantic Ocean, has personal implications for Juan, whose presence in Miami as an Afro-Cuban implicates ongoing legacies of diaspora. As Juan explains to Chiron, "I've been here a long time. But I'm from Cuba. Lot of Black folks in Cuba, you wouldn't know that from being here, though." Juan's comment about the underrepresentation of Afro-Cubans in South Florida, highlights the complex interplay and compounding of national and transnational anti-Blackness and white supremacy that comes to shape Juan's experience, or his experience as it is recalled for Chiron. As Rebecca Bodenheimer writes:

> Juan is referring to the fact that black Cubans tend to be invisible in Miami, and in the United States in general, their voices and experiences drowned out by the very vocal and largely white, anti-communist exile community. While Juan's identity as a black Cuban is tangential to the main story, this one-line statement adds a whole other layer of complexity to the film's representation of Miami.[21]

Juan's background invokes the multiplicity of Black populations in South Florida and the complexity of experience for those situated across multiple axes of oppression. In the preceding chapters, I outline how anti-Blackness in immigration policy disproportionately impacted Black émigrés, and Carlos Moore in particular gestures toward the under- and misrepresentation of Afro-Cubans in Miami, emphasizing how white supremacist ideology as it was enacted in Cuba replicated itself with the exodus of the upper classes during and following Fidel Castro's ascent to power. These compounding, transnational legacies of subjugation are called to life when Juan says that "you wouldn't know" from being in Miami that most Cubans are Black.

Moonlight suggests that broad national and international legacies inform the minute interactions shared between Juan and Chiron. This is a small moment in the film and the only mention of Juan's background viewers receive, yet it is monumental, and emblematizes the Diasporic implications of *Moonlight*. As we glean from the use of Boris Gardiner's song in the opening credits, *Moonlight* works to situate South Florida, and Miami specifically, within the Afro-Caribbean basin. Not unlike the Bahamian-South Florida connection alluded to in *Dawg Fight*, Juan's heritage demonstrates the compounding oppressions of race and nationality that inform the exclusions of Black émigrés and reflect transnational anti-Blackness. Further, as portrayed by Mahershala Ali a Black American man from the Bay Area,

Moonlight implicitly offers a Black Diasporic reflection connected, as the film beautifully demonstrates, by the sea.

Like Danticat's unnamed couple in "Children of the Sea" as analyzed in chapter 2, men are fluid, movable, flexible, while women are stagnant and disconnected from the liberatory potential of the sea. Unlike Juan and her son, Paula is bound to the domestic space, or the drug-ridden streets; in the written screenplay, McCraney describes Paula as "just a hardworking single mother in over her head." While Juan has the luxury of swimming, teaching, and parenting with kindness, Paula is, to use the language of the screenplay, drowning. Even Juan and Paula are aware of the gendered access to resources. Despite the clear care he demonstrates to Chiron, Juan does not respond when confronted by Paula when she asks if he will raise her son, recognizing his own complicity, to which Paula responds, "that's what I thought." The pair more explicitly highlight this tension as Juan finally responds, avoiding answering Paula's question: "you gon' raise him?!" to which Paula retorts "you gon' keep sellin' me rocks? Huh?" Paula makes a direct connection between Juan's dealing and her inability to be present for her son, before defiantly taking another hit and blowing smoke in Juan's face. Paula continues, identifying a common refrain that might absolve Juan's complicity, asserting: "motherfucker—don't give me that 'you gotta get it from somewhere,' nigga. I'm getting' it from you. But you gon' raise my son though, right?" She implies that while she may be a negative influence on Chiron and may be failing in her responsibilities as his mother, there are a series of communal failures that result in Chiron's victimization. Juan is enabled by the fact that he is not addicted to drugs, even though his well-being and indeed the very care that he can provide to Chiron is directly enabled by his mother's addiction.

Paula identifies Chiron's queerness to a challenge in raising him. During the same confrontation, Paula asks: "You ever see the way he walk, Juan?" suggesting that Chiron's queerness is legible in his mannerisms; as with Chiron's interaction with the principal, once again speculation about Chiron's sexuality, largely a projection from adults given his young age, goes only partially spoken. Juan quickly becomes defensive of Chiron: "You watch your damn mouth." Paula asks: "You gon' tell him why the other boys kick his ass all the time?" Once again Juan does not respond, and Paula concludes "You ain't shit." She acknowledges what she perceives as a challenge in parenting Chiron, but her language implicitly justifies the onslaughts against her son by suggesting that there is a valid reason for the physical and psychological abuse Chiron experiences throughout his childhood. Regardless, Juan is non-responsive, and although he mentors Chiron about his sexuality, the nuances of parenthood, especially given Juan's earlier self-righteousness, leave Juan at a loss.

The tense interactions between Juan and Paula surrounding her drug use lend credence to apprehensions about the under- and misrepresentation of Black women in *Moonlight*. Her pointed observation of Juan's complicity gestures toward a network of community negligence that is undergirded by white supremacy and refutes the glorification of Juan's character as a provider for Chiron.

Menaka Kannan's, Rhys Hall's, and Matthew W. Hughey's rightfully critique the film's play on archetypes of Black womanhood as contrasted with its complex examination of masculinity. Further, they problematize Juan's benevolence. They write that Paula is "a drug addict prop who serves as little more than a plot device for Chiron's boyhood and sexual anxieties as well as his tenuous economic position," and they continue noting that the two women represented in the film, Paula and Teresa, Chiron's surrogate mother, are contrasted with Teresa serving as "the Madonna figure who dotes upon Chiron and provides respite in the storm." They observe, in support of their condemnation of the film's representation of women, that neither Teresa nor Paula

> are complex nor active agents of their destiny. They have no arc. Rather, the film seems to construct gender as a zero-sum relation, whereby female agency and nuance are sacrificed on the altar of diverse representations of masculinity.[22]

I share a concern of the film's limited representations of Black women but read Paula's resistance and condemnation of Juan as a further refutation of her own reductive characterization, and a challenge to the saint-like, heroic characterization we might too easily ascribe to Juan and the other male characters in the film.

However, seeing Paula as a flattened stereotype of drug addiction and bad mothering undermines Paula's arc and how it tracks her descent into addiction and her apology to her adult son toward the end of the film. Excluding Paula's evolution, remorse, and pursuit of redemption from any analyses of female representation in *Moonlight* contributes to the flattening, and undermines the complexity, of her character as both a victim and perpetrator of the direct and indirect violence that entraps each character represented in the film. Paula directly refutes Juan's heroization even as she is complicit in her son's dehumanization, in part because of her drug addiction. The nuances of her characterization necessitate a more complex understanding than a facile gendered contrast that neglects the material consequences of anti-Blackness and societally sanctioned limited access to resources. These material consequences including and exceeding Paula's missteps degrade Chiron's normative familial connections and contributed to the construction of his surrogate family with Juan and Teresa.

To reduce Paula to a flattened stereotype overlooks the care and attentiveness she demonstrates in her early appearance in the film. In the opening chapter of the film, after Juan comes to Chiron's aid after a group of boys chased him and Juan takes him home, Paula approaches the pair angrily, asking "why didn't you come home like you supposed to? Huh?" Paula expresses outrage and concern at her son's disappearance. Once inside the house, Chiron rises to turn on the TV, and Paula, who has kissed her son's head, explaining that "Mama was just worried about you is all," asserts that Chiron's "TV privileges have been revoked," before encouraging her son to "find something . . . to read." Transitioning from Chiron's interaction with Teresa to that with Paula does not provide a neat contrast of "attentive mother" to "negligent drug addict," but rather signposts a point, preceding Paula's decline in health, wherein she was attentive to and caring for her son.

Paula, too, acknowledges her addiction and apologizes to Chiron in the concluding chapter of the film. Chiron arrives at a rehabilitation center to visit his mother, and informs her of his difficulties sleeping, at which point Paula asks if he has considered speaking to someone, "maybe somebody like ya mama," and Chiron looks at his mother pointedly, to which she replies, "yeah, it sound funny to me, too." Paula acknowledges how uncharacteristic providing support for her son feels, and in so doing begins to practice accountability for her neglectful and abusive relationship toward her son. She asks bluntly if Chiron is still dealing drugs, and when he does not answer, Paula asserts that they "didn't come all the way the hell to Georgia to have you fallin' in the same shit, Chiron." Chiron rises to leave, frustrated with the implication that Paula is attempting to parent Chiron after failing him in his youth because of her addiction. Chiron rises to leave, as Paula pleads with him to stay and listen, to which Chiron curtly replies "to you? Really, though?" Chiron mocks Paula's effort at maternal discipline and she responds, taking accountability before giving a tear-filled apology: "Lord knows I did not have love for you when you needed it, I know that. So you ain't gotta love me, but you gon' know that I love you. You hear? I'm sorry, baby. I'm so sorry." Paula's acknowledgement of her shortcomings, expression of love for her son, and apology, is expressed in the context of her revelation to Chiron that she intends to stay at the rehabilitation center, as it is now her home, and support others in their recovery process.

The film presents a paradox: Juan fractures, and substitutes Chiron's home life, which reflects the film's foiled female representation. The women in *Moonlight* are very much circumscribed to the construction of the home space, and, if we continue the analysis of how race and space make each other, including gender into this analytical matrix reveals the standard of Black, female domesticity by which both women are held up to scrutiny based on their foiling within the film. Paula fails to consistently represent maternal love and care because of her drug addiction, a fact she owns in her final scene with Chiron, while Teresa regularly provides solace and shelter for Chiron even after Juan's death; Teresa is introduced approximately ten minutes into the film, offering Chiron a place to stay, while looking defiantly at Juan as he begins to protest. She cares for Chiron, welcomes him into her home, and continues to offer him refuge when Paula kicks him out so she can spend time with a man with whom she does drugs. There is a clear difference in the domestic spaces the women occupy, and the film presents the women as the ones who set the tone for the home, and are thus contrasted based on the kind of home life they can provide for Chiron; while Teresa makes beds for Chiron, Paula yells and ejects him from the house, yet still possessively reminds him that he is *her* son, and that Teresa is not his mother.

Yet, the contrast between the care Teresa provides that Paula cannot is contextualized by the relative comfort provided to the former; it is not evident that Teresa works, and Juan's powerful position within the community as a drug dealer suggests a bit more disposable income and flexible time that would allow him to be attentive to Chiron that is not afforded to Paula as a single, working mother. Paula's eventual addiction feeds her present absence but comes to be in a compounding confluence of drug use and impoverishment that limits Paula's capacity to take care of herself and her son.

In subtle contrast to *Moonlight*, in *Dawg Fight*, women are very rarely shown or interviewed, suggesting a clear delineation between how Black men and women are expected to differently combat their experiences of systemic oppression and isolation from life-altering resources. In the documentary, a panel of women, sitting on fold-out chairs, reflect on one of the fights. One of the unnamed women declares humorously that she is "against violence, but that fight was off the chain!" in reference to the fight depicted between Mike and Chauncy. Women are almost exclusively shown on the sidelines as active spectators, with the documentary's framing of the illegal fights as a money-making mode of escape for Black men with little economic opportunities. The exclusion of women from this realm removes them as agents in this alternate economy. In fact, the female partner of a fighter who forfeits enters the ring, threatening her partner if he does not finish the fight, and lunging at his opponent. In voiceover, Dada, chuckling, observes that she "was gon' go in and finish the fight for him" while a spectator suggests that "she had more heart than he did." The unnamed woman violates an unspoken code about who fights, and community members observe her entry into the ring only as it contributes to the emasculation of her partner.

While the focus of this chapter is on the racialization and spatialization of South Florida's cultural topography as represented in media that treat Black men as their primary foci, the construction of Black masculinity, especially with its attention to violence, and repressed relationality, seems inextricable from exclusion, repression, and violence against women who are sidelined, glorified, or fall prey to the male-dominated alternate economies constructed in our white supremacist world.

Death in the Disappeared

The match between Mike and Chauncy is framed by the backgrounds of each fighter, and their fates after the fight. This framing exposes lives punctuated by exclusion and violence. Mike, a young man who was expelled from school after a fight wherein he broke a classmate's nose, declares that his life never got on the right track after that and so he must fight. His tone suggests that the fight is literal and metaphorical, or rather, that fighting in the ring is a way to fight for a better life. He goes further to say that community respect might be a reward for being a "hard" man.

Chauncy, Mike's opponent, was arrested and served an undisclosed term in prison for armed robbery and asserts that having a "rap sheet, but not a resume" has kept him from finding stable employment. Chauncy wins the fight, but later the documentary reveals that he is shot in the back of the head by his sister's boyfriend after an argument. The documentary ends with members of his family deciding to discontinue life support. While there is a sense of sadness about Chauncy's death, there is also a distinct absence of outrage. An unnamed woman, a regular spectator at the fighting events, says "that's just how it is here." Chauncy's death, as well as Tree's death at the hands of police that is reported in the ending credits, is a mundane fact in West Perrine. In *Moonlight*, Chiron's stand-in father figure is dead by the beginning of the second chapter. It is never explained how he dies, but again, brief conversations around his death demonstrate a resigned acceptance—he is never outwardly grieved, even by Teresa, who offers Chiron safe harbor after his own mother develops an addiction to drugs.

Conclusion

Moonlight and *Dawg Fight* present dynamics of gender, race, and space as inextricable and mutually constituting. Throughout this chapter, and indeed, the book in its entirety I have taken for granted, as we all should, George Lipsitz's claims in *How Racism Takes Place*. Lipsitz asserts:

> Racialized space shapes nearly every aspect of urban life. The racial imagination that relegates people of different races to different spaces produces grossly unequal access to education, employment, transportation, and shelter . . . The lived experience of race takes place in actual spaces, while the lived experience of place draws its determinate logic from overt and covert understandings of race. (7)

In this chapter, I have not, due to the limits of the genres of works I am engaging, considered exposure to environmental toxins, educational environments and opportunities, and the limited access to networks that might help improve the circumstances of a historically besieged population. One can imagine, especially when relying on contemporary research relating to stress as a result of racialized oppression, that there are increased health problems within communities like Liberty City and West Perrine that are not documented in wide-circulating media. In *Moonlight*, Chiron demonstrates a keen awareness of the ways intimacy and relationality are bound by his environment. Chiron's silence, and the psychic agony he experiences must stand in for, or gesture toward the structures we cannot see, unless we are digging; Chauncy's and Tree's deaths, and their connections to intracommunity and police violence respectively, the bloodiness and brutality of the fights themselves, and Dada's precarity in hosting the illegal fights must stand in for and gesture toward the unseen ways white supremacy and anti-Blackness have made, unmade, and remade South Florida for Black constituencies.

Coda

Between 2012, when I started work on what would ultimately become this book, and writing this short conclusion in 2022, a lot has happened; we've lost millions of lives globally to a pandemic many saw coming; we've witnessed and endured the authoritarian impulses of the state manifesting tirelessly against Black people in routinized, publicized demonstrations of violence. There are too many names that could have been added to the conclusion of the first chapter of this project; we have received warnings of our planet's impending inability to sustain our lives; in the U.S., white supremacy manifested in a storming of the Capitol and attempted overthrow of the government.

Yet the events of the past year are not "unprecedented," they're compounding reminders of more of the same willful patterns that subject minoritized groups to premature death. COVID-19 disproportionately impacts Black and Brown communities and white supremacy continues to reconstitute itself. Recently, legislators are retaliating for the uprisings of 2020 through legislation that increases penalties for protesting and shuts down discussions of racism and sexism in the classroom.

Miami continues to provide us insight into the future. When the Surfside Champlain Tower collapsed on June 24, 2021, I wished for as many survivors, and began urging my parents to sell their house in South Florida. I understand (intellectually) that encouraging them to do so is treating symptoms, but what else can we do? We won't know for a while, if ever, what led to the building's horrifying collapse, but I wondered instantly if we will see more catastrophes as our infrastructure fails with the imminent collapse of our environments. Climate change is humanmade and there will be direct and indirect consequences to the havoc we have wreaked on our planet, especially in South Florida.

The wills and whims of the past in Miami inform its present, and future. With its founding, wealthy white families sought beachfront properties, emboldened by the entitlement to the natural world that has always been enacted in Miami. Now, as we witness the increased frequency and power of hurricanes, sea level rise, and other material manifestations of climate change, the economic topography of the city is changing; the past appeals of the beachfront are now at worst, dangerous and life threatening, and at best, insurance liabilities. Wealth is moving uphill. As Valencia Gunder, founder of The Smile Trust (an organization that tackles houselessness and food insecurity in South Florida) explains:

> Here in Miami, they put wealthy communities on the outskirts [of the city] so they can enjoy the beach . . . Because of sea level rise and climate change, we know that Miami is expecting up to six feet of water, and now we're starting to see these wealthy communities start to come to the center of the city. The center of the city is where most of the under-served communities of color are housed.

Little Haiti and Overtown are particularly vulnerable to climate gentrification, but the current threat is not new—we might in reading Gunder's assessment ask why "communities of color"—though let's be clear, these are Black communities—came to be "housed" in the inner-city.[1] This recent iteration of displacement continues a Miamian pattern of moving Black people based on the whims and fantasies of the wealthy white elite.

The region seems to have always boisterously claimed: we're here for a good time but certainly not a long time, and we will build our world accordingly. It's a testament to the hubris of white supremacy that South Beach was created, built upon, and inhabited assuming we were ever meant to survive the consequences of colonial pillaging of the planet. But this hubris is amplified in, but not unique to, South Florida; Jafari Allen puts it succinctly and beautifully when he explains that "Miami is special," but it is not "exceptional." Allen continues:

> Its geography—the natural and built environment and the way folks inhabit it—is unique in the US and it is changing at a fast pace. Natural disaster and everyday natural "ruination"—hurricane and/or flooding and/or mold and/or the natural environment and decay in Miami—points out the precarity that nature presents for all of us, especially for those folks with less resources who are thrown most immediately in harm's way of not-so-natural ecological environmental racism and dumping.

The legacies of Virginia Key, Turkey Point (South Florida's very own nuclear plant), and Overtown remind me of South Florida's instructional value for the U.S., and the world. What Allen describes as its expedited timeline is a consequence of its demographic, its economies, and the happenstance of geography. It lets us know where we're headed, in terms of how we manage populations, and how the environment manages us.

Miami is a (white) controlled fantasy land, or as Julio Capo Jr. notes, a fairyland, which perfectly captures its eroticism, desirability, riskiness, and tenuous connection to material realities, especially those of its inhabitants. It reflects investors' and boosters' deepest desires and loosest inhibitions to a white, cisgender, wealthy point. These fantasies stand in for what we might otherwise call a city plan. We've been given glimpses of what a perceived loss of white control in South Florida looks like. Perhaps the most salient examples are the Mariel Boatlift and the damning, overblown productions like *Scarface* and *Miami Vice* that reflect white anxieties about Blackness, queerness, and crime. Writer Oliver Stone intended for Tony Montana to metaphorize capitalistic greed but instead showed us that aspiring to white ideals of wealth is punishable by violent death. There was no future for the Black and mixed-race émigrés that are allegedly represented in *Scarface*. Nor was there a future for Célianne, the young victim of military rape, fleeing Haiti for Miami in Danticat's "Children of the Sea." Nor was there a future in Miami for Danticat's uncle, or cousin. Yet, Miami is a city of the future, as Sheila Croucher reminds us, and reconciling how anti-Blackness robs Black people of their lives, their homes, and futures is part of what Miami can teach us.

There are more examples that have helped me understand my hometown and how Black oppression has manifested there than I include in this monograph; In *Dade County: Schools, Students, Communities, A True Story* (1993), Richard J. Strachan describes the integration of Dade County (now Miami-Dade County) schools, white flight, and personal experiences of racism as a teacher, assistant principal, and principal in Liberty City; *Forbearance: The Life of a Cocoanut Grove Native* (2003) is Thelma Vernell Anderson's detailed description of the "colored town" of Cocoanut (now Coconut) Grove and her determination to become a nurse in the segregated South. In *Lessons from the Other Side* (2004), DC Clark describes himself as "a hooked fish," detailing how racism has economically, and spatially, circumscribed his experiences in Miami.

Miami is a city of the future, and soon, so soon, it will be underwater.

I don't want this project to be my eulogy to the version of my hometown I remember, but I worry it might be. Every time I go back, it has shifted a bit: a restaurant gone, a shop priced out, a trail submerged. Given South Florida's vulnerability to climate change, and the remaking of the space to continuously displace Black people, I wonder if I'm commemorating the region I knew and have known. I deeply hope there's something left to miss.

Notes

Introduction

1. Mary Louise Pratt describes contact zones as "social spaces where disparate cultures meet, clash, and grapple with each other, often in highly asymmetrical relations of domination and subordination—such as colonialism and slavery, or their aftermaths, as they are lived out across the globe today," 7.

2. McKittrick, *Demonic Grounds: Black Women and the Cartographies of Struggle*, xvii.

3. Gosin, *The Racial Politics of Division*, 6.

4. See Kimberly Brown's, "Sniffing the "Calypso Magnolia": Unearthing the Caribbean Presence in the South (response)" (2005), Leigh Ann Duck's *The Nation's Region: Southern Modernism, Segregation, and U.S. Nationalism,* and Barbara Ladd's "Dismantling the Monolith: Southern Places—Past, Present, and Future" (2000).

5. Wolfe, "Settler Colonialism and the Elimination of the Native," 387.

6. Allen, "Afterword: "Miami's Nappy Edges: Finding Black Miami, Sin Fronteras," 3.

7. See Marvin Dunn's *The Beast in Florida: A History of Anti-Black Violence* (2013) and *Black Miami in the Twentieth Century* (1997), and Chanelle N. Rose's *The Struggle for Black Freedom in Miami: Civil Rights and America's Tourist Paradise, 1896–1968*, provide a more detailed history of Black laborers' role in Miami's inception.

8. Merrick, "Pre-Flagler Influences on the Lower Florida East Coast," 5; Peters, *Biscayne Country,* 229; 2.

9. I am referencing Benedict Anderson's *Imagined Communities* (1983); Anderson outlines the role media plays in shaping the story we tell about presumed shared national background, and how these communities can bolster practices of violent exclusion.

10. See Barbara Ladd's "Dismantling the Monolith" (2000).

11. See Claudia Milian's *Latining America: Black-Brown Passages and the Coloring of Latino/a Studies* (2013), James L. Peacock, Harry L. Watson, and Carrie R. Matthew's *The American South in a Global World* (2005), James Cobb and William Stueck's *Globalization and the American South* (2005), Jon Smith and Deborah Cohn's *Look Away! The U.S. South in New World Studies* (2004), and Andrew Gomez's "Jim Crow and the Caribbean South: Cubans and Race in South Florida, 1885–1930s" (2017).

12. A preponderance of explorations and definitions of multiculturalism exist, but most succinctly, I use multiculturalism to stand in for wide practices of celebrating the

spoils of integration and alleged learning opportunities afforded by diversity without attention to hierarchies of power that are maintained by white supremacist, heteronormative, and classist norms. See Stuart Hall's "Race, Articulation and Societies Structured in Dominance" (1980), Ruth Wilson Gilmore's "Race and Globalization" (2002), Jared Sexton's *Amalgamation Schemes* (2008), and Dylan Rodriguez's "Multiculturalist White Supremacy and the Substructure of the Body" (2011).

13. For more about tourism's role in remaking South Florida see Julio Capó Jr.'s *Welcome to Fairyland: Queer Miami before 1940* (2017), Chanelle N. Rose's *The Struggle for Black Freedom in Miami: Civil Rights and America's Tourist Paradise, 1896–1968* (2015), Gregory W. Bush's *White Sand Black Beach: Civil Rights, Public Space, and Miami's Virginia Key* (2016),and Alex Stepick and Alejandro Portes' *City on the Edge : The Transformation of Miami* (1993).

14. See MiamiandBeaches.com

15. See Marvin Dunn's *The Beast in Florida: A History of Anti-Black Violence* (2013) and *Black Miami in the Twentieth Century* (1997), Alejandro Portes and Alex Stepick's *City on the Edge: The Transformation of Miami* (1993), Alex Stepick's *This Land Is Our Land: Immigrants and Power in Miami* (2003) and *Crossing the Water and Keeping the Faith: Haitian Religion in Miami* (2013), and Guillermo Grenier's and Alex Stepick's *Miami Now!: Immigration, Ethnicity, and Social Change* (1992).

16. See Luisa Yanez's "Miami-Dade Leaders See Magic in New Name," *Sun Sentinel*, November 15, 1997.

17. Bush, *White Sand Black Beach*, 2.

18. Connolly, "Speculating," 1.

19. See Valerie Smitch's *Self-Discovery and Authority in Afro-American Narrative* (1987), Daphne Brooks *Bodies in Dissent: Spectacular Performances of Race and Freedom, 1850–1910* (2006), Eric Pritchard's *Fashioning Lives: Black Queers and the Politics of Literacy* (2017), and Hazel Carby's *Reconstructing Womanhood: The Emergence of the Afro-American Woman Novelist* (1990).

20. See "Narrative: The Road to Black Feminist Theory" (1997).

21. Allen, ibid., 4.

22. Veeser, *The New Historicism*, 71.

23. Allen, ibid., 5.

24. Baldwin, *Notes of a Native Son*, 55.

25. Here I am reminded of Junot Díaz's frequently cited speech at Bergen Community College in 2009, where the Dominican American author outlined why he felt it imperative to represent himself in literature: "You know, vampires have no reflections in a mirror? There's this idea that monsters don't have reflections in a mirror. And what I've always thought isn't that monsters don't have reflections in a mirror. It's that if you want to make a human being into a monster, deny them, at the cultural level, any reflection of themselves. And growing up, I felt like a monster in some ways. I didn't see myself reflected at all. I was like, 'Yo, is something wrong with me? That the whole society seems to think that people like me don't exist?' And part of what inspired me, was this deep desire that before I died, I would make a couple of mirrors. That I would make some

mirrors so that kids like me might see themselves reflected back and might not feel so monstrous for it."

26. de la Fuente, *A Nation for All*, 14.

27. Allen, ibid., 3.

28. Clifford, *The Predicament of Culture*, 23.

Chapter 1. To Tell a Black Story of Miami: Civil Rights and the Reverberations of Black Floridian History in *Freedom in the Family*

1. Ards, *Words of Witness*, 17. See also Hazel Carby's *Reconstructing Womanhood: The Emergence of the Afro-American Women Novelist* (1987), Carol Boyce Davies' *Writing and Identity: Migrations of the Subject* (1994), and *But Some of Us Are Brave: All the Women Are White, All the Blacks Are Men: Black Women's Studies*, edited by Akasha Gloria Hull, Patricia Bell-Scott, and Barbara Smith (1982).

2. See Portes and Stepick's *City on the Edge: The Transformation of Miami* (1993), Alejandro Portes and Ariel C. Armony's *The Global Edge: Miami in the Twenty First Century* (2018), and Elizabeth M. Aranda, Sallie Hughes, and Elena Sabogal's *Making a Life in Multi-Ethnic Miami* by Elizabeth M. Aranda, Sallie Hughes (2014).

3. McKittrick, *Demonic Grounds: Black Women and the Cartographies of Struggle*, 1.

4. Grant, *Ella Baker*, 107.

5. Stephens Due's exclusion is two-fold and indexes the historiographical stakes of this chapter. First, she spotlights the exclusion of women in discussions and investigations of the Civil Rights Movement that are as pertinent today in 2021 as they were in 2003. More recently, scholars have centered Black women's contributions to the movement. See *Want to Start a Revolution?: Radical Women in the Black Freedom Struggle* edited by Jeanne Theoharis, Komozi Woodard, and Dayo Gore (2009), *Sisters in the Struggle: African American Women in the Civil Rights Black Power Movement* edited by Bettye Collier-Thomas and V.P. Franklin (2001), *I've Got the Light of Freedom* by Charles Payne, *Ella Baker, and the Black Freedom Movement* by Barbara Ransby (2005), *How Long? How Long?* Belinda Robnett (1997).

6. Stephens Due includes the language of Martin Luther King Jr.'s communication to the Tallahassee CORE organizers and the telegram can be found in the State Library and Archives of Florida.

7. See foundational work on Black Feminist histories, theories, and storytelling by Deborah Grey White, Kimberlé Crenshaw, and Patricia Hill Collins.

8. See Doveanna S. Fulton's *Speaking Power: Black Feminist Orality in Women's Narratives* (2006) and Alice Walker's *In Search of Our Mother's Gardens* (1984) for more on non-written archives of Black women's knowledge and stories.

9. An early debate about the authenticity of Black literary production can, of course, be traced to narratives from enslaved people, or slave narratives, and the various uses of white amanuensis in Black storytelling; see Robert Stepto's *From Behind the Veil: A Study of Afro-American Narrative* (1979), William L. Andrews' *To Tell a Free Story: The First Century of Afro-American Autobiography, 1760–1865* (1986), and James Olney's "I was Born": Slave Narratives, their Status as Autobiography and as Literature." (1984)

10. See Guillermo Grenier and Alex Stepick's *Miami Now!* (1992), Alex Stepick's, Guillermo Grenier's, Max Castro's, and Marvin Dunn's *This Land Is Our Land: Immigrants and Power in Miami* (2003), Maria Cristina Garcia's *Havana USA: Cuban Exiles and Cuban Americans in South Florida 1959–1994* (1994), and Jeffrey Kahn's *Islands of Sovereignty: Haitian Migration and the Borders of Empire* by (2019).

11. Angela Ards, ibid., 9.

12. *The Struggle for Black Freedom in Miami,* published in 2015, marks the first comprehensive examination of Civil Rights history in Miami. Chanelle N. Rose observes that "Miami has been almost completely left out of the larger civil rights narrative" (3). She notes a preponderance of investigations of immigration into the city during the 1960s and 1970s without concurrent considerations of the movement. Although South Florida has been neglected in studies of the Civil Rights Movement, Northern Florida, especially Tallahassee and Jacksonville have been the subject of many examinations of the movement. See for example, James M. Fendrich's *Ideal Citizens: The Legacy of the Civil Rights Movement* (1993) and Glenda Rabby's *The Pain and the Promise: The Struggle for Civil Rights in Tallahassee, Florida* (1999).

13. Baker, *Critical Memory,* 1.

14. Rose, ibid., 17.

15. "Lena Quits $8,000 Miami Engagement Over Bias" in *JET Magazine* March 3, 1955.

16. See *Sam Rabin.* 1970 (circa). State Archives of Florida, Florida Memory.

17. The state-sanctioned destruction of Black neighborhoods (including interstate/highway development), and the complicity of Black and white landlords in Black exploitation is the central conceit of N.D.B. Connolly's *A World More Concrete: Real Estate and the Remaking of Jim Crow South Florida (2014).*

18. The Black Archives Historic Lyric Theater, see: https://www.bahlt.org/

19. Rose, ibid., 26.

20. Per Dorothy Jenkins Field, in her "Final phase of upgrades finished at Overtown's historic Lyric Theater" report in the *Miami Herald* (February 5, 2014) the renovations to the Lyric Theater were sponsored by various public and private supporters the Southeast Overtown/Park West Community Redevelopment Agency, Miami-Dade County, The Knight Foundation, Coca-Cola, Macy's, The Design Group, and Miami & Drummer Boy Sound.

21. Carey, "An Intensive Three-Weeks," 1.

22. Stephens Due does not mention which location they were testing—at its height, there were approximately 175 Royal Castle Locations, dozens of which were in South Florida, with others spread throughout the South and Midwest. The sole remaining Royal Castle (now owned by the grandson of the first Black employee of the franchise) is about ten miles (a twenty-minute drive) Northwest of the Sir John Hotel, so it is possible that in their testing, the CORE trainees ventured there. See "Miami's Last Royal Castle" published in the Miami Herald on June 30, 2019.

23. Julio Capó Jr.'s work outlines the economies of difference that model a transient permissiveness of Black, Brown, and/or queer people, but does not change the fundamental whiteness, heteronormativity, and patriarchy upon which contemporary econo-

mies, politics, and culture is structured. See also "Black Activism in a Jim Tourist City" in Chanelle Rose's *The Struggle for Black Freedom in Miami*.

24. See García's *Havana USA: Cuban Exiles and Cuban Americans in South Florida* and Alex Stepick's, Guillermo Grenier's, Max Castro's, and Marvin Dunn's *This Land Is Our Land: Immigrants and Power in Miami*, especially "Competing Elites: Cuban Power, Anglo Conversion, and Frustrated African Americans."

25. The theme of the 1964 World's Fair was, perhaps, ironically, "Peace Through Understanding." The fair was held in Flushing Meadows—Corona Park in Queens, New York City from April to October 1964 with a second season from April to October of 1965. The April 22, 1964, CORE demonstration was contested, with some organizers declaring it would be too disruptive and might affect Black folks who had been hired to work the fair. Those in favor of protesting were focused on the local NYC culture of job discrimination, police brutality, slum housing, while also targeting, as Due does, the idyllic representations of the world while ignoring systemic anti-Blackness.

26. The trial had been moved to Tampa from Miami by Circuit Judge Lenore Nesbitt on March 3, 1980—nearly two months after McDuffie's death in late December 1979. The judge claimed that the case was "a time bomb," and hoped that moving it out of Miami might increase the chances of an unbiased trial; an all-white jury ultimately tried, and acquitted, the police officers on charges ranging from manslaughter to second-degree murder.

27. López, *Unbecoming Blackness*, 157.

28. Connolly, *A World More Concrete*, 115–116.

29. See work by Marvin Dunn, Chanelle N. Rose, and N.D.B. Connolly as compared to members of the Miami school whose work is characterized by comparative attention to diversity, as opposed to treating anti-Blackness as foundational to examinations of Miami/South Florida.

30. See Joseph Caleb Jr.'s "Father's Day: In memory of my dad, Joseph Caleb" in *The Miami Herald*, June 14, 2014.

31. Stepick; Kahn, ibid.

32. Duvalier, and his administration's terror and the emigration it triggered are a focal point of the next chapter. Jean-Claude Duvalier succeeded his father, François Duvalier, in April of 1971 until 1986. Jean-Claude Duvalier's staunch anti-Communist policy garnered him support from Presidents Richard Nixon and Gerald Ford when the perceived threat of "Communist penetration" was at its height. This support continued until President Jimmy Carter's election, despite well-documented human rights violations, including the mobilization of the Tonton Macoutes, an extralegal agency tasked with maintaining the Duvalier regime and silencing dissenters by any means necessary. Duvalier's egregious human rights violations triggered massive waves of emigration from Haiti to the United States (especially New York City and Miami).

33. As of the 2020 Census, these neighborhoods are still majority white and/or "Hispanic." Palmetto Bay, for example, only has a documented 3.7% population of Black residents.

34. Drs. Kenneth and Mamie Clark's doll test with children is often cited as a prime example of how Black children can internalize white supremacist ideals, manifesting in

low self-esteem. Notably, the results of this study were used to push forward desegregation efforts, including the Brown v. Board of Education decision; unfortunately, integration into white environments has not problematized white supremacist infrastructures. More recently, Noliwe Rooks, in *Hair Raising: Beauty, Culture and African American Women* (1996) centers Black women's relationship to their hair in contexts that deride textures, colors, and practices associated with Blackness.

35. There has been notable public discourse on police brutality, in part the result of recorded and widely circulated videos and/or audio recordings of Black victims and a result of organizing by Black Lives Matter chapters across the country.

36. There are countless examinations of the culture of white terrorism in the U.S., see specifically Marable Manning's *Race, Reform, and Rebellion: The Second Reconstruction and beyond in Black America, 1945–2006* (2007), Robert Pratt's *Selma's Bloody Sunday: Protest, Voting Rights, and the Struggle for Racial Equality* (2017), and, more specific to Florida, Glenda Alice Rabby's *The Pain, and the Promise: The Struggle for Civil Rights in Tallahassee* (1999).

37. See *The FBI's War on Black America* (documentary film) (1990), Natsu Taylor Saito's, "Whose Liberty? Whose Security? The USA Patriot Act in the Context of COINTELPRO and the Unlawful Repression of Political Dissent," 81 Or. L. Rev. 1051 (2002), and Nelson Blackstock's *Cointelpro: The FBI's Secret War on Political Freedom* (1988) for examinations of surveillance of Black activists.

38. See the African American Policy Forum's "Say Her Name" Report (2015), authored by Kimberlé Williams Crenshaw and Andrea J. Ritchie, with Rachel Anspach, Rachel Gilmer, and Luke Harris.

Chapter 2. The Anti-Haitian Hydra: Remapping Haitian Spaces in Miami

1. In *Silencing the Past*, Trouillot continues "With the place of black now guaranteed at the bottom of the Western nomenclature, anti-black racism soon became the central element of planter ideology," 83; 77.

2. For more on Haiti's material existence and its representation in the global imaginary, see Myriam Chancy's *From Sugar to Revolution: Women's Visions of Haiti, Cuba, and the Dominican Republic* (2012), Gina Ulysse's *Why Haiti Needs New Narratives: A Post-quake Chronicle* (2015), Colin Dayan's *Haiti, History, and the Gods* (1995), and Raphael Dalleo's *American Imperialism's Undead: The Occupation of Haiti and the Rise of Caribbean Anticolonialism* (2016).

3. See the Migration Policy Institute's "Haitian Immigrants in the United States" report by Kira Olsen-Medina and Jeanne Batalova; the largest concentration of Haitians/ Haitian Americans in the U.S. since the 1970s have been Florida and New York, in that order.

4. This is the central premise of Carl Lindskoog's *Detain and Punish: Haitian Refugees and the Rise of the World's Largest Immigration Detention System* (2018). See also Patrisia Macías-Rojas' *From Deportation to Prison: The Politics of Immigration Enforcement in Post–Civil Rights America* (2016), Mark Dow's *American Gulag: In-side U.S. Immigration Prisons* (2005), Tanya Golash-Boza's *Immigration Nation: Raids, Detentions, and Deportations in Post-9/11 America* (2012), and Alison Mountz's and Jenna M. Loyd's *Boats,*

Borders, and Bases : Race, the Cold War, and the Rise of Migration Detention in the United States (2018).

5. In "Of Our Spiritual Strivings," the first essay in W.E.B. Du Bois' *The Souls of Black Folk* (1903), Du Bois notes that he is often implicitly asked by white people "How does it feel to be a problem?"

6. See Sant La: Haitian Neighborhood Center's "Progress and Unmet Challenges: Sant La's Profile of The Haitian Community of Miami-Dade, 2010–2015," Alex Stepick's and Dale F. Swartz's *Pride Against Prejudice: Haitians in the United States* (1997), and Thurka Sangaramoorthy's *Treating AIDS: Politics of Difference, Paradox of Prevention* (2014).

7. Sangaramoorthy, ibid., 10.

8. See more on how white supremacy privatizes allegedly public space in George Lipsitz's *How Racism Takes Place* (2011), especially "The White Spatial Imaginary," Charles Mills' *The Racial Contract* (1997), especially "Details," and Dorceta Taylor's *Toxic Communities: Environmental Racism, Industrial Pollution, and Residential Mobility,* especially "The Rise of Racially Restrictive Covenants: Guarding Against Infiltration" (2014).

9. See Carl Lindskoog, ibid., and Alison Mountz's and Jenna M. Loyd's *Boats, Borders, and Bases: Race, the Cold War, and the Rise of Migration Detention in the United States* (2018).

10. Benítez Rojo, *The Repeating Island the Caribbean and the Postmodern Perspective,* 6; 73.

11. See Regine O. Jackson's *Geographies of the Haitian Diaspora* (2011), Philippe Zacaïr's *Haiti and the Haitian Diaspora in the Wider Caribbean* (2010), and Jeffrey S. Kahn's *Islands of Sovereignty: Haitian Migration and the Borders of Empire* (2019).

12. See Hyppolite's "Dyaspora" essay in Edwidge Danticat's *The Butterfly's Way: Voices from the Haitian Dyaspora* (2001). In her introduction Edwidge Danticat describes her experience as a Haitian American as "the tenth department. Haiti has nine geographic departments, and the tenth was the floating homeland, the ideological one, which joined all Haitians living in the diaspora" (3).

13. McKittrick, ibid., 11. See also Brian Jarvis' *Postmodern Cartographies: The Geographical Imagination in Contemporary American Culture* (1998), and "Growing up White: The Social Geography of Race" from *White Women, Race Matters* by Ruth Frankenberg (1993).

14. Stepto, ibid., 67: "the idea that a landscape becomes symbolic in literature when it is a region in time and space offering spatial expressions of social structures" is also helpful here to foreground how literature set in South Florida symbolizes racialized oppression in the region.

15. See Ralph Pezzullo's *Plunging into Haiti: Clinton, Aristide, and the Defeat of Diplomacy* (2006), Alex Dupuy's *The Prophet and Power: Jean-Bertrand Aristide, the International Community, and Haiti* (2007), and Peter Hallward's *Damming the Flood: Haiti, Aristide, and the Politics of Containment* (2007)

16. Mitchell, "U. S. Policy toward Haitian Boat People," 73–74.

17. Arana and Brice, "Miami Murder Mystery: How Three Haitian Radio Hosts Were Silenced," 9.

18. Rohter, "In Miami's Little Haiti," 1994.

19. Sharpe, "The Middle Passages of Black Migration," 105.

20. Nevans, "The Repatriation of the Haitian Boat People," 273–302.

21. Mitchell, ibid., 74

22. Lindskoog, ibid.

23. Sciolino, "Clinton Says U.S. Will Continue" 1993.

24. Scholars within the Miami School note that part of Miami's appeal to Caribbean émigrés is the similarities in climate, see *This Land Is Our Land: Immigrants and Power in Miami* and Melanie Shell-Weiss' *Coming to Miami: A Social History* (2009). There is also evidence that the agricultural and climate similarities were exploited in the use of Black Bahamian labor in the foundational construction of the city as noted by real estate developer George Merrick.

25. Roberts, *Killing the Black Body,* 9; 19; 60. See also Steven Moore's "ICE Is Accused of Sterilizing Detainees" 2020.

26. Sharpe, ibid.

27. DeLoughrey, "Tidalectics," 24.

28. Monika Gosin puts forth the white supremacist parameters on "worthy citizenship" in *The Racial Politics of Division: Interethnic Struggles for Legitimacy in Multicultural Miami* (2019). Many scholars have compared the treatment of Haitian émigrés to that of Cuban émigrés with attention to their respective racial codifications—see, for example, Alex Stepick's *Pride against Prejudice: Haitians in the United States* (1997), Alan Aja's *Miami's Forgotten Cubans: Race, Racialization, and the Miami Afro-Cuban Experience* (2016), and Linda Alcoff's *Visible Identities: Race, Gender, and the Self* (2006).

29. Stepick (1997), ibid., 168.

30. Lindskoog, ibid., 16.

31. Mitchell, "The Political Costs of State Power," 85.

32. Stepick, "The Refugees Nobody Wants: Haitians in Miami," in *Miami Now! Immigration, Ethnicity, and Social Change,* 58–60.

33. Chisholm, "U.S. Policy and Black Refugees," 22–24

34. San Martín, "Immigrants' Rights in the Public Sphere," 143.

35. See Jemima Pierre's "Haiti: An Archive of Occupation, 2004" and Justin Podur's *Haiti's New Dictatorship: From the Overthrow of Aristide to the 2010 Earthquake* (2012).

36. García, ibid., 42.

37. See Lindskoog, ibid., Jana Lipman's "'The Fish Trusts the Water, and It Is in the Water That It Is Cooked,'" Cheryl Little's and Joan Friedland's "Krome's Invisible Prisoners: Cycles of Abuse and Neglect," (1996), and "Behind Locked Doors: Abuse of Refugee Women at the Krome Detention Center," (2000), "Hidden from View: Human Rights Conditions in the Krome Detention Center," (1991) and Monique O. Madan's "'There Was Blood.' Fear of Virus Fuels Fights at Krome" (2020).

38. Lipman, "'The Fish Trusts the Water,'" 121.

39. See the Everglades National Park description: https://www.nps.gov/ever/index.htm.

40. Waller, "Terra Incognita," 359.

41. Mbembe, *Necropolitics,* 70.

42. Mbembe, ibid., 66.

43. Silverstein, "Shock Corridor," 30. See also Cheryl Little's "Continuing Problems at Krome Service Processing Center," 143–152.

44. Foucault, *The History of Sexuality*, 140.

45. See *Why Haiti Needs New Narratives: A Post-quake Chronicle* by Gina Athena Ulysse (2015) and Kate Ramsey's *The Spirits and the Law: Vodou and Power in Haiti* (2011) for more on the demonization and dismissal of vodou in the global imaginary.

46. Danticat, "A Little While," 19.

47. See the "Little Haiti Housing Association: Case Study" (1999).

48. See *City on the Edge*.

49. See for example Monica Campbell's "A 'No Haitians' Job Ad Shows Discrimination Is Not Dead" (2015), "SLS Hotels to Pay $2.5M for Discriminating against Haitian Workers in Miami" (2018), and "Employees Sue Hotel in Miami Beach for Discriminatory Firing of Black Haitian Kitchen Workers" (2017).

50. Sant La Haitian Neighborhood Center's "Progress and Unmet Challenges 2010–2015," 10; 12.

51. See Marta Gierczyk's "Magic City Killjoys: Women Organizers, Gentrification, and the Politics of Multiculturalism in Little Haiti" (2020).

52. Danticat, "From Little Haiti."

53. Pierre, "Little Haiti Tenant rights in focus," 2015.

54. "Urban Renewal." § 30A-Article 6 (Miami-Dade County 2015).

55. Mele, "Neoliberalism," 600.

56. Remy, "Haitian Immigrants and African-American Relations," 15.

57. "Historic Lemon City/Little Haiti Creole District Design Guidelines."

58. "From Little Haiti" Interview.

59. Ligon, "In the Gallery of Glenn."

60. Milord, "Little Haiti on the Cusp of Big Changes."

61. Valentin, "Miami's Little Haiti."

62. Harris, "Climate."

63. Danticat, "The Soul of Little Haiti."

64. Flechas, "Magic City Innovation District."

65. Díaz, *15 Views of Miami*.

66. Fièvre, "Sinkhole," 83–90.

67. Green and Rabin, "Where's Little Haiti?" (2013). For more on the history of Lemon City, see Thelma Peters' *Lemon City: Pioneering on Biscayne Bay, 1850–1925* (1976): "By 1890, there were a few blacks in Lemon City, but there is little record of who they were" (230).

68. Roberts, ibid.

69. Charles, "This Miami Haitian artist died struggling to pay rent."

70. Little Haiti Cultural Center, https://www.miamigov.com/LHCC/About.

71. *Miami New Times*, "Libreri Mapou."

72. Potter, "Boatload of Haitians Swarms Ashore in Florida."

73. Canedy "As Cameras Roll, Haitians Dash."

74. "DHS Awards AGS Contract."

75. See Francois Pierre-Louis' *Haitians in New York City: Transnationalism and Hometown Associations* (2006).

Chapter 3. Becoming Whiteness, Rejecting Blackness: Genre, Castro, and Transnational Identity in Carlos Moore's *Pichón* and Carlos Eire's *Learning to Die in Miami*

1. Stepick, *This Land Is Our Land,* 27.

2. See Tomas Fernandez's *El Negro En Cuba, 1902–1958: Apuntes Para La Historia De La Lucha Contra La Discriminacion Racial En La Neocolonia*(1990), Alejandro de la Fuente's *A Nation for All: Race, Inequality, and Politics in Twentieth-Century Cuba* (2001), Robin Moore's *Nationalizing Blackness: Afrocubanismo and Artistic Revolution in Havana, 1920–1940* (1997), Alan Aja's *Miami's Forgotten Cubans Race, Racialization, and the Miami Afro-Cuban Experience* (2016), Monika Gosin's *The Racial Politics of Division: Interethnic Struggles for Legitimacy in Multicultural Miami* (2019), and Mirta Ojito's. "Best of Friends, Worlds Apart" (2000).

3. Aja, ibid., 148. Monika Gosin captures similar testimony in The Racial Politics of Division wherein a Black Cuban woman realizes that white Cubans speak English to her in spaces where Spanish is primarily spoken because, she speculates, they assume because she is Black that she is not Cuban, 161.

4. Monika Gosin writes more about the complexities of white Cubans choosing whiteness and its benefits. See for example: "equating Blackness with 'unworthy citizenship' became useful in the service of making claim to the nation as some Cuban Americans sought to preserve their whitened status by distinguishing 'worthy' (white) Cuban citizens from 'criminal' (black) Marielitos" (59).

5. See Borland and Bosch's *Cuban American Literature and Art: Negotiating Identities* (2009). See also Ricardo L. Ortíz's "Cuban American Literature": "Cuba and the United States have . . . loomed large in each other's collective literary imaginations since at least the early life of the US republic, and the late twentieth-century emergence of a Cuban-exile or Cuban-immigrant literary project can only serve as one moment in a much longer, richer history of both collaborative and conflictive, but decidedly mutual, and simultaneous, imaginative literary elaboration" (413).

6. See Ana Menéndez's *In Cuba I Was a German Shepherd* (2001) and Jennine Capó Crucet's *How to Leave Hialeah* (2009), for example.

7. Borland and Bosch, ibid., 2.

8. Pérez Firmat, *Life on the Hyphen*, 4.

9. Gosin, ibid., 59.

10. See more about the operation in Yvonne Conde's *Operation Pedro Pan: The Untold Exodus of 14,048 Cuban Children* (2000).

11. de la Fuente offers the best overview of Batista's demise, especially within the context of racial hierarchies. See also Robert Whitney's "The Architect of the Cuban State: Fulgencio Batista and Populism in Cuba, 1937–1940."

12. Conde, ibid., 52.

13. See Joy James' *The New Abolitionists: (Neo)Slave Narratives and Contemporary Prison Writings* (2005), Arlene Keizer's *Black Subjects: Identity Formation in the Contem-*

porary Narrative of Slavery (2004), Ashraf Rushdy's *The Neo-Slave Narrative: Studies in the Social Logic of a Literary Form,* 1999.

14. Rushdy, *Neo-Slave Narratives,* 1.

15. Angelou's oeuvre includes *I Know Why the Caged Bird Sings* (2002), *Mom & Me & Mom* (2013), *The Heart of a Woman* (1981), *A Song Flung Up to Heaven* (2002), *All God's Children Need Traveling Shoes* (1986), and many others.

16. See Valerie Smith's *Self Discovery and Authority in Afro-American Narrative* (1987), John Blassingame's "Slave Testimony: Two Centuries of Letters, Sppeches, Interviews, and Autobiographies," (1977), Lindon Barrett's "African American Slave Narratives: Literacy, the Body, Authority" (1995), and Frances Foster Smith's *Written by Herself: Literary Production by African American Women 1746–1892* (1993).

17. Moore endeavors to write himself into Diasporic community, mirroring a trope Monika Gosin has examined: "Drawing upon their Cuban identities, they also insert themselves into a larger African diasporic community to challenge moves made by some African Americans to limit what it means to be black" (162).

18. Poey, Delia and Suarez, Virgil, *Little Havana Blues,* 10.

19. Borland and Bosch, ibid., 2.

20. Aja, ibid., 146.

21. Stepto, ibid., 167

22. See, Esteban Morales Domínguez, Gary Prevost, and August H. Nimtz's *Race in Cuba Essays on the Revolution and Racial Inequality* (2013) and Danielle Clealand's *The Power of Race in Cuba: Racial Ideology and Black Consciousness during the Revolution* (2017).

23. Holt, Thomas C. "Marking-Race, Race-Making, and the Writing of History."

24. Stepto, ibid., 67.

25. Garcia, ibid., 13.

26. García, ibid., xi. See also Silvia Pedraza's *Political Disaffection in Cuba's Revolution and Exodus* (2007) and Samuel Farber's *The Origins of the Cuban Revolution Reconsidered* (2006).

27. Kennedy, "Cincinnati Democratic Dinner,."

28. Gerard, Emmanuel, and Bruce Kuklick. *Death in the Congo: Murdering Patrice Lumumba.*

29. Ortíz, *Cultural Erotics in Cuban America,* 7.

30. Poey and Suarez, ibid., 11.

31. Moore offers more forceful critiques of Castro in "Le peuple noir" (1966) and *Castro, the Blacks, and Africa* (1988). See also Omar López Montenegro's "Castro Is a Calculating Racist—Here's Why," (1993).

32. See Stephen Fay's "Walterio Carbonell," and Walterio Carbonell's *Como surgio la cultura nacional* (1961).

33. De la Fuente, ibid., 266.

34. Guerra, *Visions of Power in Cuba,* 39

35. López, ibid., 7.

36. See also Devyn Benson's *Antiracism in Cuba: The Unfinished Revolution* (2016).

37. de la Fuente, ibid., 276.

38. Chardy, "Heresy Or History."

39. The station is suspected to be blocked in the island given the nation's suppressive policies on speech and dissent. See Analysis: Cuban-American Radio Stations Influence the Cuban Community. National Public Radio, Inc. (NPR), Washington, D.C., 2000.

40. Chardy, ibid.

41. Moore Papers, Florida International University Archives.

42. Nordheimer, "Blacks Meet to Revive 50-Year-Old Search for Identity."

43. Modesto Maidique Papers. Florida International University Archives.

44. Modesto Maidique Papers, ibid.

45. Sewell, "Black Intellectuals Gather."

46. Chardy, ibid.

47. Moore, "Open Letter."

48. Martínez, The Youngest Revolution, 149.

49. Lockwood, Castro's Cuba, 128.

50. de la Fuente, A Nation for All, 18.

51. Moore, "Le peuple noir," 199.

52. Moore, "ACTING ON OUR CONSCIENCE."

53. "Carlos Eire: A Cuban-American Searches for Roots."

54. See George Lipsitz's The Possessive Investment in Whiteness (1988), Cheryl Harris' "Whiteness as Property" (1993), and Charles Mills' The Racial Contract (1997).

55. "Carlos Eire."

56. As quoted in Eire, (x). See also Emily Dickinson's The Collected Poems of Emily Dickinson (2004), 78.

57. Beyond the thematic continuities Dickinson's poem introduces, her biography, specifically her noted history of self-exile, reflect Eire's interpretation of exile from his Cuban heritage. Dickinson's self-isolation has long been a topic of discussion among literary scholars, with some, including Amy Powell and Vivian Pollak speculating that Dickinson may have struggled with agoraphobia. Pollak also speculates that Dickinson may have believed that isolation enhanced her writing, asserting: "She wanted to believe that there was value in deprivation and that her imagination of freedom was intensified by her physical confinement, in what toward the end of her life she described as a "magic Prison . . ." (25).

58. "Carlos Eire: A Cuban-American Searches for Roots."

59. "Carlos Eire."

60. "Carlos Eire: A Cuban-American Searches for Roots."

61. López, Antonio, ibid., 72.

62. See García, ibid.

63. For more on how Cubans utilized their proximity to whiteness, see Monika Gosin, Alan Aja, and Jorge Cobás and Joe R. Feagin's How the United States Racializes Latinos: White Hegemony and Its Consequences (2009).

64. "Carlos Eire."

65. See Richard Rodriguez's Hunger of Memory: The Education of Richard Rodriguez: An Autobiography, 49. For a critique of Rodriguez, see Catherine S. Ramírez "Learning and Unlearning from Ethnic Studies" (2014).

66. "Carlos Eire."

Chapter 4. Who Speaks for Miami? The White Lens in the Tropical Metropole

1. Brian De Palma's *Scarface* is likely the most prominent film about Miami's vices, but other examples include the *Cocaine Cowboys* series (2006;2008;2021), the *Bad Boys* franchise (1995; 2003; 2020), *Miami Vice* (both the TV series [1984–1989] and film [2006]), *CSI: Miami* (2002–2012), and others.

2. Lopez, *Unbecoming Blackness: The Diaspora Cultures of Afro-Cuban America*, 171. See George Lipsitz and Cheryl Harris' work on investments in whiteness.

3. Lopez, ibid., 24.

4. Mine is of course not the first analysis of these compounding experiences, nor investigation of LGBTQIA persecution in Cuba; see Jafari S. Allen's *Venceremos?: The Erotics of Black Self-Making in Cuba* (2011), Bretton White's *Staging Discomfort: Performance and Queerness in Contemporary Cuba* (2020), and María Encarnación López's *Homosexuality and Invisibility in Revolutionary Cuba* (2015).

5. See Michelle Alexander's *The New Jim Crow: Mass Incarceration in the Age of Colorblindness* (2012) and Kenneth B. Nunn's "Race, Crime and the Pool of Surplus Criminality: Or Why the 'War on Drugs' Was a 'War on Blacks'" (2002).

6. Hooks, *The Will to Change*, 17.

7. García, ibid., 187.

8. See Martin Schram's "Carter's Ad Lib Affected Policy." *The Washington Post* [Washington, D.C.] 1980: A1.

9. López, *Homosexuality and Invisibility in Revolutionary Cuba*, 2–3.

10. Peña, *Oye Loca*, 484

11. García, ibid., 70.

12. García, ibid., 69.

13. Kelly, "South Florida: Trouble in Paradise." *TIME* (1981).

14. Peña, ibid.

15. See Benigno E. Aguirre's "Cuban Mass Migration and the Social Construction of Deviants" (1994), Robert L. Bach, Jennifer B. Bach, and Timothy Triplett's, "The Flotilla 'Entrants': Latest and Most Controversial" (1982), Alejandro Portes, Juan M. Clark, and Robert D. Manning's "After Mariel: A Survey of the Resettlement Experiences of 1980 Cuban Refugees in Miami" (1985), and Alejandro Portes and Leif Lensen's "The Enclave and the Entrants: Patterns of Ethnic Enterprise in Miami before and after Mariel" (1989).

16. Sonsky, "Bye, Pal." (1989).

17. Vellon, *Great Conspiracy against Our Race*, 81.

18. Vellon, ibid., 2.

19. *Scarface*. "Creating Scarface." Universal City, CA: Universal Studios Home Videos, 2006.

20. López, ibid., 174.

21. Negrón-Muntaner, "Feeling Pretty," 92.

22. García, ibid., 68.

23. "Creating Scarface"

24. García, ibid., 15; xi; 67.

25. Alberts, "Changes in Ethnic Solidarity," 237.

26. Among others, the cast included Philip Michael Thomas as Ricardo Tubbs, Don

Johnson as Sonny Crockett, and Edward James Olmos as Martin Castillo, Saundra Santiago as Gina Calabrese, Olivia Brown as Trudy Joplin, Michael Talbott as Stanley Switek, and John Diehl as Larry Zito.

27. Rutsky, "Visible Sins, Vicarious Pleasures," 78.

28. Stepick et al., *This Land Is Our Land*, 3–4.

29. Stepick et al., ibid., 5.

30. Sanders, Steven, *Miami Vice: TV Milestones*, 27.

31. Sanders, ibid., 10.

32. Schmalz, "Miami Journal," (1989).

33. Sanders, ibid., 27.

34. Croucher, "Ethnic Inventions," 234.

35. Peña, ibid., 142.

36. García, ibid., 63.

37. Alexander, *The New Jim Crow*, 48.

38. Bagley, "Colombia and the War on Drugs," 89.

39. Alexander, ibid., 50.

40. Alexander, ibid., 51.

41. Bagley, ibid.,185.

42. *Miami Now!*, 9.

43. Dunn, "Blacks in Miami," 41–57.

44. Bagley, ibid., 190.

45. DEA (1980–1985). Department of Justice: DEA History. http://www.justice.gov/dea/about/history/1980-1985.pdf

46. Dombrink, "The Touchables," 202.

47. Peña, ibid., 143.

Chapter 5. Dawg Fight in the Moonlight: Black Masculinity in Miami

1. See also *Cocaine Cowboys*, *Cocaine Cowboys 2*, and *The U*, also created by Billy Corben.

2. Boris Gardiner. "Every Nigger is A Star" Every Nigger" (1973), Leal Productions.

3. James, "*Every Nigger Is a Star*: Reimagining Blackness," 57.

4. See Sharony Green's "Tracing Black Racial and Spatial Politics in South Florida" (2018).

5. Mohl,"Black Immigrants," 287.

6. Jan, "In Miami, Your Skin Color is a Better Predictor of Wealth than Where Your Ancestors Came from," (2019).

7. Treon Johnson was the older brother of rapper Denzel Curry, who reflected on his brother's death in the Miami Times, see Lee Castro's "Denzel Curry on Tasering Death of His Brother, Treon Johnson, in Hialeah Police Incident."

8. Kannan, Menaka, Rhys Hall, and Matthew W. Hughey, "Watching Moonlight," 290–291.

9. Connolly, *A World More Concrete*, 99

10. Connolly, ibid., 86

11. Benowitz, "Liberty City's Unique History."

12. Connolly, ibid.

13. Benowitz, ibid.

14. Ugwu, "The Hashtag that Changed the Oscars: An Oral History." (2020).

15. Even while advocating for the widespread usage of dash and body cams, many acknowledged the limitations of this use of technology. Launched in 2015, Campaign Zero, an effort to establish more strident policies to ensure police accountability in all shooting cases notes that the use of cameras is "not a cure-all. As was noted in the notorious Eric Garner, Philando Castile, and Tamir Rice cases, the presence of video evidence did not sway key officials and/or jury members to see any fault in the officer's actions, although Garner was killed when Officer Pantaleo was filmed using a chokehold, which the New York Police Department prohibits. Castile was filmed informing Officer Yanez that he had a firearm in the vehicle before following Yanez's instruction of showing his identification, and Rice was shot by Officer Loehmann within seconds of police arriving at the scene.

16. See in particular Angela Davis' "Myth of the Black Rapist" in *Women, Race, & Class* (1981).

17. Sexton, *Black Masculinity and the Cinema of Policing*, 177.

18. Bush, ibid., 21.

19. Bush, ibid., 31

20. Bush, ibid., 85.

21. Bodenheimer, "How Oscar Favorite 'Moonlight' Subtly Illuminates the Erasure of Miami's Black Cubans."

22. Kannan, Hall, and Hughey, ibid., 293.

Coda

1. "Fighting Gentrification by Making Little Haiti Great Again."

Bibliography

"Affordable Housing Units." *Haitian American Community Development Corporation.* 19 Nov. 2015.

Alberts, Heike C. "Changes in Ethnic Solidarity in Cuban Miami." *New Geographies of U.S. Immigrants*, a special issue of *Geographical Review*, vol. 95, no. 2, 2005, pp. 231–248.

Alexander, Michelle. *The New Jim Crow: Mass Incarceration in the Age of Colorblindness.* New Press, 2012.

Allen, Jafari. "Afterword: "Miami's Nappy Edges: Finding Black Miami, Sin Fronteras."" *Anthurium*, vol. 16, no. 1, 2020, p. 11, doi: 10.33596/anth.406.

Anderson, Benedict. *Imagined Communities: Reflections on the Origin and Spread of Nationalism.* Rev. ed., Verso, 2006.

Arana, Ana, and Kim Brice. "Miami Murder Mystery: How Three Haitian Radio Hosts Were Silenced." *Columbia Journalism Review*, vol. 32, no. 6, 1994, p. 9.

Ards, Angela Ann. *Words of Witness: Black Women's Autobiography in the Post-Brown Era.* U of Wisconsin P, 2015.

"Around the Unisphere at the World's Fair, Lives Changed" *New York Times.* 18 Apr. 2014.

Bagley, Bruce Michael. "Colombia and the War on Drugs." *Foreign Affairs*, vol. 67, no. 1, 1988, pp. 70–98.

Baker, Houston A. *Critical Memory: Public Spheres, African American Writing, and Black Fathers and Sons in America.* U of Georgia P, 2001.

Baldwin, James. *Notes of a Native Son.* Beacon, 2012.

Benítez, Rojo Antonio. *The Repeating Island: The Caribbean and the Postmodern Perspective.* Duke UP, 1996.

Benowitz, Shayne. "Liberty City's Unique History and Its Beginnings at Liberty Square." *The Official Site of Greater Miami*, 22 July 2020, https://www.miamiandbeaches.com/things-to-do/history-and-heritage/the-history-of-liberty-square.

Benson, Devyn Spence. *Antiracism in Cuba: The Unfinished Revolution.* U of North Carolina P, 2016.

"The Black Archives: Organizational History." THE BLACK ARCHIVES: History and Research Foundation of South Florida, Inc., 26 Mar. 2017. https://www.bahlt.org/history#:~:text=History%20%7C%20The%20Black%20Archives&text=The%20Black%20Archives%20History%20and,from%201896%20to%20the%20present.

Bodenheimer, Rebecca. "How Oscar Favorite 'Moonlight' Subtly Illuminates the Erasure of Miami's Black Cubans." *Remezcla*. 6 Jan. 2017.

Bush, Gregory Wallace. *White Sand Black Beach: Civil Rights, Public Space, and Miami's Virginia Key.* UP of Florida, 2016.

Caleb, Stanley. "Father's Day: In Memory of My Dad, Joseph Caleb." *Miami Herald.* 14 June 2014. http://www.miamiherald.com/opinion/letters-to-the-editor/article1966373.html. Accessed 29 Mar. 2017.

Campbell, Monica. "A 'No Haitians' Job Ad Shows Discrimination Is Not Dead." *Public Radio International*, 10 Mar. 2016. https://www.wgbh.org/news/2016/03/10/no-haitians-job-ad-shows-discrimination-not-dead.

Campo-Flores, Arjan, and Laura Kusisto. "On Higher Ground, Miami's Little Haiti Is the New Darling of Developers; Rising Sea Levels Are Driving Gentrification, Causing Longtime Residents to Worry about Affordability and Displacement." *The Wall Street Journal*, photographs by Angel Valentin, 22 Apr. 2019.

Canedy, Dana. "As Cameras Roll, Haitians Dash from Stranded Boat to Florida Shore." *New York Times,* 30 Oct. 2002.

Capó, Julio. Welcome to Fairyland: Queer Miami before 1940. U of North Carolina P, 2017.

Carey, Gordon. "An Intensive Three-Weeks." Core-lator 78 (Fall 1959):1.

"Carlos Eire." Interview by Robert Birnbaum. *The Morning News*, 19 Apr. 2011. Accessed 30 April 2022 https://themorningnews.org/article/carlos-eire.

"Carlos Eire." Interview by Silvana Paternostro. *BOMB Magazine*, 21 Dec. 2008. Accessed 30 April 2022. https://bombmagazine.org/articles/carlos-eire/.

"Carter's Ad Lib Affected Policy." *Washington Post* [Washington, D.C.], 15 May 1980, p. A1. Accessed 19 April 2022.

Carter, Jimmy. "Carter Pledges to Admit Cuban Refugees." *History,* http://www.history.com/speeches/carter-pledges-to-admit-cuban-refugees.

Castro, Fidel. "La Historia Me Absolverá." *Tafalla: Txalaparta*, 1999.

Castro, Lee, "Denzel Curry on Tasering Death of His Brother, Treon Johnson, in Hialeah Police Incident." *Miami New Times*, 7 May 2014, https://www.miaminewtimes.com/music/denzel-curry-on-tasering-death-of-his-brother-treon-johnson-in-hialeah-police-incident-6464586?showFullText=true.

Chardy, Alfonso. "Heresy Or History Teachings on Cuban Racism Still Outrage Exile Community." *Miami Herald*, 7 Dec. 1990, p. 1E.

Charles, Jacqueline. "This Miami Haitian Artist Died Struggling to Pay Rent. Did Gentrification Play a Role?" *Miami Herald*, 13 Dec. 2017. https://www.miamiherald.com/news/nation-world/world/americas/haiti/article189551389.html.

Chisholm, Shirley. "U.S. Policy and Black Refugees." *African Refugees and Human Rights*, a special issue of *Issue: A Journal of Opinion*, vol. 12, no. 1/2 (1982): 22–24. doi: 10.2307/1166533.

Clifford, James. *The Predicament of Culture: Twentieth-Century Ethnography, Literature, and Art.* 2nd ed. Harvard UP, 2002.

Cocaine Cowboys. Directed by Billy Corben, performances by Jon Roberts, Mickey Munday, Jorge "Rivi" Ayala, 2006.

Conde, Yvonne M. *Operation Pedro Pan: The Untold Exodus of 14,000 Cuban Children*. Routledge, 2000.

Connolly, N.D.B. *A World More Concrete: Real Estate and the Remaking of Jim Crow South Florida*. U of Chicago P, 2016.

Connolly, N.D.B. "Speculating in History." *Anthurium*, vol. 16, no. 1, 2020, p. 9. doi: 10.33596/anth.364.

Corben, Billy, *Dawg Fight*: Rakontur, 2015.

"Creating Scarface." *Scarface*. Dir. Brian De Palma. Perf. Al Pacino. Universal Studios, 1983; re-released 2008. DVD.

Croucher, Sheila L. "Ethnic Inventions: Constructing and Deconstructing Miami's Culture Clash." *Pacific Historical Review*. vol. 68, no. 2, 1999, pp. 233–251. doi: 10.2307/3641986.

Cuban Adjustment Act, § 104–114, 1996.

Danticat, Edwidge. "A Little While." *The New Yorker*. 1 Feb. 2010.Accessed 30 April 2022 https://www.newyorker.com/magazine/2010/02/01/a-little-while

Danticat, Edwidge. *Brother, I'm Dying*. Alfred A. Knopf, 2007.

Danticat, Edwidge. "Children of the Sea." *Krik? Krak!* Soho, 1995. 3–29.

Danticat, Edwidge "In My Opinion: The Soul of Little Haiti." *The Miami Herald* (FL), 29 Sept. 2019, p. 1A.

Danticat, Edwidge. "From Little Haiti, Miami: The Writing of Edwidge Danticat." Interview by Jonathan Bastian. *Aspen Public Radio*. PRX, 29 Jan. 2015. Accessed 29 Nov. 2015. https://beta.prx.org/stories/73827.

Danticat, Edwidge. *The Butterfly's Way: Voices from the Haitian Dyaspora [sic] in the United States*. Soho, 2001.

DEA (1980–1985). *Department of Justice: DEA History*. Accessed 29 Apr. 2014. http://www.justice.gov/dea/about/history/1980–1985.pdf

de la Fuente, Alejandro. *A Nation for All: Race, Inequality, and Politics in Twentieth-Century Cuba*, U of North Carolina P, 2001.

DeLoughrey, Elizabeth. "Tidalectics: Charting the Space/Time of Caribbean Waters." *Span: Journal of the South Pacific Association for Commonwealth Literature and Language Studies*, vol. 47, 1998, pp. 18–38.

"DHS Awards AGS Contract to Support Krome Detention Center." Akima Global Services. AGS, 15 May 2014. http://www.akimaglobal.com/2014/05/13/dhs-awards-akima-global-services-contract-to-support-krome-detention-center/. Accessed 27 Nov. 2015.

Díaz, Jaquira. *15 Views of Miami*. Burrow P, 2014.

Dombrink, John. "The Touchables: Vice and Police Corruption in the 1980's." *Law and Contemporary Problems*, vol. 51, no. 1, 1988, pp. 201–232.

Dubois, Laurent. *Haiti: The Aftershocks of History*. Metropolitan, 2012.

Du Bois, W.E.B. *The Souls of Black Folk Essays and Sketches*. U of Virginia Library, 1996.

Due, Tananarive, and Patricia Stephens Due. *Freedom in the Family: A Mother-Daughter Memoir of the Fight for Civil Rights*. Ballantine P, 2003.

Dunn, Marvin. "Blacks in Miami" in *Miami Now!: Immigration, Ethnicity, and Social Change*. UP of Florida, 1992, pp. 41–57.

Edelman, Lee. *No Future: Queer Theory and the Death Drive.* Duke UP, 2004.

Eire, Carlos. *Learning to Die in Miami: Confessions of a Refugee Boy.* Free P, 2011.

Eire, Carlos. *Waiting for Snow in Havana: Confessions of a Cuban Boy.* Free P, 2006.

"Everglades National Park." *National Parks Service.* U.S. Department of the Interior, 24 Nov. 2015. Accessed 28 Nov. 2015.

Field, Dorothy Jenkins. "Final Phase of Upgrades Finished at Overtown Historic Lyric Theater," *The Miami Herald.* 5 Feb. 2014.

Fièvre, M. J. "Sinkhole" in *15 Views of Miami,* edited by Jaquira Diaz. Burrow, 2014. 83–90.

Firmat, Gustavo Pérez. *Life on the Hyphen: The Cuban-American Way.* U of Texas P, 2014.

Flechas, Joey, "Magic City Innovation District; Miami Receives $3 Million from Little Haiti Developers Who Sparked Gentrification Fears." *The Miami Herald.* 2 Mar. 2021.

Foucault, Michel. *The History of Sexuality.* Pantheon, 1978. Print.

Garcia, Maria Cristina. *Havana USA: Cuban Exiles and Cuban Americans in South Florida, 1959–1994.* U of California P, 1996.

Gierczyk, Marta. "Magic City Killjoys: Women Organizers, Gentrification, and the Politics of Multiculturalism in Little Haiti." *Anthurium,* vol. 16, no. 1, 2020. doi:10.33596/anth.409.

Glissant, Édouard. *Faulkner, Mississippi.* Farrar, Straus and Giroux, 1999.

Gosin, Monika. *The Racial Politics of Division: Interethnic Struggles for Legitimacy in Multicultural Miami.* Cornell UP, 2019.

Grant, Joanne. *Ella Baker: Freedom Bound.* Wiley, 1998.

Green, Nadege, and Charles Rabin. "Where's Little Haiti? It's a Big Question." *Miami Herald.* 13 Oct. 2013. Accessed 26 Nov. 2015.

Grenier, Guillermo J, and Alex Stepick. *Miami Now!: Immigration, Ethnicity, and Social Change.* Gainesville: UP of Florida, 1992.

Guerra, Lillian. *Visions of Power in Cuba: Revolution, Redemption, and Resistance, 1959–1971.* U of North Carolina P, 2012.

Harris, Alex. "Climate is Sea rise turning high ground into a hot commodity? Miami is the first city to study whether 'climate gentrification'—redevelopment driven by consumer preferences for higher ground as sea levels rise—is driving residents out of historically black and poor neighborhoods like Little Haiti." *Miami Herald,* 18 Dec. 2018, p. 1A.

Harrison, Faye V. "From the Chesapeake Bay to the Caribbean Sea and Back: Remapping Routes, Unburying Roots." *Caribbean and Southern: Transnational Perspectives on the U.S. South,* edited by Helen Regis, 2006. U of Georgia P, pp. 7–33.

"Historic Lemon City/Little Haiti Creole District Design Guidelines." *City of Miami: Planning and Zoning,* 2013.

Hodges, Timothy. *East of Overtown* (pitch). Found in *Black Archives of South Florida,* circa 1981. Accessed 22 June 2016.

"Holocaust Memorial Miami Beach: History." *The Holocaust Memorial of Miami Beach.* Accessed 26 Mar. 2017. https://holocaustmemorialmiamibeach.org/about/history/#:~:text=History%20of%20the%20Holocaust%20Memorial&text=In%201984%2C%20a%20small%20group,a%20private%20non%2Dprofit%20organization.

Holt, Thomas C. "Marking-Race, Race-Making, and the Writing of History." *The American Historical Review* 100.1 (1995): 1–20. Web.

hooks, bell. *The Will to Change: Men, Masculinity, and Love.* Simon & Schuster, 2005.

Hughes, Langston. *Montage of a Dream Deferred.* Holt Publishing, 1951.

Hurston, Zora Neale. "Letter to the Editor." "Letter to the Orlando Sentinel." *The Orlando Sentinel,* 11 Aug. 1955. Accessed 26 Mar. 2017. http://teachingamericanhistory.org/library/document/letter-to-the-orlando-sentinel/.

James, Erica Moiah. "Every Nigger Is a Star: Reimagining Blackness from Post–Civil Rights America to the Postindependence Caribbean," *Black Camera: The Newsletter of the Black Film Center/Archives,* vol. 8, no. 1, 2016: 55–83.

Jan, Tracy. "In Miami, Your Skin Color is a Better Predictor of Wealth than Where Your Ancestors Came from." *Washington Post.* 27 Feb. 2019.

Jarvis, Brian. *Postmodern Cartographies the Geographical Imagination in Contemporary American Culture.* Pluto, 1998.

Kadlec, David. "Zora Neale Hurston and the Federal Folk." *Modernism/Modernity* Vol. 7:3, Sept. 2000. Pp. 471–485. Web.

Kannan, Menaka, Rhys Hall, and Matthew W. Hughey. "Watching Moonlight in the Twilight of Obama." *Humanity & Society,* vol. 41, no. 3, 2017, 287–98.

Kelly, James. "South Florida: Trouble in Paradise." *TIME: Paradise Lost?* 23 Nov. 1981.

Kennedy, John F. "John F. Kennedy Address on October 6, 1960 Democratic Dinner in Cincinnati, Ohio." Democratic Dinner. Cincinnati, OH.

Kopan, Tal. "What Donald Trump has said about Mexico." *Cable News Network.* 31 Aug. 2016.

Lemaire, Sandra. "Fighting Gentrification by Making Little Haiti Great Again." *Voice of America News,* 2018.

"Libreri Mapou Won Best Haitian Bookstore in Miami New Times' 2000 Best Of Issue." *Miami New Times.* 11 Oct. 2000.

Ligon, Glenn. "In the Gallery of Glenn." Interview by Staxton Foley. 18 Dec. 2012. Accessed 29 Nov. 2015. https://staxtonfoley.wordpress.com/2012/12/18/chapter-3-in-the-gallery-of-glenn/.

Lindskoog, Carl. *Detain and Punish: Haitian Refugees and the Rise of the World's Largest Immigration Detention System.* U of Florida P, 2018.

Lipman, Jana K. "'The Fish Trusts the Water, and It Is in the Water That It Is Cooked': The Caribbean Origins of the Krome Detention Center" *Radical History Review,* vol. 115, 2015, pp. 115–141. doi:10.1215/01636545-1724742.

Lipsitz, George. *How Racism Takes Place.* Temple UP, 2011.

Listokin, David. "Case Study Little Haiti Housing Association" Fannie Mae Foundation, 2000. 321–346.

Little Haiti Cultural Center Website. Accessed 26 Nov. 2015.

López, Antonio. *Unbecoming Blackness: The Diaspora Cultures of Afro-Cuban America.* NYU P, 2012.

López, María Encarnación. *Homosexuality and Invisibility in Revolutionary Cuba: Reinaldo Arenas and Tomás Gutiérrez Alea.* Tamesis, 2015.

Lowe, John. "Calypso Magnolia: The Caribbean Side of the South." *South Central Review,* vol. 22, no. 1, pp.54–80.

Lowe, John Wharton. *Calypso Magnolia: The Crosscurrents of Caribbean and Southern Literature.* U of North Carolina P, 2016.

Maidique, Modesto Papers. Florida International University Archives.

Martínez, Elizabeth S. *The Youngest Revolution: A Personal Report on Cuba.* Dial P, 1969.

Mbembe, Achille, and Steve Corcoran. *Necropolitics.* Duke UP, 2019.

McClennen, Sophia A. "Inter-American studies or Imperial American studies?" *Comparative American Studies,* vol. 3, no. 4, 2005, 393–413.

McKittrick, Katherine. *Demonic Grounds Black Women and the Cartographies of Struggle.* U of Minnesota P, 2006.

Mele, Christopher. "Neoliberalism, Race and the Redefining of Urban Redevelopment." *International Journal of Urban and Regional Research,* vol. 37, no. 2, 2012: 598–617.

Merrick, George E. "Pre-Flagler Influences on the Lower Florida East Coast," *Tequesta* 1, March 1941.

Milord, Joann. "Little Haiti on the Cusp of Big Changes." *The Miami Herald.* 14 Nov. 2014.

Mirabal, Nancy Raquel. "'Ser De Aquí': Beyond the Cuban Exile Model." *Latino Studies,* vol. 1, no. 3, 2003, pp. 366–82.

Mitchell, Christopher. "U.S. Policy toward Haitian Boat People, 1972–93." *The Annals of the American Academy of Political and Social Science,* vol. 534, 1994, pp. 69–80. doi: 10.1177/0002716294534001006.

Mitchell, Christopher. "The Political Costs of State Power: US Border Control in South Florida," *The Wall Around the West: State Borders and Immigration Controls in North America and Europe,* edited by Peter Andreas and Timothy Snyder. Rowman & Littlefield, 2000.

Mohl, Raymond A. "Black Immigrants: Bahamians in Early Twentieth-Century Miami." *The Florida Historical Quarterly,* vol. 65, no. 3, 1987, pp. 271–297.

Moonlight. Directed by Barry Jenkins, perfomances by Trevante Rhodes, André Holland, Janelle Monáe, Ashton Sanders, Jharrel Jerome, Naomie Harris, Mahershala Ali, Lionsgate, 2016.

Moore, Carlos. "Acting On Our Conscience: A Declaration of African American Support for the Civil Rights Struggle in Cuba." 9 Nov. 2009.

Moore, Carlos. *Pichón A Memoir: Race and Revolution in Castro's Cuba.* Lawrence Hill, 2008.

Moore, Carlos. Assorted documents from the Florida International University Archives.

Moore, Steven. "ICE Is Accused of Sterilizing Detainees. That Echoes the U.S.'s Long History of Forced Sterilization." *The Washington Post.* 26 Sept. 2020.

Natambu, Kofi. "POEM FOR ARTHUR MCDUFFIE: MAY, 1980." *Obsidian* (1975–1982), vol. 7, no. 1, 1981, pp. 66–66.

National Public Radio: Fresh Air. "Carlos Eire: A Cuban-American Searches for Roots." 22 Nov. 2010.

Negrón-Muntaner, Frances. "Feeling Pretty: West Side Story and Puerto Rican Identity Discourses" (2000)." *The Great American Mosaic: An Exploration of Diversity in Primary Documents,* 2014, pp. 288–89.

Nevans, Mary Frances. "The Repatriation of the Haitian Boat People: Its Legal Justification under the Interdiction Agreement between the United States and Haiti." *Temple International and Comparative Law Journal,* vol. 5, no. 2, 1991, p. 273.

Nordheimer, Jon. "BLACKS MEET TO REVIVE 50-YEAR-OLD SEARCH FOR IDEN-TITY." The New York Times. 1 Mar. 1987.

Obejas, Achy. "Race in Cuba: The Root Interviews Carlos Moore." *The Root*. 29 July 2010.

Olsen-Medina, Kira, and Jeanne Batalova. "Haitian Immigrants in the United States." *Migration Policy Institute*. 12 Aug. 2020. https://www.migrationpolicy.org/article/haitian-immigrants-united-states-2018.

Ortíz, Ricardo L., *Cultural Erotics in Cuban America*. U of Minnesota P, 2007.

Peña, Susana. *Oye Loca: From the Mariel Boatlift to Gay Cuban Miami*. U of Minnesota P, 2013.

Peters, Thelma. *Lemon City: Pioneering on Biscayne Bay, 1850–1925*. Banyan Books, 1976.

Pierre, Jeffrey. "LITTLE HAITI Tenant rights in focus as investors eye area." *The Miami Herald*, 9 July 2015, p. 6NC.

Pierre, Jemima. "Haiti: An Archive of Occupation, 2004." *Transforming Anthropology*, vol. 28, no. 1, 2020, pp. 3–23.

Podur, Justin, and William I. Robinson. *Haiti's New Dictatorship: The Coup, the Earthquake and the UN Occupation*. Pluto P, 2012.

Pollak, Vivian R. *A Historical Guide to Emily Dickinson*. Oxford: Oxford UP, 2004.

Potter, Mark. "Boatload of Haitians Swarms Ashore in Florida." *Cable News Network*. 30 Oct. 2002.

Portes, Alejandro, and Alex Stepick. *City on the Edge the Transformation of Miami*. U of California P, 1994.

Pratt, Mary Louise. *Imperial Eyes: Travel Writing and Transculturation*. Routledge, 2007.

"Progress and Unmet Challenges: Sant La's Profile of The Haitian Community of Miami-Dade, 2010–015." Sant La Haitian Neighborhood Center. 16 Mar. 2015.

Remy, Gemima M. "Haitian Immigrants and African-American Relations: Ethnic Dilemmas in a Racially-Stratified Society," *Trotter Review*, vol. 10, no. 1, 1996. Article 5.

Renick, Ralph, *WTVJ*. Quoted in *Cocaine Cowboys*. Magnolia Home Entertainment, 2007.

Roberts, Dorothy E. *Killing the Black Body: Race, Reproduction, and the Meaning of Liberty*. Pantheon, 1997.

Rohter, Larry. "In Miami's Little Haiti, Fears of Assassination" [NYC, New York]. *The New York Times*, 20 Mar. 1994.

Rose, Chanelle N. *The Struggle for Black Freedom in Miami: Civil Rights and America's Tourist Paradise, 1896–1968*. Louisiana State University P, 2015.

Rutsky, R. L. "Visible Sins, Vicarious Pleasures: Style and Vice in "Miami Vice." *SubStance*, vol. 17, no. 1, 1988, pp.77–82.

San Martín, Mariana. "Immigrants' Rights in the Public Sphere: Hannah Arendt's Concepts Reconsidered." *Societies without Borders*, vol. 4, no. 2, 2009, pp. 141–57.

Sanders, Steven. *Miami Vice: TV Milestones*. Wayne State UP, 2010.

Sandler, Nathaniel. "Map Of South Florida Shows How Racially Segregated We Are." *WLRN*. 6 Sept. 2013. Web. 29 Mar. 2017. http://wlrn.org/post/map-south-florida-shows-how-racially-segregated-we-are.

Sangaramoorthy, Thurka. *Treating AIDS: Politics of Difference, Paradox of Prevention*. New Brunswick, New Jersey: Routledge, 2014. Web.

Scarface. Directed by Brian De Palma, perfomance by Al Pacino. Universal Studios, 1983.

Schmalz, Jeffrey "Miami Journal; Sun Sets on Show That Redefined a City." *The New York Times*, 18 May 1989.

Schomburg, Arthur. "The Negro Digs Up His Past." in *The New Negro*, edited by Alain. Simon & Schuster, 1997, pp. 231–237.

Schumacher, Edward. "Retarded People and Criminals are included in Cuban Exodus." *New York Times*. 11 May 1980.

Sciolino, Elaine. "Clinton Says U.S. Will Continue Ban on Haitian Exodus." *The New York Times*. 14 Jan. 1993. Accessed 27 Nov. 2015.

Sewell, Dan. "Black Intellectuals Gather in Miami for Negritude Conference." *Associated Press*. 26 Feb. 1987.

Sexton, Jared. *Amalgamation Schemes: Antiblackness and the Critique of Multiracialism*. U of Minnesota P, 2008.

Sexton, Jared Yates. *Black Masculinity and the Cinema of Policing*. Palgrave Macmillan, 2017.

Sharpe, Jenny. "The Middle Passages of Black Migration." *Atlantic Studies*, vol. 6, no. 1, 2009, pp. 97–112.

Silverstein, Ken. "Shock Corridor" [NYC, New York]. *The New Republic*. 19 Aug. 2019.

Smiley, Calvin John, and David Fakunle. "From 'brute' to 'thug:' The Demonization and Criminalization of Unarmed Black Male Victims in America." *Journal of Human Behavior in the Social Environment* 26.3–4 (2016): 350–66.

Smith, Jon, and Deborah Cohn. *Look Away! The U.S. South in New World Studies*. Duke UP, 2004.

Sonsky, Steve. "Bye, Pal." *Miami Herald*, 21 May 1989.

Stepick, Alex. "Haitian Boat People: A Study in the Conflicting Forces Shaping U.S. Immigration Policy." *Law and Contemporary Problems*, vol. 45, no. 2, 1982, pp.163–196.

Stepick, Alex, and Dale F. Swartz. *Pride against Prejudice: Haitians in the United States*. Allyn and Bacon, 1998.

Stepick, Alex. *This Land Is Our Land Immigrants and Power in Miami*. U of California P, 2003.

Stepto, Robert B. *From Behind the Veil: A Study of Afro-American Narrative*. U of Illinois P, 1979.

Stetler, Carrie. "Junot Diaz: Man in the Mirror." *NJ.com*, 26 Oct. 2009.

Stover, Johnnie M. *Rhetoric and Resistance in Black Women's Autobiography*. Orange Grove, 2009.

Telles, Edward Eric. *Pigmentocracies: Ethnicity, Race, and Color in Latin America*. U of North Carolina P, 2014.

Trouillot, Michel-Rolph, and Hazel V. Carby. *Silencing the Past: Power and the Production of History*. Beacon, 2015.

"Urban Renewal." § 30A-Article 6 (Miami-Dade County 2015). Web. Accessed 25 Nov. 2015.

Vagianos, Alanna. "John Lewis: Women Did All 'The Heavy Lifting' During Civil Rights Movement." *The Huffington Post*. 23 Sept. 2016. Accessed 26 Mar. 2017.

Veeser, H. Aram. *The New Historicism*. Routledge, 1988.

Vellon, Peter G. *Great Conspiracy against Our Race: Italian Immigrant Newspapers and the Construction of Whiteness in the Early 20th Century*. NYU P, 2017. Print.

Waller, Nicole. "Terra Incognita: Mapping the Detention Center in Edwidge Danticat's *Brother, I'm Dying* and the US Supreme Court Ruling Boumediene v. Bush." *Atlantic Studies*, vol. 6, no. 3, 2009, pp. 357–69.

The WPA Guide to Florida: The Federal Writers' Project Guide to 1930s Florida. Pantheon Books, 1984.

Wolfe, Patrick. "Settler Colonialism and the Elimination of the Native." *Journal of Genocide Research*, vol. 8, no. 4, 2006, pp. 387–409.

Yanez, Luisa. "MIAMI-DADE LEADERS SEE MAGIC IN NEW NAME." *Sun-Sentinel*, 1997.

Yerkovich, Anthony, creator. *Miami Vice*. Michael Mann Productions and Universal Television. 1984.

Index

Tatiana D. McInnis is instructor of American studies and humanities at the North Carolina School of Science and Mathematics.